POLITICAL COMMUNICATIONS
Why Labour Won the General Election of 1997

Edited by

IVOR CREWE
University of Essex

BRIAN GOSSCHALK
MORI

JOHN BARTLE
University of Essex

FRANK CASS
LONDON • PORTLAND, OR

First Published in 1998 in Great Britain by
FRANK CASS PUBLISHERS
Newbury House, 900 Eastern Avenue
London IG2 7HH

and in the United States of America by
FRANK CASS PUBLISHERS
c/o ISBS, 5804 N.E. Hassalo Street
Portland, Oregon 97213-3644

Website http://www.frankcass.com

British Library Cataloguing in Publication Data

Political communications: why Labour won the general
election of 1997
1. Great Britain. Parliament – Elections, 1997 2. Labour
Party (Great Britain)
I. Crewe, Ivor II. Gosschalk, Brian III. Bartle, John
324.9'41'0559

ISBN 0-7146-4923-6 (cloth)
ISBN 0-7146-4482-X (paper)

Library of Congress Cataloging-in-Publication Data

Political communications : why Labour won the general election of 1997
/ edited by Ivor Crewe, Brian Gosschalk, John Bartle.
    p.   cm.
  Based on a conference held at the University of Essex in September
1997.
  Includes bibliographical references and index.
  ISBN 0-7146-4923-6 (cloth). – ISBN 0-7146-4482-X (paper).
  1. Elections–Great Britain–Congresses. 2. Great Britain.
Parliament–Elections. 1997–Congresses. 3. Communication in
politics–Great Britain–Congresses. 4. Labour Party (Great
Britain) I. Crewe, Ivor. II. Gosschalk, Brian. III. Bartle,
John, lecturer.
JN956.P65   1998
324.941'0859–DC21   98-38304
                                                             CIP

Typeset by Vitaset, Paddock Wood, Kent
Printed in Great Britain by
Bookcraft (Bath) Ltd, Midsomer Norton, Somerset

Contents

Notes on Contributors

John Bartle is Lecturer in Government and British Academy Post-Doctoral Fellow at the University of Essex. He has published articles in the *British Journal of Political Science* and *British Elections & Parties Review* on British voting behaviour.

Jay G. Blumler is Professor Emeritus of the University of Leeds, where he directed its Centre for Television Research from 1963–89, and of the University of Maryland, where he was a Professor of Journalism from 1983–95. He is a fellow and past president of the International Communications Association, research consultant to the Broadcasting Standards Commission, founding co-editor of the *European Journal of Communication* and a member of the editorial board of Political Communications. He has published numerous books on political communication.

Adam Boulton has been presenter and political editor of Sky News since 1989 and before that was presenter and political editor of TV-AM. He is a founding member of both companies.

Ivor Crewe is Vice Chancellor and Professor of Government at the University of Essex. He is the author of numerous books and articles on British parties, elections and public opinion. He has been a co-organiser of every post-election Political Communications conference at the University of Essex since 1983.

David Denver is Professor of Politics at the University of Lancaster. He is the author of *Elections and Voting Behaviour in Britain* (1994) and (with Gordon Hands) *Modern Constituency Electioneering* (1997). He has also edited (again with Gordon Hands) *Issues and Controversies in British Electoral Behaviour* (1992). He convenes the elections group of the Political Studies Association and is a frequent commentator on elections in the press, radio and television.

Daniel Finkelstein has been director of the Conservative Party Research Department since October 1995. His role includes running the Shadow Cabinet Secretariat, advising the party leader on policy and strategy and managing the party's briefing, policy development and opinion research work.

Ivor Gaber is Professor of Broadcast Journalism at Goldsmiths College, University of London, and an independent radio and television producer. During the 1997 election campaign he was a member of *Channel Four News* election campaign team; he was also the results editor for ITN on the election night programme. He has written broadly in the area of political communications and is currently completing a book, with Steven Barnett, on the production of political news.

Rachel Gibson is Lecturer in Politics in the European Studies Institute, University of Salford. She is currently involved in a research project (with Stephen Ward) examining political parties and the Internet. Other publications include work on power distribution within parties and on anti-immigrant politics in western Europe.

Peter Goddard is a teacher and research assistant in the Department of Communication Studies at the University of Liverpool working for a project funded by the Economic and Social Research Council on political marketing in the 1997 general election. He has published articles about the development of situation comedy on British television in the 1950s.

Brian Gosschalk is Managing Director of MORI. He is a past chairman of the Social Research Association and a council member of the World Association of Public Opinion Research (WAPOR). He worked at the BBC and with David Butler prior to joining MORI in 1979 to specialise in social and political research. He is co-editor (with Ivor Crewe) of *Political Communications: The General Election Campaign of 1992.*

Philip Gould has been strategy and polling advisor to Tony Blair and the Labour Party since 1994. During that period he has conducted over 300 focus groups in the political and public affairs field. He has worked in a strategic and polling capacity in national elections across the world, including the Clinton presidential campaigns of 1992 and 1996.

Michael Gurevitch is Professor at the College of Journalism at the University of Maryland. He has written books and journal articles and contributed chapters on the subject of political communications. His most recent book is *The Crisis of Public Communication* (with Jay Blumler). He is the co-editor of *Mass Communication and Society* (1977), *Culture, Society and the Media* (1982), and *Mass Media and Society* (1995). He is currently a member of the editorial board of Political Communications.

Gordon Hands is Head of the Department of Politics at the University of Lancaster. He is co-author (with David Denver) of *Modern Constituency Electioneering* (1997). He has also edited (again with David Denver) *Issues and Controversies in British Electoral Behaviour* (1992). He has written widely on British electoral politics and political sociology.

Steve Hilton was Conservative Central Office campaign co-ordinator for the 1992 general election campaign and joined Saatchi & Saatchi in May 1992 to help set up Saatchi & Saatchi Government Communications Worldwide. He joined M&C Saatchi in 1995, and ran the Conservative Party's 1997 election advertising campaign.

Richard Holme (Lord Holme of Cheltenham) is a politician, publisher and businessman. He was made a Liberal Democrat life peer in 1990 and was chairman of the Liberal Democrats' general election campaign team in 1997.

Alison Holmes was the Campaign Planning Manager of the Liberal Democrats' election campaign in 1997 and now works for the BBC.

David McKie, formerly political correspondent, parliamentary correspondent, leader writer and deputy editor of the *Guardian*, is now a *Guardian* columnist.

Austin Mitchell is a former political scientist (Nuffield College, Oxford) and television journalist (Yorkshire Television) who has been Member of Parliament for Grimsby since 1977.

Colin Munro is Professor of Constitutional Law at the University of Edinburgh, which he joined in 1990, having previously taught at the Universities of Birmingham, Durham, Essex and Manchester. He is the author of *Studies in Constitutional Law* (1987) and books and articles on public law and media law.

Stephen Perkins joined the Independent Broadcasting Authority (IBA) as Radio Programming Officer, working on factual programme issues including election broadcasting. In 1988 he became Regional Officer – East of England for the IBA and subsequently the Independent Television Commission (ITC), returning to London in 1995, as Senior Programme Officer. He is now responsible for the ITC's factual programmes department, specialising in current affairs and elections.

Chris Powell is Chief Executive of BMP DDB. He joined BMP just as it started, in 1969 as a partner and shareholder. He became Joint Managing Director in 1975 and Chief Executive in 1986. Besides commercial clients, he and the agency have worked with the Labour party across four general elections. He is a past president of the industry's trade body, the Institute of Practitioners in Advertising.

Margaret Scammell is a Senior Lecturer in Communication Studies at Liverpool University, having previously worked as a journalist in the provincial and national press and for Channel 4 Television. She has published *Designer Politics: How Elections are Won* (1995) and is currently working on an edited volume on journalism studies.

Holli A. Semetko is Professor of Communications at the University of Amsterdam. Her books include *The Formation of Campaign Agendas* (1991) and *Germany's Unity Election* (1994).

Colin Seymour-Ure is Professor of Government at the University of Kent at Canterbury. He has written about a variety of aspects of media and British elections since first contributing a chapter about the press to *The British General Election of 1966* by David Butler and Anthony King.

Richard Tait has been Editor-in-Chief of Independent Television News (ITN) since 1995. He has editorial responsibility for all ITN's news and current affairs programmes on ITV, Channel 4, Channel 5 and Independent Radio News. He began his television career at the BBC, where he edited *The Money Programme* and BBC Television's 1987 general election results programme. Before becoming Editor-in-Chief of ITN, he was Editor of *Channel Four News* from 1987–95.

Stephen Ward is a Lecturer in Politics in the European Studies Research Institute at the University of Salford. He is currently involved in a research project (with Rachel Gibson) examining political parties and the Internet. His other research interests include environmental politics and the European Union, on which he has published a number of articles.

Robert M. Worcester is Chairman of MORI. He has been an Honorary Visiting Professor in the Graduate Centre for Journalism at City University since 1989, Visiting Professor of Government at the London School of Economics since 1992, and Visiting Professor of Marketing at University of Strathclyde, Glasgow, since 1996. He is a past president of the World Association of Public Opinion Research (WAPOR). He inaugurated the series of the post-election Political Communications conferences in Britain.

Preface

This is the fifth book in a continuing series examining political communications in British general elections. Like its predecessors for the 1979, 1983, 1987 and 1992 elections, it has a dual purpose: first, to provide an analysis of the media, the parties and the opinion polls in the campaign and, second, to make available the reflections of some of those who participated in it.

The book is based on a conference held at the University of Essex in September 1997 which brought together, for a weekend's intensive review of the campaign, academics, politicians, journalists, pollsters and many other practitioners of political communication.

Given the size of the conference – 45 contributions and 160 participants – it was unfortunately not possible to publish all the papers and talks in this volume. Many that do not appear here have been published in Charles Pattie *et al.* (eds), *British Elections & Parties Review*, Volume 7. We are grateful to all the contributors to the conference.

The conference was held under the auspices of the Elections, Public Opinion and Parties Group of the Political Studies Association. We wish to acknowledge the generous financial support received from the Economic and Social Research Council, the Arthur McDougall Fund, the Political Studies Association and the University of Essex, and the office facilities provided by MORI. We owe an enormous debt of gratitude to Jackie Mutlow, who managed the day-to-day preparations for the conference almost single-handedly. We are also grateful to Nicola Carnaby, Daniel Crewe, Paul Hughes and Rosie Packer for their assistance. We also acknowledge the ordinary participants at the conference whose knowledgeable and often witty interventions brought the best out of the speakers and have encouraged us to plan a similar conference and book after the next election.

Ivor Crewe
Brian Gosschalk
John Bartle

List of Figures and Tables

List of Abbreviations

AC	Appeals Cases
All ER	All England Law Reports
ALR	Australian Law Reports
Alta. LR	Alberta Law Reports
APOPO	Association of Professional Opinion-Polling Organisations
BARB	British Audience Research Board
BDB	'Britain Deserves Better'
BNP	British National Party
BSE	Bovine Spongiform Encephalopathy ('Mad Cow Disease')
Cm	Command Paper
Con.	Conservative Party
DLR	Dominion Law Reports
DUP	Democratic Unionist Party (Northern Ireland)
EBB	Entrepreneurs for a Booming Britain
EMU	European Monetary Union
EOI	Economic Optimism Index
ERM	European Exchange Rate Mechanism
IBA	Independent Broadcasting Authority
ICM	International Communications and Marketing
ILR	Independent London Radio
ISP	Internet Service Provider
ITC	Independent Television Commission
ITN	Independent Television News
Lab.	Labour Party
Lib. Dem.	Liberal Democrats
MORI	Market and Opinion Research International
NDP	National Democratic Party
NI Lab.	Northern Ireland Labour Party
NILR	Northern Ireland Law Reports
NLND	'New Labour, New Danger'
NLP	Natural Law Party
NOP	National Opinion Polls
ORB	Opinion Research Business
PC	Plaid Cymru (Welsh nationalists)
PEB	party election broadcast
PPB	party political broadcast
PTC	Public Service, Tax and Commercial Union
PUP	Progressive Unionist Party (Northern Ireland)

Ref.	Referendum Party
RPA	Representation of the People Act 1983
RSL	Research Services Ltd
SC	Sessions Cases
SCP	Scottish Conservative Party
SDLP	Social Democratic and Labour Party (Northern Ireland)
SDP	Social Democratic Party (merged with Liberal Party in 1988 to form Liberal Democrats)
SF	Sinn Féin (Northern Ireland)
SLD	Scottish Liberal Democrats
SLP	Socialist Labour Party
SLT	Scots Law Times
SNP	Scottish Nationalist Party
SSA	Scottish Socialist Alliance
UDP	Ulster Democratic Party (Northern Ireland)
UKIP	United Kingdom Independence Party
UUP	Ulster Unionist Party (Northern Ireland)
WLR	Weekly Law Reports
WWW	World Wide Web

Introduction

Elections invariably generate instant explanations, which have a habit of turning into myths. The 1997 election is no exception. Instant diagnosis jelled swiftly into received wisdom. The Labour landslide, it is widely assumed, was caused by Mandelson's 'Magnificent Millbank Machine'; the *Sun*'s switching of sides to Labour; the Referendum Party's splitting of the Conservative vote; the Conservatives' position on Europe; tactical voting; Tony Blair's personality and John Major's apparent lack of one.

Some of these assumptions are false; some are only partly true. Now the dust has settled and the numbers have been crunched, it is appropriate to separate myth from reality and review theories of voting behaviour and assumptions about campaigns in the light of the result.

THE 1997 ELECTION OUTCOME

How should we describe the 1997 election result? The usual label is 'Labour landslide', in the sense that it produced the largest Labour majority (179) and the largest number of Labour MPs (419) in history, with the largest swing (10.3 per cent) since 1945, twice that of the Conservatives' victory in 1979 (5.2 per cent). However, analysis of the votes cast rather than seats won alters this perspective; Labour's share of the vote, at 44.4 per cent, was better than any election since 1970, but – note – lower than in any election from 1945–66, including those it lost in the 1950s. Taking turnout into account, we see that only 30.9 per cent of the registered electorate – less than one in three – came out and voted Labour. This hardly amounts to a mass mobilisation for political renewal.

'Lib Dem Breakthrough' perhaps? Again, only in one sense. The Liberal Democrats increased their number of seats to 46, their largest total since 1929, becoming a serious parliamentary group for the first time since the 1920s. But, again, if votes rather than seats are the focus, the Lib Dem share, at 17.3 per cent, was 1 per cent down on 1992, and fell for the third election running, following its 26 per cent peak in 1983. Then, however, 26 per cent delivered 23 seats; this time 17 per cent delivered twice as many. Then the electoral system punished the Liberal/SDP Alliance savagely; this time it was much more lenient.

'Conservative Catastrophe' is the most accurate description. In 1997 the Conservatives received their lowest share of the vote (31.5 per cent) since 1832, and saw the smallest number of MPs (165) elected since 1906.

There was a complete wipe-out in Scotland and Wales, leaving the Conservatives without any seats in these countries. There was also a clearout of Conservative MPs in the big cities outside London: no seats were held in Newcastle, Leeds, Hull, Bradford, Nottingham, Leicester, Manchester, Liverpool, Sheffield or Bristol, and just one in Birmingham.

Even so, the Conservative percentage of the vote (at 31.5 per cent) did not ebb as far as Labour's did in 1983 (28 per cent). In 1983, under Margaret Thatcher, the Conservatives had a 16 per cent lead and an overall majority of 144. In 1997, Labour, under Tony Blair, had a 13 per cent lead but an overall majority of 179. Evidently, the electoral system was working for Labour and against the Conservatives, an issue we return to later.

TURNOUT

The left and centre like to depict 1997 as a dramatic turning point in British political history – a watershed comparable with 1945 and 1906. 'Were you still up when Portillo went down?' they ask of election night. But the turnout, at 71.3 per cent, was the lowest since 1935 – when there was no television, no computer-based canvassing and women had been enfranchised for less than two decades.

The low turnout is a puzzle. All the elements for a high turnout were present: a long build-up to the election with six weeks of intensive media coverage; the emergence of the Referendum Party, providing a new, nation-wide party; as well as a record number of candidates. The weather on election day was fine, the electoral register was new, and there was the clear and determined desire to turf out the government.

Why, then, such a low turnout? This was not caused by Conservative abstentions: the turnout fell least in safe Conservative seats and most in safe Labour seats. There is no definitive answer, but a probable explanation is a combination of factors. New Labour's move to the ideological centre led to a sharp drop in the percentage of voters seeing a large difference between the parties. Sleaze created disillusion with politicians of all parties, and Labour had abandoned its safe seats in order to concentrate, ruthlessly, on the marginals it needed to win. There was virtually no campaign on the ground in Labour's traditional heartlands.

EXPLANATIONS FOR THE RESULT

The fundamental feature of the Conservative disaster is the extent to which the election campaign itself was irrelevant. If there had been a nation-wide strike of journalists – a news blackout from the day the election was announced – the result would have been virtually the same.

Most voters, including those who had decided to switch to Labour from the Conservatives, had made up their mind well before the campaign. The party choice of the minority who left it until the campaign to decide was largely self-cancelling but, if anything, favoured the Liberal Democrats at the expense of Labour. Indeed, the 31.5 per cent Conservative vote was higher than at any time before or after the election in 1997. Thus, all explanations which assume that features or characteristics of the campaign itself were crucial, fail.

Labour's superior organisation ('Mandelson's Magnificent Millbank Machine')

The average Labour lead over the Conservatives in the opinion polls during the campaign fell from 22 per cent in weeks one and two; to 21 per cent in week three; to 18 per cent in week four; to 17 per cent in week five; to 15 per cent in week six; to 16 per cent in the final days; and finally to 13 per cent in the actual election. This amounts to a 'loss' of 2.25 million Labour supporters over the campaign. Analysis of performance in the target seats shows that Labour's share of the votes rose 12.5 per cent points in 100 target seats but by 13.6 per cent in non-target seats!

Labour's campaign machine failed to mobilise anything like full Labour support. Arguably, it consolidated Labour's pre-campaign position, and was effective as a 'banana-skin' avoidance machine, and helped catalyse effective tactical voting (see below).

The Murdoch Press

The 1997 election was certainly an historical landmark, in that for the first time since 1945, the majority of newspapers, including all the tabloids, supported Labour. Moreover, the Conservative press that stayed loyal was distinctly lukewarm, as David McKie demonstrates in this volume in his chapter analysing press allegiance.

There is no evidence that the switch of the *Sun* and *News of the World* threw the election to Labour. In fact, support for Labour declined slightly in the polls after these tabloids publicly endorsed Tony Blair.

The main impact of the press occurred much earlier in the parliament. The disillusion of traditional Conservative newspapers with the government in general, and John Major in particular, precluded a revival of Conservative support among readers of the tabloids of the kind that marked the 1987 and 1992 elections. Labour did not win because the *Sun* backed it; rather, the *Sun* backed Labour because Labour was going to win.

'The Referendum Party lost it for the Conservatives'

The Referendum Party ran candidates in most seats (547), together with the UK Independence Party, taking 3.1 per cent of the vote, but up to 9 per cent in some rural and seaside seats with large numbers of elderly people. Its vote share exceeded the Labour or Lib Dem majority in 19 seats lost by the Conservatives.

The common assumption is that these were natural but disillusioned Conservatives, who would have stayed loyal in the absence of the Referendum Movement or if the Conservative government had taken a more resolutely anti-European position. This is not the case, however. Referendum Party voters were more likely to have voted Conservative in 1992, but not overwhelmingly; around half did so. The Conservative vote did not fall most where Referendum Party candidates did best; rather, the Liberal Democrat vote did. The Referendum Party's support was a symptom, not a cause, of the Conservative disaster. The intervention of this new party led to a net loss of only three Conservative seats.

TACTICAL VOTING

One feature of the campaign that *did* matter was tactical voting. To a greater degree than ever before, determined anti-Conservatives worked out which party in their constituency had the best chance of defeating the local Conservative candidate and voted accordingly, irrespective of their normal party allegiance. Where this was not obvious they relied on constituency polls, where available. The *Observer*/ICM poll of 16 Conservative seats on the Sunday before polling was particularly influential, for example, in Michael Portillo's and William Waldegrave's seats.

Tactical voting turned what would have been an emphatic Labour victory into a landslide. It lost the Conservatives 43 additional seats, gave the Lib Dems 46 instead of 28 and Labour 419 instead of 394, and an overall majority of 179 instead of 131.

1997 AND MODELS OF VOTING BEHAVIOUR

The campaign itself was largely irrelevant. All the events, incidents and media hullabaloo of the campaign counted for little. The Conservatives were well beaten long before – but when exactly, and why?

The monthly opinion polls show that the Conservative government was doomed almost as soon as it was so unexpectedly elected in April

1992. Its fate was sealed on 16 September 1992, 'Black Wednesday', when Britain was forced to abandon the European Exchange Rate Mechanism and, in effect, to devalue sterling.

Before Black Wednesday, the Conservatives were marginally ahead in the polls, at 42–43 per cent. Almost overnight, however, their position was transformed – and doomed. Thereafter, Conservative support never exceeded 33 per cent and Labour always enjoyed a double-digit lead.

From 1993, Conservative Party support was always below 30 per cent and Labour's lead was always above 20 per cent. From summer 1994, when Tony Blair became Labour leader, the Labour lead was consistently above 25 per cent, until the beginning of 1997, when there was a tiny narrowing of the gap to 20 per cent. Poll data were corroborated by unprecedented Conservative disasters in by-elections, local elections and Euro-elections.

The normal pattern is for the government to suffer a short-lived dip in popularity in the middle 18 months of the parliament, lose a few by-elections, only to recover strongly in its final year as party loyalties reassert themselves and voters respond to a government-induced economic boom. But the Major government presided over the longest, deepest slump this century. The failure of the Major government to recover fatally undermines two long-established models of voting behaviour.

First, the party-identification model. This theory assumes that most voters have a deep-seated party loyalty, based on enduring social identities such as class and ethnicity, which are inherited from their parents, confirmed in youth and strengthened with age. In mid-term elections, when the Westminster government is not at stake, voters will forswear their party allegiance as a safe protest, especially for the Lib Dems and nationalist parties, but at a general election, party loyalty resurfaces.

Evidently, this did not happen in 1997. Party loyalties had become too weak and the long-term trend in partisan dealignment continued apace. Conservative identifiers did not return to the fold but strayed – the majority of them all the way over the hill to Labour. They had been fatally weakened by the failures of the Conservative government, the ambivalence of the Tory press and class dealignment, i.e., the diminishing impact of social-class background on voting behaviour.

In 1997 class-based voting was weaker than at any time since 1945, with Labour achieving its highest ever level of support among the middle class (ABC1s), and affluent, (ex-)Conservative-voting London suburbs, such as Finchley, Wimbledon, Southgate, Harrow, and Surbiton, returning Labour or Liberal Democrat MPs.

Second, the economic model of voting collapsed. The 1997 election showed that the economy does not necessarily matter above all else. Everybody knows, or rather thought they knew, that voters reward governments when times are good and punish governments when times are bad. By all the usual indicators, times were exceptionally good in May 1997, with 3 per cent annual growth, historically low inflation, steadily falling unemployment, a long bull run in the City, a reviving property market and TESSA (Tax-Exempt Special Savings Account) and demutualised building society windfalls in people's pockets. Yet the government presiding over the best economic news and healthiest economy for two generations suffered a resounding defeat. Moreover, it was hit hardest where the economy was steaming ahead fastest – in London and the South-East.

Why, then, did the economic model fail? It was not because voters failed to recognise the economic upswing. Economic optimism did slowly return in the final year. Indeed, econometric analysis shows that without the economic recovery, the Conservatives would have done even worse: instead of 31.5 per cent of the vote and 165 seats, they might have received just 26 per cent of the vote and a mere 120 seats.

The model failed for two reasons: first, because voters refused to give the Conservatives the credit. As Danny Finkelstein's chapter in this volume emphasises, 'The feelgood factor' only half operated. Voters felt good about the economy but not about the government. The Conservatives had lost their priceless electoral asset: a reputation for economic competence. It was destroyed on 'Black Wednesday'.

Second, because the economy had ceased to be a problem, voters' concerns turned to other problems, notably spending on health, education and pensions, on which voters were massively dissatisfied with the government. In recession, such as in 1992, voters perhaps care more about taxes than spending; in booms, such as in 1997, the opposite applies.

BIAS OF THE ELECTORAL SYSTEM

A combination of tactical voting and the tendency to lose most where they were strongest led to a disproportionately severe defeat for the Conservatives.

Disproportionality between votes and seats is a well-known feature of the British first-past-the-post electoral system, but is often justified on the grounds that it produces an overall majority for the winning party and thus strong government; so voters are given the choice between a strong Conservative or a strong Labour government.

However, the electoral system is now so stacked against the

Conservatives that in reality that claim can no longer be made. Assuming a uniform national swing:

- if Labour and Conservative had an equal share of votes, Labour would get 79 more seats;
- for the Conservatives to win as many seats as Labour, they would need to be 6.7 per cent ahead;
- Labour could win an overall majority even if 1.5 per cent behind in the popular vote;
- but the Conservatives would need to be 10 per cent ahead for a bare overall majority.

This bias has occurred because Labour and the Lib Dems now distribute their votes much more efficiently across constituencies, owing partly to anti-Conservative tactical voting and partly to the fact that Labour seats are smaller in size and have lower turnouts: in 1997 9,000 fewer people voted in Labour than in Conservative seats. To win the next election by a single seat, the Conservative Party needs an 11.5 per cent swing – even more than Labour achieved in 1997.

The Labour government has enjoyed a prolonged honeymoon in office, while William Hague has found his first year as Conservative leader a challenging experience. Perhaps the Conservatives will reverse their long-standing opposition to proportional representation; it may be the factor most likely to save them from another defeat at the next election.

This book, the fifth in a series dating back to 1979, examines the interaction of politicians, spin-doctors, the media, pollsters and pundits, and how these impact on the public. The art and science of political communications at the end of the twentieth century are examined by those directly involved in the campaign itself, as well as by academic scholars. The television debate that never took place, the role of the Internet and the issues involved in regulating the media are three of the topics explored in this book. Conventional wisdom on voting behaviour was turned upside down in the 1997 general election, the outcome of which will go down in history as being as remarkable as that of 1906.

New election, New Labour, new government, new century.

John Bartle
Ivor Crewe
Brian Gosschalk

PART I:

PARTY STRATEGIES

1

Why Labour Won

PHILIP GOULD

The election of the Labour government on 1 May was the end of a journey. Not just for me, and for those in the Labour Party who had been working so long to get Labour elected – 18 years certainly gives new meaning to the notion of a long campaign – but to many at the special post-election conference also. For four elections Labour electoral failure has been scrutinised, dissected and analysed. For Labour, almost, but never quite, a corpse, this procedure has always been less academic review, more autopsy.

As Labour stumbled from defeat to defeat it was never quite alone. The psephologists were always there: not quite participants, but never just observers, dedicated followers of failure, always wanting to make sense of yet another defeat, always willing to speculate that, yes, it was possible that one day Labour might win. If nothing else it was comforting to know that, even as we lost, somebody cared.

Not that we took their advice. In the aftermath of 1992 we were advised that leadership had not been a decisive issue, that tabloid attacks had had no effect, that we could raise tax without fear of electoral damage, that few Conservative voters would switch directly to us without stopping first at the Liberals. Needless to say we based our strategy on precisely the opposite precepts and just managed to scrape home. I am sure, however, that if we had let Major out-gun us on leadership, had told Murdoch to jump in a ditch, had hiked up taxes and left Tory switchers to the Liberals, we would have won by a landslide.

I would hate to think that Labour's magnificent victory in May 1997 would put this small army of political pathologists out of work. For there is a new corpse on the table, younger certainly, smaller definitely, but capable, of giving analysts many years of dissecting pleasure. Already the first pathological study, 'Is Conservatism dead?', is published, and I am confident that there will be many more to come.

It is invidious to mention names but I would like to make special mention of Ivor Crewe, for his early and emphatic understanding of the smashed link between voter aspiration and Labour reality; of Roger

Jowell, for his understanding that, despite huge voter changes, the values still existed within the electorate that could sustain a Labour majority; and of Nick Moon, who was spot-on to the exact percentage point with his last private poll for the Labour Party. It is a pity his published polls were not quite so accurate, but you cannot have everything.

So after 18 years and hundreds of books, thousands of articles and hundreds of thousands of memos we finally got there. How did we do it?

The Labour victory of 1997 was the end of a journey that started in the 1950s with the first failed attempt at modernisation, which culminated in Gaitskell's failure to change Clause IV of the party's constitution. That was the crucial Labour failure, both the starting point of a period of modernisation that ended with the May 1997 triumph, and a defeat that condemned Labour to a 30-year struggle before it was able to gain final, ascendant victory.

Gaitskell's failure meant that Labour failed to become a modern party just as Britain was starting to modernise. It meant also that Wilson's governments were always essentially a fudge, balancing both wings of the party, not free to modernise Britain, because Labour had yet to modernise itself.

Wilson's defeat saw the ascendancy of the left and Labour's move from fudge to fundamentalism. This was a process which led directly to the defeat of 1983, which was without question the defining event of postwar Labour politics. 'Defining' is not a word used lightly, for it was this election, and the events leading up to it, that seared into the electoral consciousness of almost every voter in Britain an image so negative, so destructive, so alienating that it has taken 14 years, three leaders and a totally remade party to eradicate it.

The election of 1983 was the greatest betrayal by a progressive party of its supporters, and in particular its working-class supporters, that modern democratic politics has witnessed. It was not just that Labour was not listening. It was Labour declaring unrestrained war on the values, the instincts, the ethics of the great majority of hardworking, decent, ordinary voters. Labour unleashed upon its potential supporters the political equivalent of a first-strike nuclear attack, something incidentally it would not countenance in the event of genuine military attack from a mortal enemy.

The effect of this period and this defeat was devastating. Nothing about subsequent Labour politics can be understood without appreciating its full and awful damage. Like a freeze frame on a video, Labour's identity was frozen in time. Labour was the party of extremism, of union domination, of strikes, of roaring inflation and punitive taxation, of soft defence, of massive public ownership, of incompetence, of indiscipline, of disunity.

This negative Labour identity stuck, burrowing deep into the psyche of the British electorate, and casting a shadow of fear that was never truly removed until Labour had won and Tony Blair was in Downing Street.

It seemed that nothing could shift it – neither the extraordinary courage of Neil Kinnock nor the campaigning brilliance of Peter Mandelson. In 1987 we edged forward a couple of per cent, a tiny increase, but probably enough to secure the future of the party. In 1992 we achieved, again, only a tiny increase in the vote, despite the far-reaching changes of the Policy Review.

This time the Conservative majority was down to 20 seats and the enemy was in sight. But although we were now tantalisingly close, we were still separated from victory by a chasm.

This actual account of focus groups conducted in 1992 after the general election defeat illustrates the point:

1. *Labour is judged by its past*
Phrases associated with the party are:
   - winter of discontent
   - union influence
   - strikes
   - inflation
   - disarmament
   - Benn/Scargill
   - Brent/Islington
   - miners' strike/three-day week

2. *Labour's values are negative, aimed at depriving people of:*
   - wealth, in the form of taxes
   - choice in education and health
   - ownership, in the form of council houses

3. *Labour is hostile to:*
   - people who have money/savings/even pensions.
   - people who want to start their own businesses; and
   - people who want the best for their kids.

4. *Labour is no longer the party of 'ordinary working people'*
People are saying,
'I've left the Labour Party and the Labour Party has left me.'
'It's obvious isn't it: the better you are doing, the more money you have got, the more likely you are to vote Tory. It's hardly surprising.'

This was Labour's political landscape in 1992, and it had not substantially changed by the summer of 1994, when Tony Blair became leader. John Smith helped Labour, and he certainly healed Labour, but he did not transform perceptions of Labour. I conducted focus groups throughout this period and the identity of Labour was simply not improving. In the spring of 1994, just before John Smith's tragic death, levels of voter identification between the two parties were still running neck and neck.

The response of the new Labour leadership to this was categorical. Labour could not win an election unless it was effectively razed to the ground and rebuilt.

Rebuilding Labour had four components:

- a new party
- new campaigning principles
- new campaigning organisation
- new political purpose.

Making Labour a new party was the core, the absolute heart, of Labour's strategy; both for electoral success and success in government. This meant if not a new name, then at least a new designation. It meant shock not stealth, summed up by a completely uncompromising slogan: New Labour, New Britain. It meant the ditching of the old Clause IV of the party's constitution – which had, in theory, committed the party to wholesale nationalisation – and a doubling of membership, as well as new positions on business, the family, trade unions and crime. New Labour was our key to election victory. In the last few weeks of the campaign, as doubts grew, it was New Labour that saved us; New Labour that gave nervous voters the confidence to make the final jump.

But New Labour was not enough, and it certainly was not all we could offer. The new party was built on a set of ten new campaigning principles. These were:

1. **Concede and move on**: This was a subtle instinct, but it was an important one. It was to accept that on privatisation, on crime, on markets, the issue was settled. We decided to accept it and move on to new battles.
2. **New dividing lines**: This meant not accepting the political landscape as it stood. We wanted to remake the political map by establishing new dividing lines, new prisms through which politics was perceived. Not tax and spend, but save and invest; not private versus public, but partnership between the two.

3. **Take their ground (or rather take our own ground back)**: We would become the party of business, of the family, of responsibility, of enterprise, of getting on, of aspiration, of the people.
4. **Balance the positive with the negative**: We believed that negative hits would simply not get covered unless they were connected to a positive story. The electorate would not accept negative attacks unless they were balanced by positive messages and themes.
5. **Work with the news, rather than against it**: Broadcasting news has its own agenda and it is pointless fighting it. Shape the agenda certainly, but also exploit the agenda that is in place.
6. **Never compromise on trust**: Trust is completely indivisible. You cannot be a bit trusted. On any issue involving trust, we were emphatic. On tax, on public expenditure and on crime, we did not fudge.
7. **Put substance before style**: At a simple level this recognised that the electorate wanted real policy, real change, real commitment. They wanted always to look below the surface. But there is a deeper point too. In modern communications, rhetoric unmatched by reality is unlikely to be effective: words spoken have to be matched by deeds done. That is why the change to Clause IV was so effective, as was – at a lower level – the balloting of our manifesto. Real events, real battles, real tension, genuine uncertainty: that is what is necessary to persuade the modern voter.
8. **Remorseless, unceasing focus on 1992 Tory voters**: We never deviated from this; they were always our target.
9. **Neutralising tax as an issue**: This was a fetish for us. We were certain that we had lost elections in the past partly because of tax, and we were determined not to let it happen again this time.
10. **Small, concrete promises**: In the face of the cynicism and mistrust that was the predominant mood of the pre-election voter, small, costed, achievable promises were essential to gain trust. They were small only to us, of course. To the voter they were huge: real changes to those crucial areas of their lives that they considered were beyond changing.

A new party meant new principles, but also a new campaigning organisation. We restructured our campaigning around a war-room in which all campaign operations and all campaign personnel were in the same physical space; opposition activity was constantly monitored; attacks were instantly rebutted; dialogue with the electorate was constant. From top to bottom, voter feedback was built into the system.

But all this would have been useless without political purpose and a political project. This was the fundamental first base from which we all started. In notes for the leadership election in 1994, Tony Blair wrote: 'We have to renew Britain as a strong society – one-nation socialism – but do it for the modern world.' These two themes, renewal and modernity, and cohesiveness and community, have dominated Labour's discourse over the last few years. Together they have always been New Labour's big idea. The three years prior to 1 May 1997 saw the interweaving of these four pillars of new Labour: (1) building a new party; (2) implementing new campaigning principles; (3) creating a new campaigning organisation; (4) developing our political project. This was the political revolution that was New Labour.

Labour was not alone in its journey. The Conservatives were on a journey of their own. In the 1950s they caught the popular mood for affluence and post-war aspiration; in the 1980s they identified directly with the hard-nosed ambitions of a new working class, exemplified by probably the most successful postwar policy: the sale of council houses. The Conservatives became the party of the aspiring working class, of the new middle class, of the people. But two things undid them.

In the first place, they confused winning elections with support for their values. This support did exist but only to a degree. The main reason that the Conservatives won was because Labour was not electable. That meant that health, education and the state of society, all vital issues for the electorate, were neglected by the government.

Second, in their desperation to retain power, they did two things. They expanded the economy so quickly that the crash was devastating, attacking their middle class and rising working class with a venom and ferocity of which early Labour would have been proud. And they lied about tax, about the state of public finances and the point at which the recession was likely to end.

This combination, of a nation fearful about the state of education and health, and brutally hurt by soaring interest rates, negative equity and the constant threat of repossession of their houses, left the middle classes of middle England bruised and betrayed. If the European Exchange Rate Mechanism (ERM) debacle and the constant Tory divisions over Europe are added in, this can fairly be described as the greatest betrayal in modern politics by a Conservative Party of its middle-class supporters.

This was the state of the two parties opening the race in 1994, just as Tony Blair became leader. Here was a Labour Party drenched with the imagery of the past, of extremism, of downward mobility, of working-class betrayal, but a party about to completely transform itself. And there was a Conservative Party which had been successful in the eyes of the electorate for many years, but now resented – even hated – for their betrayal of the middle class.

For Labour the campaign started the moment Tony Blair was elected leader of the Party. We had several worries. The first was time. Three years seemed too long to sustain an opinion poll lead that was so large. How could we retain momentum, how could we avoid getting stale?

The second was the concern that, at the death, hope would be beaten by fear, and that the voters would say, as they had always done: better the devil you know. The third was the economy. Perceptions of economic strength never stopped rising, and by the end over 70 per cent of the electorate thought that the economy was strong. We felt sure that at some point this would turn into votes. Finally, we had huge respect for our opponents: for their resources, for their previous successes, for their expertise. We always had a secret sense that whatever the evidence to the contrary, the Tories somehow had a secret plan that would work.

Our campaign had three broad phases. The first was the Clause IV period from October 1994 until the summer of 1995. This was to establish that Labour was new. The second was the period of definition: one nation, stakeholding and young country, from October 1995 until the spring of 1996. This was intended to establish our big themes of social inclusion, community, one-nation patriotism and renewal. The third was the period of the manifesto: this was designed to demonstrate that Labour had policies, that these policies were new and that the party endorsed them.

These three phases were not solo appearances. The Tories started to react. They started with a half-apology in late winter 1996 with 'It hurt but it worked', which was exactly on the right track. It was followed by a kind of hobbling half-campaign about Britain being best in Europe. This campaign, focusing on the country's economic success, was strategically exactly right. Apology and economic achievement, these should have been the foundation of the Tory campaign. They were – for about a fortnight.

Then the Tory campaign became derailed. They went onto the attack far too early, dislodging no voters and alienating their support base. They developed 'New Labour, New Danger', which conceded that we had changed. To us this was like rain in a drought. They stopped focusing on the economy and started to attack Tony Blair as evil incarnate – surely the biggest marketing debacle since the launch of new Coke.

We knew that the Tory advertising was losing them support so we focused on rebuttal, 'Same old Tories: same old lies', and positive communication of the pledges. This was much criticised at the time, but we knew that we were meeting the voter mood, whereas the Tories were clashing with it.

We expected a massive Tory tax attack at the beginning of January, but were met with 'It will all end in tears'. If anything this campaign alienated the voters more than the last. Conversely, we started the year with a positive statement of our vision and policies.

February did, however, see the voters getting nervous. For the first time switchers were confronted with the prospect of Labour winning and they started to panic. Our response to this was twofold: first reassurance, mainly in the form of the tax pledge. This, after New Labour itself, was, I believe, the single most important initiative of the campaign. Second, we decided to go positive.

We knew that the relentless negativism of the Tories was entirely counterproductive, and we decided to feed off this failure by producing nothing but positive posters for the whole of the rest of the campaign. By now we had settled on our campaign theme, 'Britain Deserves Better', developed in part because it was able to retain its validity, however strong the economy.

When the campaign proper started we thought we would win, but had no certainty as to by how much. I was aiming for a 10 per cent margin and 100 seats, but I was not sure we would get it.

Blair won the first day. I found Major calm and convincing outside Number 10 Downing Street, but the voters did not – they found him complacent. We decided to stay as positive as possible for as long as possible. Tony Blair was almost always positive in the opening period, exposing the negativism of Major. But increasingly we were outflanked by Ashdown, whose message of higher taxes to fund improvements in education was starting to break through by the middle of the campaign.

Although our lead was holding, the voters were always nervous, and their nerves intensified as we came under attack on trade unions, devolution, privatisation and air-traffic control. The Tories were of course in awful shape, as wave after wave of sleaze rocked their campaign. But in the early days sleaze was working to the disadvantage of both main parties, tarnishing the image of politicians. Only later was this to change.

In this middle campaign period the electorate were getting increasingly uneasy and nervous. We had to decide at what point to make the turn and move through the gears: both by being more assertive and more attacking. Major had an immediate boost from his 'don't bind my hands speech' on 16 April (although this quickly faded) and it was time to move. Tony Blair let rip at first in Scotland on 17 April, and then again in Stevenage on 22 April. The turn worked; all Labour's internal numbers started to move up.

The end of the penultimate week was dominated by pensions, following the Conservatives' decision to pour petrol on the flames of our fifth-term attack. This brought home to the voters the horror of another Conservative term, and gave us momentum going into the final week.

We expected a strong finish from John Major, but instead he faded and Tony Blair went up yet more gears, crying out against complacency ('This is not a landslide country,' he said), and storming the electorate through a succession of public meetings. Meanwhile Paddy Ashdown, after a good campaign, had lost his message and had no final week story. We were on the pitch almost alone.

But, almost until the last, the voters were nervous. The strike-ridden Winter of Discontent of 1978 and fear of old Labour were still haunting them. And then it happened. On the final Sunday before polling day, a group of women said, with one voice: that is it, I have talked to my friends and they are going to vote Labour, and I am going to vote Labour too. In the last weekend, the nation decided: hope would defeat fear.

It was the same on Monday, Tuesday and Wednesday (I was leaving nothing to chance). Caution and fear had gone: the voters were decided and confident. Late on Wednesday morning I packed my bags and left Millbank for the final time, walked to my wife's office and promptly fell asleep on the sofa after muttering something about a huge majority. For the first time in many, many years I could relax.

2

Why the Conservatives Lost

DANIEL FINKELSTEIN

This chapter will look at some of the strategic reasons why the Conservative Party lost the last general election, although at times during the campaign one might have been forgiven for believing that strategy, even politics, had nothing to do with it.

During the few weeks of the campaign itself a Scottish MP, who had previously resigned as a minister having been accused of threatening someone with an axe, was forced to resign his candidacy in a further scandal. The Scottish Party chairman, mooted as a replacement, had to stand down having been accused by colleagues of homosexual relationships with other Conservative activists. Two former government ministers were embroiled in the Harrods so-called 'cash-for-questions' affair. A Parliamentary Private Secretary was photographed in a park embracing a 17-year-old Soho nightclub hostess. A white-suited war hero BBC journalist, Martin Bell, decided to stand against the Tatton Conservatives with the help of David Soul from *Starsky and Hutch*. And, of course, there was the rebellion over European Monetary Union (EMU).

With all this going on, at times it seemed that the only strategy the campaign could cling to was: 'I am glad you brought that up because it is just what we wanted to talk about.' I believe that when forced back upon this, we implemented the strategy with verve, enthusiasm and skill. In particular, John Major showed his presence and quality with some superb performances. Yet disunity and scandal is hardly a recipe for victory.

Damaging though all of these events were, and impossible though they made it to develop and implement a successful campaign, they are not the real explanation of our defeat. I would like to offer four such reasons.

First, the result was a vote against Conservatives, not Conservatism. Our research showed that the basic attitudes of most voters have changed very little over the last decade. And although there are, and always have been, important differences, their instincts are generally very similar to those of most Conservative activists. Yet millions of people thought hard about how to defend our legacy and our common outlook and then went out and voted for Labour.

Why? Because, rightly or wrongly, they saw us as arrogant, smug, sleazy, weak, incompetent and divided. They desperately wanted a change and were prepared to take a risk to achieve it, although Tony Blair understood, as Neil Kinnock did not, that there were very strict limits to the willingness to take risks.

Second, it was not just us that they disliked for being Conservative, it was themselves they disliked. They began to see voting Conservative as something one only did if one was greedy. It was something one did for oneself, not for the country. This feeling had already begun to take hold in 1992 and is one of the explanations for the fact that opinion polls in 1992 underestimated our support.

In the 1980s people felt that by voting Conservative they were doing something for the country and not just themselves. We had a project (curing the 'British disease' of high inflation, over-regulation and poor industrial relations) that they thought was worthwhile. By 1992 they had begun to feel that the project was complete and that we did not have a new one. The only reason they could think of to vote for us was to protect their personal economic position from Neil Kinnock and his tax plans. They were embarrassed about this and did not tell the pollsters. Yet on the day they came out and voted Conservative once more.

When the government was forced to raise taxes temporarily to keep public finances sound after sterling left the European Exchange Rate Mechanism (ERM), the voters turned on us in fury. Whatever we did later we could not counter the fact that, as they saw it, we had betrayed their one reason for voting for us. It was a reason they had in any case been rather hesitant and defensive about. With hindsight, from the end of 1992 the government was probably doomed.

Yet perhaps some of the losses could have been reduced if we had succeeded in establishing a clear mission for the final term. The criticism that the government did not know what it stood for is wrong. So is the suggestion that it ran out of ideas. The Major government was creative and imaginative in many policy areas, and even at its end it produced an exciting and fresh manifesto.

However, after three terms, with a very small majority, a cynical press and a great deal of disunity, the challenge of rethinking and selling our purpose – 'why' we were needed rather than 'what' we stood for – proved impossible. It is the task for Opposition, which William Hague is taking up with vigour.

The result of this failure is that voters were left with New Labour's project – one that has been spectacularly successful. The project is to id of the awful Tories'. The voters wanted this project to succeed. every time Blair made a U-turn, the public cheered him and every time he stamped on a dissident they cheered him. They may or may not have liked certain decisions in themselves, but they could see they were necessary to achieving their shared goal.

The importance of having a purpose, a mission, that the public shares can best be illustrated by looking at the example of privatisation. Both British Telecom (BT) and British Rail (BR) privatisation were necessary and wise measures. Unfortunately, when they were proposed both were quite unpopular. Yet there was a difference between them. BT's privatisation, though unpopular as an individual policy, actually contributed something to Margaret Thatcher's popularity. The reason is that voters understood its purpose – to help cure the British disease – and were prepared to support policies they did not much like very much in order to further a purpose they did like. When BR privatisation began voters hadn't the same clear understanding of its purpose and so it was simply and straightforwardly unpopular.

Without a clear and fresh purpose, the Conservative Party in 1997 was like the Winter of Discontent running for office – we were the problem the voters were trying to solve.

The third reason for the defeat of the Conservatives was our failure to come to grips with New Labour. The fall of the Berlin Wall, four election defeats, the intellectual victory of Thatcherism, class changes in Britain and the leadership of Tony Blair have changed the Labour Party for ever. We did not adjust to this properly. Notwithstanding a decision to pursue a single, simple strategy ('New Labour, New Danger'), we made a whole range of inconsistent and often unconvincing attacks on our opponents. These included saying they were jackdaws ('Good', replied the voter) and that they haven't really changed ('They have', replied the voter). Often we appeared to be arguing that New Labour was a good thing, and that the public only needed to worry about 'old' Labour.

The fourth reason for defeat was the successful use by the Labour Party of certain campaign techniques. The media's obsession with these techniques was rather ridiculous. Sometimes they seemed to believe that we were both using computers to generate lines of argument. They were often more interested in reporting on the rapidity of rebuttal than on its content. I do not believe that any of this was anywhere near as important or impressive as the reporting suggests. Nevertheless it did have some impact on the result.

The financial problems the Conservative Party faced in 1992 absorbed the energy and time of the Central Office team for a long period after the election. When Brian Mawhinney arrived in 1995, preparations were behind schedule. He moved rapidly to create a new team and made important changes which will have lasting beneficial effect. In particular, he ensured that departments were far better integrated.

One consequence of our financial position was that the party spent money late on billboard advertising while Labour spent it early on staff and polling. A huge part of Labour's apparent superiority in terms of, say, rapid rebuttal was that they had a great deal more staff.

The Conservative Party was not, of course, the only group of people who lost the 1997 election. Our defeat was merely the most spectacular. The polling industry suffered another defeat. Their predictions were only a little better than in 1992 and for much the same reason. Most (ICM was an exception) failed in 1992 to account properly for the failure of Conservative voters to admit they were going to support us. They were saved from great embarrassment in 1997 only by Labour's landslide victory and by uneven swings.

Deciding whether ICM or their rivals got it right is vital in any analysis of the impact of the election campaign. The ICM version of the campaign is that the parties ended up pretty much back where they were when the election was called. During the campaign Labour's lead fell when John Major tackled EMU head-on, but then it rose again. The non-ICM version is that there was a late swing away from Labour in the last couple of days of the campaign.

Leaving statistical debates to one side, ICM's version seems much more credible to those of us at the centre of the campaign in the last week. It is certainly what we thought was happening.

Though it is less clear-cut, the election campaign defeated the broadcasters too. They, too, failed to adapt to New Labour. They accepted without demur the tactic of briefing heavily on stories that were later withdrawn, denied or had little substance. The emphasis that many programmes now put on covering news before it happens means that it is extremely difficult to subject any proposal to critical scrutiny. This problem, which is far worse with Labour in office, still defeats them. The broadcasters need to make changes.

Certainly, the Conservative Party needs to change, and under William Hague's leadership we have already begun to do so.

3

'Sausages or Policeman?' The Role of the Liberal Democrats in the 1997 General Election Campaign

RICHARD HOLME and ALISON HOLMES

1 April. 7.30 a.m. Punch and Judy? The general election had moved not to the seaside but to Church House, Westminster. John Major and Tony Blair (as Punch and Judy puppets created by the makers of *Spitting Image*) were entertaining journalists and crews over coffee from a miniature House of Commons – all bells and bats. It was the opening press conference of the Liberal Democrat election campaign.

A nice visual idea – and an expression of the Liberal Democrats' key election strategy, to differentiate itself from both the other parties, made easier in this case by the long period of 'hard pounding' between Tory and Labour which had characterised the run-up phoney war to the election proper.

Did the use of Punch and Judy cut across the other major Liberal Democrat strategy of positive campaigning? Perish the thought. After all it was April Fools' Day. Even before the first 8 a.m. press conference began, the Liberal Democrats looked different and acted differently. Ours became the campaign to watch for innovation and energy. Vincent Hanna immediately and typically caught the spirit of the event with his insightful question to Paddy Ashdown – and, by extension, to the party: Would the Liberal Democrats be the sausages or the policeman of the campaign?

This chapter will briefly outline the approach of the Liberal Democrats to the 1997 general election campaign. Our analysis is divided into three parts. The first sets out the view which the party took of the political climate in the 1992 parliament and the prospects for maximising the impact of our vote. The second looks at the creation of our strategy for the actual campaign and the positioning of the party to play to its perceived strengths. The third describes the implementation of that strategy during the course of the six long weeks of the campaign.

We conclude that the Liberal Democrats were able to take maximum advantage of a potentially difficult political climate. The campaign created a new space in which to argue the party's position and policies more clearly to the electorate than at any time since its creation. This election represents the party's move from being the beneficiary of the protest vote to becoming the home of a positive vote. In the terms posed by Vincent Hanna, we argue that the party succeeded in being the policeman of the 1997 election, bringing honesty, strength and confidence to a stage fraught with insecurities and false expectations, rather than being the squeezed-out sausages.

Let us first examine the context in which the Liberal Democrats prepared for the campaign. Almost from the close of poll in 1992 the tide had begun to turn against the Conservative government. They won the campaign but were fatally wounded in the fight. They struggled through the subsequent five years but always from the position of weakness.

However, since Conservatives were the incumbents in many of the seats we hoped to gain, we could not presume on their continued weakness and we watched vigilantly for signs of recovery.

The Labour Party, on the other hand, were devastated by the 1992 defeat and initially could not make hits – even on a weakened Tory government. But their fortunes began to change and, as inexorably as they moved onto our issues and policy territory, they climbed higher in the polls. The 'Blair revolution' changed the Labour Party from the inside out, presenting the Liberal Democrats with a new challenge. The pundits began to credit 'New Labour' with squeezing our vote and to predict – as so often before – our demise.

Almost the first act by the Liberal Democrats in the 1992 parliament was to abandon so-called 'equidistance'. The shift from a position which had proved so confusing during the 1992 campaign was significant to our ability to find a voice both in terms of our grassroots campaigns and our positioning as a party. 'No quarter for the Tories – no let up on Labour' was the line presented to the Glasgow conference in 1995 and seemed to have an energising effect on Liberal Democrats. It unified the party and allowed it to campaign positively at all levels on a focused and exclusively Liberal Democrat agenda.

The key component of our strategy was to target the most vulnerable seats. In the aftermath of the 1992 election one thing became clear. Campaigning in our best prospect seats needed to begin much earlier and needed resources – however limited the party's means – as soon as possible. 'Targeting' became the watchword of the party, and the first strategic decision of the 1997 election, made almost three years earlier, was that funding in those seats would start immediately. This decision to 'front-load' an already constrained election budget meant, even more than usual, that the campaign itself would have to be very 'lean'.

Regions were encouraged, where possible, to part-fund target seats, and the central operation created matching money schemes to make this more feasible and provide guidance. Many individual constituencies also undertook matching fund projects with the central operation. Each target seat was regularly measured against agreed criteria and required to produce a development plan for a minimum of two years. This was designed to cover every item of expenditure and include detailed plans for fund-raising over that period.

A process of funding, training and encouraging a cadre of target seats also produced an ethos of spreading best practice throughout regions and seats. The party had viewed the 1992 election as a 'developmental campaign' and that was not lost as we moved towards the 'targeting campaign'. Individuals, groups and regions all got involved in raising our party's standards across the board.

The length of the parliament, however, did begin to take its toll. Regions with few prospects grew increasingly concerned as resources for even some basic functions migrated towards regions and seats with higher hopes of success. This did not sit easily with our fundamental principle of equality. Post-election recriminations began to be a real possibility if the disparities in funding in the run-up to the election did not pay off in terms of real gains.

The party's message also needed to be more focused to deal with the 'Nobody knows what they stand for' problem. Education remained the priority. The party recognised it was the most widely known of the party's policies and remained high in public consciousness and on the political agenda. Health was also seen as an area in which the Conservative government had damaged their already weak position, and the Labour Party were increasingly not interested in defending the issue as its 'cost police' cracked down on any areas of potential spending.

So in parallel we began to develop our policies of honesty about taxation, which built on our 1992 position of 1p on tax for education and played to people's common sense realisation that better services were unlikely to be delivered without being paid for. Our advocacy of this position, which had the danger of having us portrayed as the high-tax party, nevertheless succeeded both in placing a burr beneath Labour's saddle and in assisting in our strategy of differentiation.

The environment also seemed, over time, to be one policy issue which both the other parties had abandoned. Despite – or perhaps because of – the party's difficulties in Newbury where David Rendel, the by-election victor in 1993, was supporting the bypass in the face of opposition from various environmental groups, the party's green credentials were worth making an issue where possible.

As the policy and campaigning agenda became more clear the acronym of the Liberal Democrat campaign became 'CHEESE'. This stood for Crime, Health, Education, the Economy, Sleaze (used for anti-Tory campaigning) and the Environment. In other words, we were determined to concentrate on issues which the public felt strongly about and the party had highlighted as core to our appeal.

As a matter of principle the party did not use polling to check, change or alter our policies. The party did, however, for the first time use polling to enable us to be more specific with our messages and to concentrate the campaign on those areas of policy which found more resonance with the electorate.

Approximately midway through the parliament the party also began, for the first time, to undertake a polling operation in individual target seats. This work was invaluable as we worked through our agreed agenda. Education and health moved further and further towards centre-stage and we planned accordingly.

The target seat polling information was then incorporated within a new programme of polling. We referred to this as our target voters in target seats – TVITS – strategy. The mythology of the third party vote has long included the truism that the third party does well in the 'Celtic fringe' or nonconformist parts of the country. This is despite evidence which suggests that during the course of the 1981–88 Liberal–SDP (Social Democratic Party) Alliance the vote was very evenly spread throughout the country. However, the grain of truth contained in the truism held sway – with many inside the party as well as outside.

The first task was to interrogate the information about our target seats to find any demographic similarities which may not be obvious in terms of their geography. This procedure uncovered several characteristics which helped shape various messages more specifically. Thus we found a high proportion of undecided voters in these seats to be women who, in turn, had a high propensity to be interested in our education message. The fact that as a result we won Twickenham and Richmond Park may not, with hindsight, have been a surprise to many, but we also won Sheffield Hallam, which makes these groupings more interesting.

This targeted polling led us to take a strategic decision about the relative electoral significance of questions on various issues as they affected the country, as opposed to how they affected the family. For example, Europe consistently appeared on the list of issues people felt were important for the country. However, when asked about issues that were important to their families, Europe invariably fell significantly or dropped off the list altogether. The ranking also varied according to gender.

In this context the Conservatives could be said to have fought a campaign of government on the national issues (frightened perhaps of their record on more family-oriented issues). The Labour Party fought a campaign between the two lists, wanting to look credible on issues of statesmanship and frightened of the cost implications of fighting solely on social issues. Liberal Democrats de-emphasised issues such as constitutional reform and Europe, assuming that our position was well known, and concentrated on health and education and honesty in taxation.

Pollsters and pundits regard voting intention as statements of fact – albeit temporary. Our view of undecideds was purely pragmatic. For our party, in campaigning terms, the large number of undecideds as well as many 'soft' Labour voters were seen as being as open to persuasion, as were potential 'voters on the move'. Therefore, we developed a new range of literature which included more fine-tuning for those households where voters were looking around to be persuaded. The Liberal Democrat agenda had a great deal of potential with this group if we got our information to them. This proved to be fruitful ground for conversion locally.

The number of women who entered the election period as undecideds was also of great importance to us as a party. Our agenda appealed directly to the priorities expressed by women. Our job was to ensure those women heard our message on the issues they put high on their agenda.

We needed to find more and better ways of maximising our vote and the impact of our vote. Over the course of the parliament we had learned how to beat the system effectively. As a party, we knew we could gain more seats despite the electoral system. However, the evidence also seemed to suggest that, as we gained better results in terms of seats, we could be opening ourselves to a potential reduction in the overall vote.

The general election context meant that we needed to target for seat maximisation but to lose as few votes as possible in the process. An election in which the government was steadily on the way out but in which the official opposition party was unable to propose anything to the electorate for fear of reprisal, gave space for both of those propositions to work in favour of the third party.

What, then, of the campaign itself?

The analysis of the political climate only sets the context for the campaign. The task before the Liberal Democrats was to build a campaign within that context which was credible to the media and to use all our resources, both human and financial, to reinforce that credibility. There is a delicate balance in the relationship between the way in which the media portrays the party nationally and our perceptions of our own ability to win our target seats. When that relationship is working, each constituency campaign is able to reinforce the national message and thus give it strength. When it breaks down, each constituency becomes isolated and distances itself from the national campaign, thus harming itself and the national campaign at the same time.

The theme we adopted was 'Make the Difference'. This appealed strongly to the core constituency of party activists and workers since it gave them a feeling of purposive evangelism. It also was a summary of and a framework for our sharper policy positions to the electorate, as well as a statement of style. The key to memorability for the Liberal Democrats was to be different.

The party spent roughly £2.75 million centrally on the election in 1997. We had spent approximately £2.2 million in 1992. If we take central and constituency expenditure together, the total dedicated spend on the election in 1997 was around £5 million, a fraction of the sums spent by Labour and the Conservatives.

The only effective way to deal with such a disparity in spending between the parties was to concentrate, that is, to target not only our seats but every element of our campaign, and always play to our strengths.

The first and foremost of these strengths was obviously our party leader. Every poll, every focus group and every instinct told us that Paddy Ashdown was the most popular and most trusted leader of the three main parties. He entered the election as the oldest party leader, but that suggested experience and understanding. The popularity he gained in the 1992 election was generally sustained through the parliament and clearly evident again throughout the 1997 election. Given that John Major was more popular than his party – slightly – and Tony Blair was seen, particularly by women, as an unknown quantity, we could only welcome the inevitable comparison of leaders.

However, in the light of the fact that analysis of past election coverage, and particularly of third parties in British politics, indicates that the leader of the party gets the overwhelming share of the coverage, the general election team decided that we needed to extend our profile to other leading figures who would complement the leader and broaden the image of the party.

A key item on the agenda of our high-level meetings with broadcasters, both centrally and regionally, was to discuss spokespeople and requirements throughout the campaign to facilitate getting our other leading spokespeople on air and give the leader more space to concentrate on national events.

However, the trend towards televisual campaigns or presidential politics seemed inexorable, and therefore the leader's campaign would be crucial to the way in which our campaign was perceived. We began his series of visits a full year before the election, building on his 'beyond Westminster' programme in the early years of the parliament. These visits served three purposes: the first was to provide media opportunities for the party in mid-term to highlight what would be our campaigning issues – health and education. The second was to enable target seat candidates to gain regional profiles on those issues and highlight their ongoing campaigning work. Third, we were able to provide test runs for visits during the election.

The 1992 Ashdown campaign had been famous for the leader's whirlwind tour. This was deemed necessary for both the party and Ashdown, since the election was the first under his leadership. The second election for both did not demand such a schedule, and given the likelihood of Paddy Ashdown becoming a grandfather during the course of the election it seemed more and more inappropriate, despite his superabundant energy, to undertake anything so gruelling for all concerned. However, we also made other variations not only to the leader's tour but the way we included a supporting cast in other events – thus supporting our wider team. We reserved the 'whirlwind' for the last week in order to build on the accurate perception of gathering momentum.

Paddy Ashdown attended most morning press conferences. He missed approximately one a week, often taking those from Scotland or Wales. He undertook approximately two to four constituency visits in any one day, with two highlighted for attention. We reduced the number of rallies from 11 in 1992 to nine in 1997 – three of which were in the last week, reflecting the different tempo of this campaign. At the same time we increased the number of rallies staged by the central party for colleagues. In 1992 there were no rallies not addressed by the leader; in 1997 there were four. In this way, and by the careful placement of leading figures in main interviews, we were able to enhance the profile of colleagues such as Roy Jenkins, David Steel, Shirley Williams, Charles Kennedy, Menzies Campbell, Malcolm Bruce, Alan Beith and Emma Nicholson, while not overusing the leader.

We added another type of event to the daily schedule which would play to Paddy Ashdown's strengths, as well as to the polling evidence of the attitudes of our target audience. This event was termed an 'open circle'. It consisted of 15–20 people all linked by an interest in a particular issue. For example, a health open circle would obviously have doctors and nurses but would also include ambulance drivers, medical students, nursing home administrators and NHS trust managers. We tested the event in several party political broadcasts before the election and they received a good response from the public, in particular women and the increasing number of people who felt that politicians did not listen. In the course of the election these events were somewhat difficult to cover and did not always convey exactly the sense we had achieved in the run-up to the campaign. We dropped the final event of this kind, but the general impression remained of a leader willing to talk to real people in small groups about issues of concern which they knew well as professionals in the field under discussion.

The other innovation was developed literally in response to the length of the campaign. This type of event became known as the 'opt out'. This enabled Paddy Ashdown to make an extended visit of a more personal nature to an area and get involved in depth in issues of concern which the party had highlighted in its manifesto, while not bringing hordes of journalists to yet another site for the photo-opportunity.

Our campaign became known for these types of innovations. 'Election Call with John Cleese' was memorable. In an event captured on television, he telephoned people who had responded to the television broadcast he made for the party before the election. We also held 'An Afternoon with Peter Ustinov and Shirley Williams', which also took the media by surprise. Our regular briefings on other issues such as small businesses and with sections of the media such as women and the ethnic minority press also moved the party towards wider audiences.

Advertising was always going to be limited on our stretched budget. In the event, the fleet of mobile poster vans, the 'Super site' at Vauxhall Cross (a special poster site where we displayed our posters temporarily for the media), regional advertising and the broadcasts formed a coherent if limited whole. Each type of media supported other events. No activity stood in isolation but worked with other areas of the campaign. Mobile posters became press events for target seats and regional media. The Super site supported the launch of the campaign and the Punch and Judy motif of the first week. Regional advertising helped support the rally operation and the broadcasts supported the Punch and Judy theme, the open circle events and the leadership of the campaign.

This different style of event and approach seemed to find resonance with the electorate. If the broadcasts are any indication, what became known as 'the Ashdown movie' was by a long way the most watched PEB of the campaign, and in the week it was shown came 31st of all programmes transmitted, according to BARB. It was an unashamed attempt to bring out the humanity and diverse experience of a very atypical politician.

Our campaign had a core daily structure based around the press conference and the leader's activities, but this election saw more innovative events and more variety. Each event in and of itself was not crucial to the outcome or as turning points, but as part of the whole they formed a campaign which had energy and communicated a positive sense of the party. This strategy proved successful as the other two parties stalled in the polls and our party began to move up. The stalemate of Punch and Judy politics granted the policeman enough space and the media granted enough air time for the campaign to be creative and energetic and hammer away on the positive agenda the party had for the electorate.

The greatest single challenge of a gruelling campaign is to stay 'on message'. Relatively early in 1997 hints and leaks suggested a long campaign. Easter, the change of the clocks and seasonal shifts in weather all clouded the indications, but the Conservatives appeared to take a strategic decision to grind the electorate (and the other parties) through a long costly campaign. The 'pending period' as stipulated in broadcasters' guidelines had varying start dates but most moved into a near-campaign mode from the new year.

This produced various problems for the Liberal Democrats. The first was the workload, given the increase in volume of political news and programming which had to be supported and co-ordinated. The second was our own ability to staff an upgraded operation. Our professional staff are supplemented during campaigns by volunteer members of the general election team. This volunteer effort was not available to the party until the 'proper' four-week campaign. This created the related problem – physical exhaustion. Running on such a lean machine meant that staying on message was a battle against sleep as much as anything else, especially as the campaign wore on. The final problem was financial. Having paced the campaign to this point we were forced to sustain our highest level of spending up until the campaign proper finally started.

The reality of this situation meant that the 'extra' two weeks at the front of the campaign were fuelled more by imagination and quick thinking than funded, orchestrated events. We began to spread out various planned campaign events such as the leader's bus and posters over a longer period. It was not ideal, but the length of time before the campaign proper meant that when the general election plan took over it was detailed enough to sustain the effort.

From Punch and Judy to polling day we were well on message – and the central command, communication and central management capability was institutionalised in a communication centre, into which all information flowed and from which decisions, initiatives and the 'line' flowed out.

Apart from the drama unfolding in Tatton, the other preoccupying issue was that of the leaders' debate. In the 1992 campaign we opened with the 'Ashdown challenge' which included the invitation to the other two leaders to a three-way debate. The broadcasters and other political parties were not interested and the idea disappeared without trace.

In the run-up to the 1997 campaign the Liberal Democrats again supported the idea of a debate and discussed this at various meetings with broadcasters during the planning of the campaign. At no early stage did the broadcasters engage in serious negotiations on the idea. It was assumed that it would not happen unless the Prime Minister agreed and most felt he would not agree unless he was in trouble during the campaign. This attitude meant that it could not be taken forward.

This campaign, however, was different. The Conservatives began to show interest in the idea and broadcasters began to compete to find the formula which would persuade John Major. This Tory-led approach made progress difficult as negotiations got serious. There was a moment when a compromise formula involving Paddy Ashdown as a full participant was almost reached but then the process expired, not least from lack of time, in bickering and backbiting.

There are two other broadcasting issues which created the climate of those six weeks. The first is the interpretation of the 1983 Representation of the People Act (RPA). The third party in British politics undoubtedly benefits from the protections offered under this act. The increase in coverage for our party and its policies gives the voter, who normally sees less of the third party given the prejudices of the media, access to more information and background to the issues being discussed.

If 'news' values were allowed to be determined by news organisations alone, the agenda on which the Liberal Democrats fought this campaign might well not have been given a voice. More important, the issues on which people consistently wanted to know more about what the political parties were offering would not have found an airing. The other two parties were involved in a conspiracy of silence. The media often require a yes/no answer to involved questions of policy. This does not encourage sensible debate. Which party discussed the environment? Which party honestly discussed spending priorities? Which party explained its taxation policies? Some political parties would do a deal with their political enemy if it meant that both could remain silent on difficult issues. Both major parties adopted this strategy over Europe in 1997. However, by ensuring that the third party has a significant voice, the RPA is a strong defence against this process.

The ability of the Liberal Democrats to stay with our agenda, or stay on message, enabled us to differentiate ourselves from the other political parties. We offered a different style, a different approach and a more relevant agenda. This was rewarded with voter confidence.

A second broadcasting issue related to the allocation and content of PPBs (party political broadcasts). It will remain an issue throughout the 1997 parliament and is of particular importance to smaller parties.

Party political broadcasts began as part of the BBC's duty to inform and educate. The parties are granted time and by and large allowed to do anything they wish with this time. The 1997 election campaign period was significant on this front in two ways. The rules were changed in the run-up to this election in terms of the allocation of broadcasts, and it was the first occasion on which a broadcast was banned. These two developments are worrying.

The Liberal Democrats and its predecessor parties have spent considerable time and money on party political broadcasts while watching this system develop over the years. We were concerned to see that parties with no electoral support could effectively buy PPBs. We were also disturbed by the banning of an election broadcast by the anti-abortion coalition. This prohibition was imposed by a broadcasting committee whose procedures are opaque and not subject to further appeal. This state of affairs could represent a serious threat to free political broadcasts.

Commentators often lament the onset of the 'Americanisation' of British politics. But in the United States these characteristics are primarily due to the fact that it has neither a public service ethic in political broadcasting nor 'free' television time for election broadcasts. The duty to educate and inform and the duty to be balanced are the only defence against 'Americanisation'. If they are usurped by commercial demands and the obsession with viewing figures, the country will deserve the shallow debate that will result.

In conclusion, we believe:

First, Liberal Democrats, judging by both press coverage and polling evidence, fought a well-respected campaign, which enhanced the party's reputation and that of its leader. The campaign gave it a clearer position and policy profile and, most importantly, provided the context and backing for victory in 46 seats, exceeding our highest estimates and representing the best third-party result since 1929.

Second, the policy of targeting which has been part of the party's development over the past 40 years, first in local government and then in all elections, was wholeheartedly pursued and served us well. The party's co-efficient of seats won to votes cast has steadily improved in general elections.

Third, the management of the campaign, and consequently its message, was tighter and better integrated than before, with an effective back-up of internal communication to the campaigning party and external communication via the media to the electorate.

Finally, although many people had expected us, entering the election with support estimated by the opinion polls at 10–11 per cent, in the face of a very smooth, careful and lavishly funded New Labour campaign, to be squeezed out – to be the sausages in fact – in the event we were the policemen, increasing the vote share to 17–18 per cent, winning many seats and conducting a straightforward, convincing and trustworthy campaign.

e Role of Labour's Advertising in the 1997 General Election

CHRIS POWELL

Labour's poll lead entered double figures in September 1992 and reached its zenith – just under 40 points – in December 1994, shortly after the election of Tony Blair as the new leader. Labour's campaign strategy, therefore, addressed itself to the maintenance of this lead.[1]

This chapter attempts to provide an analysis of the role played by advertising in the campaign. It is virtually impossible to isolate the effect of advertising as distinct from other elements of the campaign. However, we will argue that the selection of advertising messages – and in particular the focus on taxation – was important in crystallising a decision to vote Labour among our key target of switcher voters.

The run-up to the 1997 election was highly propitious for Labour. The early 1990s bore witness to the deepest and broadest-hitting recession since the Second World War, which in turn created widespread disillusionment with the Conservatives (see below). The emergence of New Labour coincided with the descent of the Conservative Party into sleaze and scandal. In the opinion polls, Labour overtook the Tories on both voting intention and economic competence just a few short months after the 1992 election.

However, despite these favourable conditions, two issues gave cause for concern: first, the improvement in the 'feel-good factor', which threatened to make switcher voters 'stick with the devil they knew'. Second, among switcher voters, support for Labour was vulnerable to Tory attack.[2] Indeed, even quite close to the election, several opinion polls indicated that a large proportion of them claimed that they might yet change the way they intended to vote.[3]

OUR STRATEGIC TASK

In order to hold on to the fragile support of the Tory switchers, Labour's campaign needed to do three things:

1. exploit Tory weaknesses (chiefly their economic record);
2. neutralise any (latent) Tory strengths (the re-emergence of economic optimism and the superior rating of John Major above his party);
3. exploit our strengths (Tony Blair, five pledges).

Research indicated that 'economic issues' should form the backbone of the campaign. Nevertheless, attacking John Major and exploiting Labour strengths had an important role to play.

At the core of the advertising campaign lay an assumption that among switchers, final voting behaviour would be heavily influenced by their perception as to which party would improve (or present least risk to) their personal prosperity. This assumption was based on three separate strands of evidence.

First, both quantitative and qualitative evidence from the 1992 general election indicated that, while Labour led the Tories in areas such as health and education, people doubted Labour's economic competence, and worried that taxes and interest rates might go up: this was crucial in their decision to vote Tory.

Second, statistical modelling by David Sanders suggested that voting intention correlated closely with people's perceptions of the economy and their own circumstances. Data from 1979 to 1994 indicated that there was a strong relationship between Tory voting intention, their perceived economic competence and people's perceptions of how well off they were likely to be in the next 12 months. Sanders argued:

> The theoretical interpretation of this is simple ... If I am pessimistic about my economic prospects, I am more inclined to seek to change the status quo that has produced my pessimism.[4]

Finally, statistical modelling undertaken by Stan Greenberg and others in the run-up to the 1997 election consistently found that economic issues had the most significant effect on switchers' voting intention.

LABOUR'S ADVERTISING STRATEGY

Therefore, in summary, our advertising strategy was as follows:

Target audience: 'switcher voters' in marginal seats – primarily those who had voted Conservative in 1992;
Behavioural objective: strengthen their resolve to vote Labour;
How to get them to do this: primarily – persuade them that they will be

worse off economically if they vote Tory than
if they vote Labour;
but also – attack John Major
– provide positive reasons to vote
Labour

There were three components to the campaign:

Focus on tax

Taxation was selected as the focus for our economic attack. Our qualitative research showed that while many switcher voters were feeling worse off, they had a decidedly hazy understanding of how government economic policy had affected them personally, particularly since they were aware that the basic rate of income tax was lower than it had been in previous years.

There was a clear role for advertising to re-educate people about tax: to point out that the Tories had increased the burden of taxation on ordinary people by raising indirect taxes. When prompted, switcher voters found the way in which the Tories had imposed 'hidden taxes' particularly galling: 'giving with one hand and taking away with the other'.

In addition, taxation (unlike interest rates or inflation) was wholly within the government's control. Voters could therefore easily link a party (the Conservatives) with an unwanted outcome (higher taxes). Lastly, the issue of taxation hit a particularly raw nerve with Tory switchers, who felt angry that the Tories had broken their 1992 election promises on tax.

The tax campaign, therefore, aimed to get people to think about tax in a new way to consider indirect as well as direct taxes. The advertising had three main thrusts:

1. Tories' tax record (22 tax rises since 1992);
2. Tory broken promises on tax (22 tax rises and VAT on fuel);
3. future Tory tax plans (VAT on food).

Attacking John Major

The Tories considered John Major to be their biggest asset. Certainly, evidence from the polls showed that while he lagged behind Tony Blair on all measures, he was nevertheless rated more highly than his party. We were concerned that John Major had the potential to gain ground: the Tories had made it clear that they would be trying to make the most of the Prime Minister's 'honest John' image. Therefore, an important part of the campaign consisted in 'disarming' John Major.

Our qualitative research suggested that he was most vulnerable to charges of dishonesty. Switcher voters felt strongly that John Major had broken his election promises and felt angry and betrayed as a consequence. Our 'two-faced' posters aimed to dramatise John Major's duplicity.

The positive campaign

Most of the positive advertising ran in the final weeks of the election campaign. Its purpose was twofold: to give people a clear rationale for voting Labour by demonstrating the positive benefits offered by a change of government. Second, to reassure people that Labour's policies were sensible and moderate. Once again, taxation was an important issue: Labour's pledge not to increase income tax rates was given more weight than the other four pledges in our pre-election poster campaign.

ADVERTISING AND BROADCASTING ACTIVITY

Spending

This was vastly greater than any previous election and the advertising ran for a full year up to the election itself. The two main parties had spent a bit over £5 million in 1987 and about £6.5 million between them in 1992. In 1997, together with the Referendum Party, they spent a total of around £27 million (see Figure 4.1). Reassuringly, despite the expenditure of over £13 million on advertising, the Tories barely made a dent in the polls. Reassuringly, it seems that elections still cannot be bought.

Posters

The Conservatives spent about £11 million on poster advertising from May 1996 up until the election itself. The Labour Party spent just under £6 million across the same period. Both parties spent at roughly the same time, but with Labour at a lower rate. Figure 4.2 demonstrates that expenditure was concentrated in the period from January 1997 to the election itself.

Press

In the national press the Referendum Party was by far the biggest spender, with a spend of just under £7 million. The Conservatives spent

Figure 4.1: Total spending on advertising, 1996/97

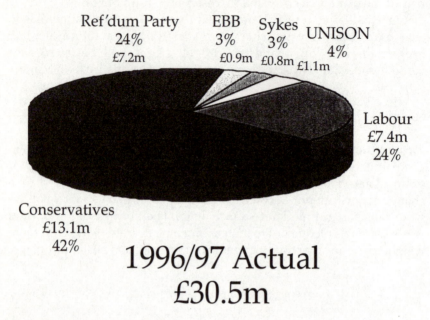

Ref'dum Party
24%
£7.2m

EBB
3%
£0.9m

Sykes
3%
£0.8m

UNISON
4%
£1.1m

Labour
£7.4m
24%

Conservatives
£13.1m
42%

1996/97 Actual
£30.5m

Source: PPL/BMP/Register Meal.

just over £2 million and Labour £1.3 million. One of the features of this election was the considerable expenditure by parallel groups: the public-sector trade union UNISON spent about £1 million, the Trade Union Congress and National Union of Teachers each spent about £0.5 million in support of Labour. Paul Sykes (a Eurosceptic businessman) and Entrepreneurs for a Booming Britain (EBB) also spent about £1 million in support of the Conservative Party. Figure 4.3 sets out the expenditure of all those parties, organisations and people who spent more than £0.5 million on press advertisements.

Much of the expenditure by Labour, the Tories and supporting groups was in the last week, with £3 million being spent in that period and Paul Sykes being the largest advertiser (see Figure 4.4).

Figure 4.5 summarises spending in the final week by both major 'sides' and the Referendum Party. Overall in that last week the 'Blue' advertisers (Conservatives plus allies) spent over half the money with the 'Red' advertisers (Labour plus allies) spending about a third.

Television

One of the factors often overlooked in the elections is the importance, and worth, of the broadcasts. Even given the extraordinarily heavy

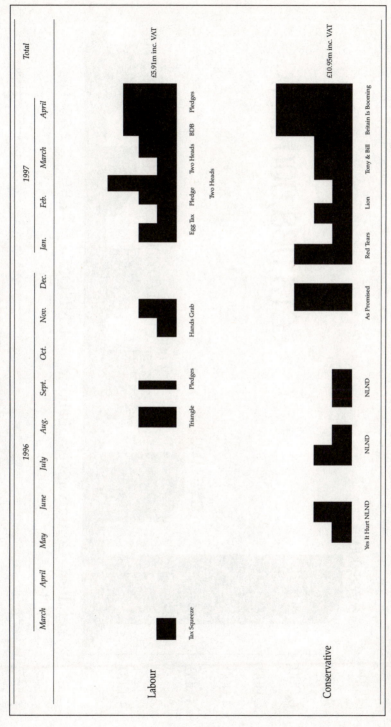

Figure 4.2: Political poster advertising, 1996/97

Source: BARB.

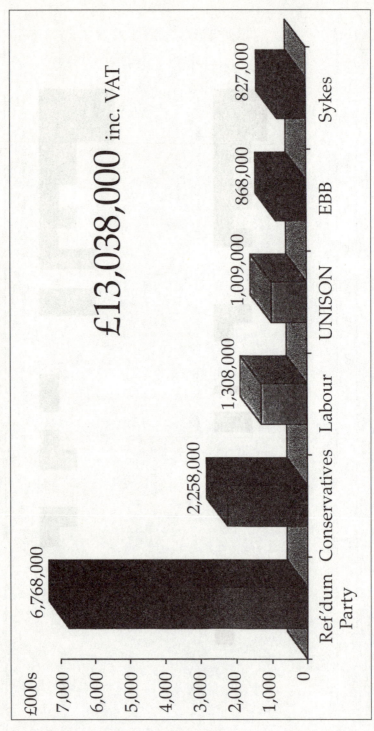

Figure 4.3: Spending in the national press, 1996/97

£13,038,000 inc. VAT

Source: BMP/Register Meal.

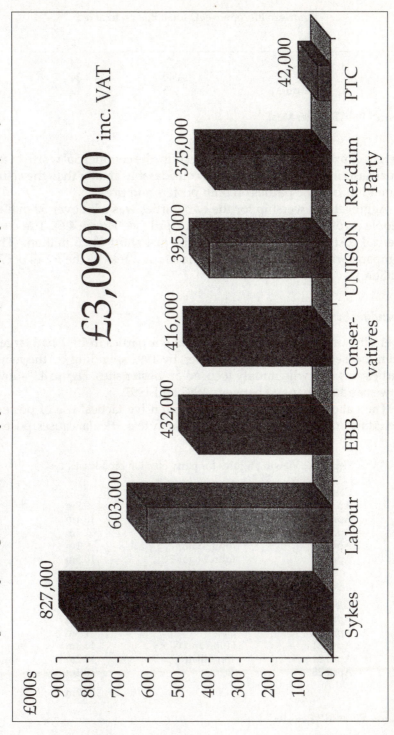

Figure 4.4: Spending in the national newspapers: election week (Thursday 24 April–Thursday 1 May 1997)

£3,090,000 inc. VAT

£000s

Sykes	827,000
Labour	603,000
EBB	432,000
Conser-vatives	416,000
UNISON	395,000
Ref'dum Party	375,000
PTC	42,000

Source: BMP/Register Meal.

Figure 4.5: Election week: total blue vs. total red

	£	%
Blue	1,675	54
Red	1,040	34
(Ref'dum)	375	12

Source: BMP/Register Meal.

weight of print advertising in this election, the commercial worth of the broadcasts in the last four weeks is considerably greater than the actual expenditure of the parties on both posters and press.

Aggregate viewership for the two parties was a bit over 50 million people across the five broadcasts, in April (see Figure 4.6). The commercial cost of this air time would be just short of £5 million. (This compares with a poster spend in the last four weeks by the Tories of £2.9 million.)

Spending by medium

Spending on advertising by the two major parties in 1987 had largely been focused on the press. However, by 1997 spending by the major parties was overwhelmingly focused on poster sites. Figure 4.7 shows how spending changed between 1992 and 1997.

The Labour campaign also made extensive tactical use of posters, including one-off posters to attract publicity to particular causes, posters

Figure 4.6: Viewing figures for party election broadcasts, 1997

Conservative

April 9	Future Voxpops	9.7m
April 16	Tree With No Roots	10.1m
April 22	John Major 1	12.1m
April 25	John Major 2	9.1m
April 29	John Major 3	10.5m
		51.5m

Labour

April 10	Business	10.8m
April 15	Dog	11.3m
April 21	Hope and Glory	10.3m
April 24	Tony Blair	10.2m
April 28	Taxi	10.1m
		52.7m

Source: PPL/BMP/Register Meal.

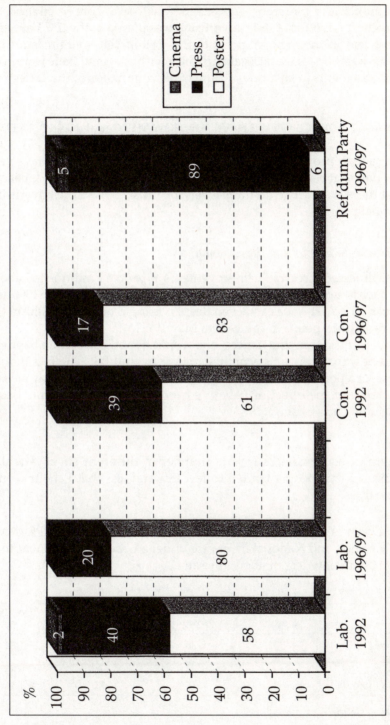

Figure 4.7: Advertising spending by medium, 1992 and 1996/97

Source: PPL/BMP/Register Meal.

at Conservative conferences and on ad-vans to rival Conservative poster launches. Advertorial style advertising was placed in the IPC Women's press and in the regional press in the 'cotton-belt' marginals (of the north-west). Space was also taken in the Jewish press and there were even advertisements in lavatories ('Now wash your hands of the Tories').

WHAT EVIDENCE DO WE HAVE FOR HOW THE CAMPAIGN WORKED?

We cannot 'prove' the effect of the advertising. Indeed, we have very few data that pertain specifically to the advertising. However, we believe that there is evidence on three levels for the success of the advertising campaign.

Attitudes to Labour and the economy

We witnessed discernible improvements in people's attitude to Labour on such issues as tax and standard of living towards the end of 1996 and in early 1997. This was achieved despite rising economic optimism (an increase of 15 points in the year to May 1997).[5]

Under these circumstances, one would hypothesise (from Sanders' findings) that Labour's economic ratings would fall. The fact that, at least for a period of about six months, they did not do this may well be evidence of the effect of Labour's campaigning on economic issues (including advertising).

Tax

There is also evidence from a number of different surveys which indicated that people tended to feel less and less that Labour would raise taxes:

Q. Do you think you and your family would pay more in all forms of taxation and National Insurance under a Labour government than you do now, less or about the same?

	Jan. 1992 (%)	Sept. 1994 (%)	Sept. 1995 (%)	Dec. 1996 (%)
More	57	38	42	34
Less	6	12	11	9
Same	32	38	36	41
Don't know	5	16	11	16

Source: Gallup.

Attitudes to taxation	Dec. 1993 (%)	June 1996 (%)	Oct. 1996 (%)	Feb. 1997 (%)
Likely to raise income tax	−18	−15	−9	−4
Likely to raise VAT	n.a	+18	+29	+30
Keep taxes at right level	n.a	+6	+6	+8

Note: A positive score indicates a Labour advantage.
Source: NOP.

In February 1997, three separate polling companies suggested that voters believed that the Tories were more likely to raise taxes than Labour.

Gallup conducted a survey in March 1997 which probed voters' fears if Labour were elected. This was a repeat of a study initially commissioned in August 1996. The March data showed that tax had fallen to fourth place in the ranked list of concerns, from second place at the time of the original study. The salience of the tax issue had been reduced.

Standard of living
Polling evidence also shows that people continued to believe that Labour would improve their standard of living:

Party most likely to improve my standard of living:

June 1996 (%)	Oct. 1996 (%)	Feb. 1997 (%)	April 1997 (%)
+18	+21	+15	+17

Note: A positive score indicates a Labour advantage
Source: NOP.

Even throughout the campaign period, Labour's lead on 'improving standard of living' averaged 17 points, despite the fact that 68 per cent of people believed that the economy was strong or fairly strong.

Attitudes to John Major and Tory broken promises

The message that John Major had broken his promises on tax was particularly persuasive for switcher voters. Over half, 58 per cent claimed that this message made them more inclined to vote Labour (compared with 31 per cent for the sample as a whole and 49 per cent for constant Labour voters).[6]

Despite the fact that John Major's overall rating rallied slightly as the campaign progressed, his 'trust rating' fell away:

Blair lead over Major:

	mid Feb. 1997 (%)	end April 1997 (%)
Good Prime Minister	+22	+19
Trust more	+7	+13

Source: NOP.

Indeed, of all the 'anti-Tory' reasons for voting Labour, broken promises was the most potent, according to a poll carried out on the Friday and Saturday after the election.

	Very important in voting decision (% agree)
The Tories broke too many promises	75
It was just time for a change	65
The Tories were sleazy and corrupt	62
Major's government was accident prone	53
Major was a weak leader	43

Source: Gallup.

Attitudes to the advertising

Recognition
At the outset of the campaign, the Tories, with their 'Demon Eyes' advertising, clearly had the edge over Labour in terms of public and media visibility. However, at the end of 1996, Labour regained the initiative with its 'Hands campaign' and the Tories' record. This is all the more impressive when we take into account the fact that the Tories spent twice as much as Labour on advertising.

Among Tory switchers the recognition figures were as follows:

	% recognise
Next time VAT on food	40
22 new taxes	32
New Labour, Euro Danger	30

Source: ORB.

Another survey showed that the Labour Party enjoyed the highest recall of any poster advertiser in April – substantially higher than the Tories.

Adults	Labour ads	Tory ads
% recognise	72	59
% like	45	34

Source: RSL.

Relevance and persuasiveness of message
Two pieces of quantitative evidence suggest that Labour's campaign more accurately tapped into how people felt than the Tories' advertising.

First, the 'Enough is Enough' slogan found particular resonance with switcher voters.

Q. Thinking about the two campaigns, which seems more true to you?

	All	Constant Labour	Defectors to Labour
Enough is Enough	48	77	83
New Labour, New Danger	24	4	2

Source: NOP.

Second, research by Bates Dorland endorsed the use of the slogan 'Britain Deserves Better'.

> Labour's communication strategy is spot on ... 'Britain deserves better' is exactly what the majority of voters are currently thinking ... Even the majority of Tory voters (58 per cent) believe that Britain deserves better.
> Only a tiny minority buy into the claim that 'Britain is booming'.[7]

In this election we were able to obtain minute-by-minute data of the Party Election Broadcasts which is shown on the following chart.

Figure 4.8 shows that, while on ITV, because of the scheduling, viewers were turning on during the course of the PEB in order to watch the next programme, more people were turning on and staying with the Labour broadcast than they were with the Tory broadcast. Conversely, on BBC 1 most people were changing to watch programmes on other channels. However, across this period the Labour audience declined by only 1 per cent, but the audience for the Conservative Party Election Broadcast declined by 12 per cent.

Style and tone of campaign
People felt much more sympathetic to the way in which Labour campaigned, as indicated by Gallup in their political tracking report.

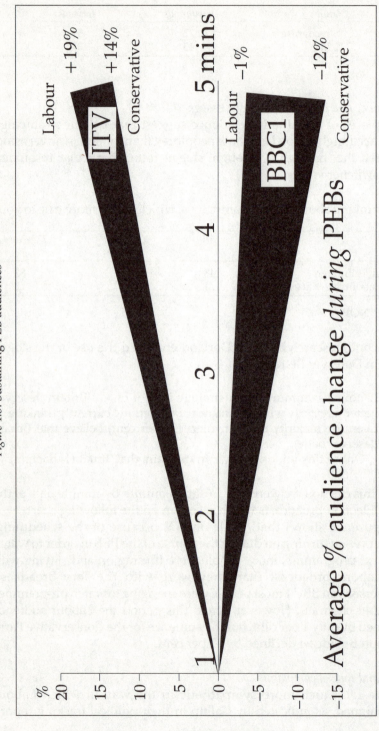

Source: BARB.

Figure 4.8: Sustaining PEB audiences

The 62 per cent of people whose opinion of Labour improved as a result of their campaign is higher than their share of the vote (44 per cent).

Q. Irrespective of how you finally voted, please tell me whether your opinion of the main parties went up or went down as a result of the way they fought the election.

	Tories (%)	Labour (%)
Up	13	62
Down	61	14
Neither	21	19

Source: Gallup.

CONCLUSIONS AND KEY LEARNING

From the success of Labour's campaign, three key principles emerge, which should inform future election campaigns.

Prosperity is the key

People's voting behaviour is governed by self-interest. There was a recognition in this campaign that personal prosperity (and the fact that the Tories damaged it) needed to have a central role. We hypothesise that at the next general election, people will be equally self-interested.

People don't forget broken promises

The fact that John Major and his government had broken their election promises (particularly on tax) was the primary source of anger for disillusioned Tory switchers. We would suggest that being seen to honour its election pledges will be a key determinant of future success for Labour.

'Slagging' doesn't work

Attacks based on 'new facts' are found to be acceptable and even useful by the electorate. For instance, that the government had imposed 22 new taxes was regarded as a legitimate advertisement that helped to explain to people why they felt, as they did, disgruntled at their financial plight.

Tory attacks – 'New Labour, New Danger' and so on – were seen, by contrast, as 'slagging', just a way of being rude about the other side without any addition to the debate. As such, this was seen as negative advertising that reflected badly on the Tories especially as, after 18 years in government, this is the most they had to say for themselves.

NOTES

1 Source: Gallup 9000 series.
2 Fully 75 per cent of defectors to Labour claimed that their support for Labour was fairly or very weak; 75 per cent of consistent Labour supporters claimed that their support was strong or fairly strong (NOP, October 1996).
3 22 per cent of Labour, Lib. Dem. and undecided voters claimed there was a chance they might vote Tory (NOP, 26 March).
4 David Sanders, 'The Economy, Political Forecasting and the Marketing of Political Parties', paper delivered at a Conference on Political Marketing, Churchill College, Cambridge, March 1995.
5 Source: Gallup.
6 Source: NOP, February 1997.
7 Audience Selection Omnibus, 4–6 April 1997.

The Conservative Party's Advertising Strategy

STEVE HILTON

M&C Saatchi began work on a strategy to re-elect the Conservatives in January 1996. We were immediately confronted with a fundamental dilemma: the vast chasm between image and reality. The economic realities were good: a fantastic economy which, on paper, represented the best record of any government seeking re-election for generations. The political image, however was bad: 'sleaze', 'disunity', 'time for a change'.

So we faced a contradictory background: no incumbent government with such a good record had ever lost an election; but neither had an incumbent with such a long period in office or such levels of unpopularity ever won. Which would prove more powerful; economic reality, or political image?

In theory, this was the ideal task for advertising image-makers: it was political image that needed changing, not the facts. We approached the task by choosing as our central strategic proposition the faithful Tory slogan: 'Life's better with the Conservatives, don't let Labour ruin it.'

We intended to begin our campaign in March 1996, in advance of the local council elections. We were going to start with the positive message, telling people that 'life is better'. This endeavour was not greatly assisted by the fact that the bovine spongiform encephalopathy (BSE) story broke in the week of our launch. Our first party political broadcast told an expectant country that people in other countries admired Britain. Perhaps they did, but the bulletins that immediately followed the PPB led with the news that virtually the whole world was refusing to eat our beef. Not the most auspicious start.

In May, we launched our first poster campaign. The intention was to communicate Conservative economic achievements in a credible way, which went with the grain of public opinion and acknowledged the pain that had been involved in creating Britain's economic success. We launched the 'Yes it Hurt, Yes it Worked' campaign in May – thanks to BSE, more than two months after we had intended to begin full campaigning.

The amount of attention given to the campaign by the media, and its sheer weight, meant that the message certainly got through to our target audience of Conservative defectors and first-time voters. But our research showed that while they agreed life was better than a few years previously, they did not give credit for these economic achievements to the Conservative government.

We seemed to be gripped in an intellectual vice, where voters perceived, rightly or wrongly, that: 'The Conservatives have done badly [the ERM debacle/tax increases etc.]' and 'Even if they convince me they have done well [the facts of economic success]', 'Labour would not ruin it'.

They thought 'Labour would not ruin it' because: 'The Conservatives are safe', 'Labour have copied the Conservatives', therefore 'Labour are safe'.

So our problem lay in choosing a credible way to undermine what 'New Labour' meant to people. In drawing up our strategy, we identified at least six different lines of attack that were then in use by Conservative spokesmen – often on the same day, or even in the same interview! Some strategic clarity was required.

We set ourselves three criteria for any anti-Labour message. Not only should it deter our target audience from voting Labour, but it also had to be clear and credible. On the basis of these criteria, we rejected the existing lines of attack one by one. We could not argue that Labour had not changed: this was not credible. We could not argue that while Tony Blair may have changed, the Labour Party would revert to its old ways if elected. This was neither clear nor, we discovered in research, credible. And, most importantly, we could not argue that Labour were copying the Conservatives: this was no deterrent to voting Labour. As we have seen, this argument had the opposite effect, serving to confirm that it was safe to vote Labour.

So we agreed on a formula which again, in the style of 'Yes it Hurt, Yes it Worked', attempted to go with the grain of public opinion. We argued that while Labour had indeed changed, New Labour was newly dangerous – in new ways. Thus emerged 'New Labour, New Danger'.

The advertising style we chose to communicate this strategy was a deliberately emotional one. This is because we knew that our target audience was expressing support for Labour for mainly emotional reasons. We saw the battle as being a battle for control of one word: 'new'. We believed that if Labour's meaning prevailed ('new' = fresh, different, innovative), then Labour would win. But if our meaning prevailed ('new' = experimental, risky and dangerous; it could blow up in your face), then we would win.

But by the end of a summer of campaigning, it was clear that we were making no impact on voting intention. Labour's version of 'new' was winning. This could either have been because the electorate simply didn't believe what we were saying, or that they believed it but didn't care.

Our research suggested that it was the latter. The proportions agreeing that a Labour government would increase taxes, mortgages and inflation to name just a few evils, were precisely in line with the figures we encountered in the equivalent period in 1992. Unlike 1992, however, these views were not being translated into Conservative voting intention. This is why many of us managed to stay so cheerful, and in the view of many commentators, ludicrously optimistic. We knew that our target audience agreed with our arguments. It was only a matter of time, we consoled ourselves, before they would acknowledge this in their voting intention.

But the headline voting intention figures remained stuck, with the Conservatives struggling to get near 30 per cent and a huge Labour lead all the way through the party conference season. The Conservative Party conference, based on the theme 'opportunity for all', provided a temporary boost, but this was dissipated by the seemingly inevitable 'events, dear boy, events' as soon as normal Westminster service was resumed. In the particular case of the Conservative Party, of course, it tended to be Euro-events that did the dissipating, right up until polling day – with the odd day of sleaze thrown in for good measure.

It is important to point out, however, that despite these formidable pressures, for much of the campaign we maintained, if anything, greater strategic discipline than in 1992. We also had a strong and united team at Central Office and Number 10. But what lessons can we draw from the experience?

First, it is essential to recognise the power of events, and their consequent domination of the daily news agenda. As the 1992 experience showed, political advertising works best when it sets and then dominates the media agenda. It was the carefully crafted and planned 'tax bombshell' advertising, launched on 6 January 1992, that put the issue of tax centre stage for the entire 1992 election campaign.

But when unplanned events come to dominate, political advertising struggles to be heard. So our advertising messages, powerful though we believed them to be, were often simply drowned out by the daily diet of sometimes real, sometimes invented – but always exaggerated – splits, rows and gaffes. I cannot recall more than one or two periods with consecutive days of respite.

Think of the advertising expenditure needed to balance the front and inside pages of every daily newspaper and the top stories in every news bulletin over a 14-month period. There is no question that advertising, while playing a vital role in communicating a chosen message directly to the target audience without media interference, cannot work as well when it is fighting the news agenda as when it is leading it.

The second lesson involves the relative importance of political and economic factors in deciding modern elections. In the 1960s and 1970s, conventional wisdom argued that, in Britain, oppositions don't win elections, governments lose them. The 1980s turned that around: the new conventional wisdom was that governments didn't win elections, oppositions lost them. In the same way, I believe that the 1992 and 1997 elections turned conventional wisdom on its head.

It used to be said that economic realities always trump political image in deciding elections. This is the famous 'Essex model', or 'Heseltine's law' as we naturally preferred to call it. But in 1992 the Conservatives won an election in the middle of a recession, and in 1997 we lost in the middle of a boom. In other words, political image defeated economic reality on both occasions.

But if the difficulty for the Conservatives was political image, why couldn't the notorious image-makers, with all their black arts, fix the problem? The answer is fairly obvious. Political image itself is based on political realities. These translate into simple, basic perceptions about parties. So just as with any consumer brand, a political brand image is based on perceptions of the product. As every piece of research has shown, the traditional Conservative brand image was built on two simple perceptions about the party. The Conservatives were seen by voters as 'efficient, but uncaring'.

On the other hand, for four elections in a row, the Labour Party's brand image was based on the opposite perceptions: 'caring but incompetent'. The Conservative brand positioning trumped Labour's every time.

But it is a clear finding of all the polling evidence that following the events of 'Black Wednesday' in September 1992, when sterling was forced to leave the ERM, one of those fundamental Conservative brand characteristics was damaged in the eyes of voters: the party's reputation for competence. From then on, the Party came to be defined in voters' minds by the remaining perception alone: the Conservative Party's traditional, but in previous circumstances electorally benign, reputation as 'uncaring'. Meanwhile the Labour Party actively sought to attach the 'incompetent' tag to the Conservatives.

At the same time New Labour's prime campaigning focus from 1992 onwards was to replace 'incompetent' with 'efficient' as its leading brand characteristic, while retaining their traditional perceived characteristic as 'caring'. So the 1997 election, in voters' eyes, became a contest between 'incompetent and uncaring' and 'efficient and caring'. For the first time in 18 years, through a determined and impressive act of political will, Labour had gained the winning combination of perceptions.

And the truth is that image-making cannot help in these matters. Because the removal of the Conservative reputation for 'efficiency' was based on a real event – sterling's ejection from the ERM – advertising and public relations alone were powerless to re-instate it.

Equally, Labour's acquisition of the 'efficient' characteristic was based on real, hard policy 'events'. Image-making alone would not have won Labour the 1997 election. I bow to no-one in my admiration for Peter Mandelson's professionalism and communications skills. But it was only when his and his colleagues' skills were applied to a transformed political reality that they bore electoral fruit.

There is a further, final lesson to be drawn, and it is a more cultural one. Over 18 years, the Conservative Party changed the culture of our country. But the party itself failed to adapt to those changes. So by 1997, as William Hague has said, the party 'had lost touch with some of the people we always said we represented', displaying 'more than a hint of arrogance and conceit'.

So put in the simplest possible terms, some of our traditional supporters just said: 'New Labour aren't that bad.' And every third party they could hear agreed with them that Labour 'weren't that bad'. In the face of this, in the face of the media communicating almost exclusively negative messages about the Conservative Party, in the face of severe damage to the Conservative brand, it is perhaps not surprising that our election defeat was as heavy as it was.

In conclusion, for political advertising, there is one simple salutary lesson. It is directed particularly at those who argue that modern elections can in some way be 'bought' by heavy advertising expenditure. The general election of 1997 simply shows that advertising, on its own, cannot make all the difference.

PART II:

CAMPAIGNING AND OPINION POLLS

6

The Media and the Polls: Pundits, Polls and Prognostications in British General Elections

ROBERT M. WORCESTER

There is a love–hate relationship between the media and the polls. Over the past 50 years, polls have transformed political reporting. As a boy in the United States, I can recall the radio interviews reporting from the hustings, the sincere interviews with the county chairmen who, when asked by the polite radio journalist, reported that morale was good in the wards, that the public mood was shifting to his (always his) candidate, and that on election day justice would be done. David McKie, former Deputy Editor of the *Guardian* and one of the few journalists who really took the time and trouble to understand the uses and limitations of polls, reported that he had researched the election reporting of the British press prior to the introduction of systematic polls, and found that the *News Chronicle* always reported a last-minute swing to Labour, while equally sincerely the Beaverbrook papers were reporting a last-minute swing to the Tories.

Polls have changed all of that, although there is considerable licence given still to politicians to get away with the time-worn clichés: 'The only poll that counts is the poll on election day' (*I am losing*); 'That's not what I am finding on the ground' (*It is not what my agent is admitting*); 'We'll have to wait and see' (*I haven't a clue*); 'I never comment on opinion polls' (*… except when they are in my favour*); and, 'Our canvass returns tell a different story' (*They would, wouldn't they?*).

In the period in between the 1992 and 1997 British general elections, every BBC broadcast of poll findings, on the relatively rare occasions on which they were broadcast, carried a 'health warning', recalling that in the previous election 'the polls were wrong', planting the ideas in the listeners' and viewers' minds that polls were not to be trusted, that they were of limited use at best and wildly misleading at worst, and that a better guide, broadcast without similar health warnings, were the claims of the politicians that their party was far ahead, or even worse, that their private polls were providing a more rosy picture somehow than were the public polls so heavily discounted by BBC commentators acting under the BBC's own *Producers' Guidelines*.

VOODOO POLLS, FOCUS GROUPS AND CANVASS RETURNS

There are many ways in which the ordinary voter can send a message to the political elite, from sounding off in pubs and workplaces in the hopes that such signals will be picked up, writing letters to MPs and seeing them in their surgeries, writing letters to editors and being interviewed on radio and television vox pops and on phone-ins and in opinion polls. Of these, only opinion polls reach out systematically and objectively to assess public opinion.

The limitations of self-selecting samples, whether they be letters written to MPs or radio phone-ins, are well known to students of psephology, but not necessarily to the listener or viewer, reader or even untrained journalist or broadcaster. Two examples from the past will suffice to make the point. The first, Tony Benn in his argument in the House of Commons against Britain's participation in the Falklands War. Brandishing a handful of letters that supported him (and those who did would of course be those who wrote – a self-selecting sample), he avowed 'Public opinion is swinging massively against the war!' A MORI (Market and Opinion Research International) poll a few days later in the *Economist* showed that 83 per cent of the British public favoured sending the Task Force to the Falklands. The second example considers the case of 'Desmond', writing a letter to the *Evening Standard*, pleased that 'his side' won in a BBC Radio 4 phone-in poll, having 'voted' 157 times himself.

These 'voodoo polls' are open to cynical manipulation – one former chief whip recently admitted that he had on occasion organised colleagues to phone in to rig the results[1] – and should not be given any credence whatsoever. Yet such vox pops continue to be taken seriously, or at least to be reported, by the media generally, and even conducted by the BBC itself. (Was it too much to hope that the fiasco of the *Today* programme's 1996 'Personality of the Year' poll would teach the Corporation a lesson? Apparently so, for the BBC programme *You Decide* now exclusively relies on a phone-in for its assessment of British public opinion.) Other examples abound, and the trend to the use of such voodoo polls seems to be growing in Great Britain, while declining in the United States, having been there discredited and abandoned by the serious broadcasters and newspapers.

The 1997 election brought a rich crop of voodoo polls and straw polls, occasionally written up as if they were a credible measure of public opinion. In perhaps the worst instance, since the misleading report appeared in a normally reliable and accurate newspaper, the *Guardian* reported a phone-in 'poll' from the *Worcester Evening News*, giving Labour 73 per cent support in the key marginal, as 'according to a telephone poll', putting it together with a report of the entirely reputable HSBC (Hong Kong Shanghai Bank) James Capel panel, conducted by ORB.[2]

Equally alarming was the *News of the World*'s do-it-yourself poll in Basildon,[3] which some commentators naturally assumed was by MORI since we had conducted that paper's poll the previous week. On a base of '1,000 locals quizzed', the sub-headline blazoned '52% will back New Labour' – but this turned out to refer to the figures *before* repercentaging, with the don't knows running second on which basis they reported 'the Conservatives trailed in a poor third' – a classic reporting blunder which no polling company would be likely to let their clients make with their data. The figures should have read Labour 71 per cent, Conservative 20 per cent! *Private Eye* later carried a leaked report of the *News of the World*'s methodology:

> The *Screws* [*News of the World*] did not commission a professional poll to get these 'stunning' results: it sent local hack Vanessa Large and some news agency bods to question voters. But it proved difficult for them to find 1,000 people who would talk as local blue rinses did their best to dodge the seedy hacks.
>
> Eventually they found an audience who didn't object to answering questions – a stream of people leaving Towngate Theatre. It was only after dozens of them had responded that Large noticed how all were Labour supporters … not surprising as they were leaving the local Constituency Labour Party's weekly meeting.
>
> So the hacks did what all hacks do in an emergency: they went to a pub where they conducted an extremely scientific and in-depth poll, reaching the conclusion that Basildon would probably vote Labour.[4]

Another offender was the *Daily Record*, which led their election day round-up of the polls with their own phone-in poll: 'A massive 64 per cent of readers backed Labour in a *Daily Record* poll', with the figures in a prominent panel.[5] Beside these examples, the inevitable light-hearted marketing exercises such as the Thornton's lollipop 'poll' or the 'Beerometer' in the Marquis of Granby pub seem comparatively harmless.

More amusing, though potentially dangerous as its prominent headline was the only political coverage on the front page, was the *Daily Mirror* story on 11 April. Headed 'New Poll Sensation: Labour "Bloody Miles Ahead"', it stated: 'A shock *Mirror* poll has sensationally revealed that Labour are "very likely" to win the election by a massive landslide. The poll, conducted by a quick show of hands yesterday round the *Mirror* newsroom, confirmed that absolutely nobody gives John Major and his hopeless Tory cronies a cat in hell's chance.'[6]

Not much better than voodoo polling is the misuse of focus groups as a source for quantitative data. There is nothing wrong in principle with focus groups, which are a valuable research tool for exploring issues in depth and for developing quantitative questionnaires. The media could certainly make interesting and constructive use of them in reporting an election; the *Guardian* (ICM) and to a lesser extent the *Sunday Times* (NOP) did so. But they are not a substitute for opinion polls, as the *Financial Times* tried to make them in 1997,[7] and certainly not capable of contradicting the polls, as the *Independent*'s reporting tried to suggest.[8] Lucy Kellaway (writing in the *Financial Times*) hit the nail on the head when she wrote: 'One of the silliest aspects of this remarkably silly election campaign has been the great enthusiasm for the focus group.'[9]

It was, however, the self-same *Financial Times* which commissioned and gave extensive space to reports of focus groups run by an advertising agency. In one article they percentaged the responses of 79 people who were representative of nothing other than they had been willing to take part in these focus groups, reporting not even the group findings but telephone re-interviews of their 'panel' packaged as 'a new survey of the mood of "floating" voters in marginal constituencies'.[10] Laura Marks, chair of the Association of Qualitative Research Practitioners, wise in the use of focus groups to discern the 'whys' of what people are thinking, and alert to their mis-use (as utilised by the *Financial Times* and other newspapers and broadcast media) to attempt to forecast voting behaviour, pointed out their limitations on BBC Radio 4's *Today* programme. Kellaway observed: 'The appeal of focus groups is that they are cheap and immediate. But not only are the samples so small that they don't mean a thing, they do not even reflect the views of the members of the groups ... They can be useful if what is wanted is new ideas ...'[11]

Of course, much greater users of focus groups are the parties themselves, for whom – if properly used – they can be of considerable value in campaign planning. A *Private Eye* report of leaked focus group findings from the Conservatives' private polls shortly before the election gives a good idea of one of the established methods, using projective techniques to help group members articulate their underlying ideas.

This is according to the new breed of Tory number-crunchers who have abandoned the rigour of conventional polling for the psephological equivalent of astrology. Their system involves asking focus groups daft questions such as: 'If John Major were a biscuit, what kind of biscuit would he be?'

The Prime Minister turns out to be a Hob Nob – oaty, conventionally English, a safe choice; while Blair is a Bath Oliver – a deeply pretentious biscuit; a toff trying to look plain. The Labour leader figured even lower in the public estimation when the researchers got into the bathroom. The question: 'What kind of toilet paper do you think Tony Blair would use?' got the cynical reply: 'He'd *say* he uses recycled, but he really uses Andrex.'[12]

Private Eye underestimated the potential value of this sort of research to an astute political strategist; and similar techniques could also have been used to broaden the media coverage of the election (rather than the way the *Financial Times*, in particular, did use them). But, fascinating though this brief insight into the Tory research methods might be, the 'leaking' of private polls, which political journalists reported extensively during the 1997 general election with little attempt made by the media to ascertain their veracity, is another even more pernicious form of political manipulation and spin-doctoring.

This arose in 1997 to a greater degree than at any previous election, leaking findings both from 'private' polls and from focus groups done by and for the political parties. In previous elections there has been the occasional leak, or spin, from party spokesmen claiming that results from their own 'private' polls were somehow different from the results of public polling done often by the same organisation. The Code of Conduct of the APOPO Group, which comprises all the major polling organisations, calls for its members to clarify any misleading references to polls they have conducted when leaked by party spokesmen.

ICM's Nick Sparrow directed the private polling for the Tory party, and what his polls for the Conservatives were saying first reached a peak of speculation on 31 January, when they were brought into play by the Prime Minister himself, who was frequently quoted as saying he never commented on poll findings. According to Peter Riddell in *The Times* the following day, Mr Major 'broke a cardinal rule of politicians: never claim that your secret opinion polls tell a better story than published polls unless you are prepared to back that with the facts'.

Riddell's column said the Prime Minister 'provided no evidence for his assertions. Conservative Central Office staff later refused to disclose any details, claiming that they were private'. Riddell went on to say, 'It would be surprising if what the private Tory polls showed was different … there is no reason to doubt current polls pointing to a Tory share of about 30 per cent … Mr Major was whistling in the wind. Worse, he was making precisely the mistake he himself criticises in others of selectively using polls when it suits him.'[13]

David Butler comments that 'It is a good rule never to believe anything that the parties say publicly about their canvass returns – or their private polls. One should even disbelieve what they say privately and in good faith; the capacity for self-deception grows as the campaign advances.'[14]

Yet Major persisted with his claims: 'The difference out on the doorstep with what we are seeing in the opinion polls is very striking indeed – very striking. This election is there to be won, of that I have not a shred of doubt and I believe that we are going to win it ... The polls are rubbish.' Bob Wybrow of Gallup responded: 'A leader has to put on a brave face and given that we were wrong about him in '92, he has a slight edge but the position is different this time.' He also compared Mr Major to the Labour leader, Michael Foot, in the 1983 election: 'Foot was saying "no, no, the polls have got it wrong. I have been at meetings up and down the country". Everyone knows what happened in 1983.'[15]

Peter Kellner put the case for paying more attention to the polls than the politicians: 'Labour and Conservative politicians are trying hard, both on and off the record, to persuade anyone who will listen that the race is closer than the polls are saying. Labour is trying to guard against complacency, while the Tories are seeking to revive morale. Both stances are understandable, but neither has anything to do with the truth ... Don't let the spin doctors persuade you otherwise, even – perhaps especially – when the spin doctors of both main parties are in agreement.'[16]

POLITICAL COMMUNICATION AND THE POLLS

But serious polling, mostly conducted for the news media, should offer a genuine channel for political communication. Just over six people in ten, 63 per cent, say they were aware of any national opinion polls in this election, down sharply from 89 per cent at the last election, when there were more polls over a shorter period, with certainly more coverage on the BBC than in this election. Many more men, 73 per cent, than women, 54 per cent, were aware of having heard poll findings in the previous week (18–25 April) including two-thirds of those aged 45 and over and three-quarters of middle-class respondents, but only just over half, 55 per cent, of working-class electors. Nearly all, 94 per cent, of those aware of having seen any polls recalled that the Labour Party was in the lead. The public seem to want to continue to hear poll findings, and remain interested in what the polls are saying, despite the persistent sniping from the media and the spin doctors; while interest in the polls was less in 1997 than in 1992, the fall was in line with the more general drop in interest in election coverage.

Table 6.1: Interest in the election

Q. *How interested would you say you are in each of the following?*	1992 %	1997 %	*% Change 1992–97*
'Very' or 'fairly' interested			
News about the election	60	52	−8
What the opinion polls say about the election	40	33	−7
Party election broadcasts	36	32	−4
Politicians' speeches	43	40	−3
'Not at all interested'			
News about the election	14	22	+8
What the opinion polls say about the election	25	28	+3
Party election broadcasts	32	36	+4
Politicians' speeches	28	30	+2

Fieldwork: 25–28 April 1997.
Base: 997 British adults aged 18+.

Source: Robert M. Worcester and Roger Mortimore, *British Public Opinion: The British General Election of 1997* (London: MORI, 1997).

A week after the election, five in six people said they recalled what opinion polls were saying, and over half recalled them as saying it would be a Labour landslide. I forecast that this knowledge affected some people's behaviour. I believe that it explains:

1. the low turnout, as core-value Tories knew they did not have to vote against those core values to get what they wanted: the government out of office and John Major replaced;
2. the significant increase in the number of Liberal Democrats elected on 1 May, as some of those core-value Tories who had voted for the Conservative Party in 1992 were aware of the impending landslide for Labour and saw their Liberal Democrat vote not as a 'wasted vote', but as a 'double vote', voting to get the Conservative government out of office and John Major replaced, and reducing Labour's overall majority and building a third force in parliament as a sheet anchor against Labour excesses; and
3. the non-Conservative vote for the Referendum and other third parties, as people knew that their vote for third parties would not jeopardise the removal of the Tory government from office.

Table 6.2: Public awareness of the polls

Q. *From what you can remember, what did the opinion polls, published on the day of the election, predict the results would be?*

	%
Was not aware of the polls/Don't know	17
Aware:	
A large majority for Labour (majority of more than 100 MPs)/Landslide for Labour	54
A medium-sized majority for Labour (majority of 51–100 MPs)	14
A small majority for Labour (majority of up to 50 MPs)	3
No overall majority for either party	–
A small majority for the Conservatives (majority of up to 50 MPs)	–
A medium-sized majority for the Conservatives (majority of 51–100 MPs)	0
A large majority for the Conservatives (majority of more than 100 MPs)	0
Majority for Labour (don't know what size)	3
Majority for Conservatives (don't know what size)	–
Can't remember	9

Fieldwork: 7–8 May 1997.
Base: 1,192 British adults 18+ interviewed by telephone.

Source: Robert M. Worcester and Roger Mortimore, *British Public Opinion: The British General Election of 1997* (London: MORI, 1997).

BANNING POLLS

Banning polls during elections gets scant support. Only 16 per cent of the public believe that polls should be banned during elections, down sharply from the last election, while more than three people in four do not. Who are those who would ban the publication of opinion polls (other than some politicians of course)? Those opposing a ban (78 per cent) are more likely to be men, younger (82 per cent of under 35, 77 per cent of 35 and over) and more likely to be middle class (82 per cent) than working class (75 per cent). We should note that this figure compares with one person in five who would ban party election broadcasts, 15 per cent who would ban all coverage of the election on radio and television, and one in ten who would ban all coverage of the election in newspapers!

But then when asked who they trusted to tell the truth, over half, 55 per cent, said they trusted pollsters; only 12 per cent trusted government ministers (somewhat fewer than the 15 per cent who said they trusted journalists).

Table 6.3: Banning of election coverage

Q. *During an election campaign, do you think there should or should not be a ban on ...?*

	% 'should be a ban'			
	1983	1987	1992	1997
Party political broadcasts of the election on television and radio	14	25	24	20
Publication of opinion polls	22	25	24	16
All coverage of the election on television and radio	13	24	21	15
All coverage of the election in newspapers	9	16	13	10

Fieldwork: 25–28 April 1997.
Base: 997 British adults aged 18+.

Source: Robert M. Worcester and Roger Mortimore, *British Public Opinion: The British General Election of 1997* (London: MORI, 1997).

THE PUNDITS

During each election the news media seek out those who have some claim to be able to read the runes and are willing to attend radio and television studios, write articles for the press and otherwise pronounce on what the election is all about, what the impact will be of political events, and try to foretell the future. Not content to report the past, the media seek those who by their academic training or position can somehow read tea leaves, gaze into crystal balls, ascertain Tarot cards' meaning or otherwise peer into the public's mind to see what the electorate will do come that day when the electorate decides which party will take power over the lives of Her Majesty's subjects for the next four or five years.

David Butler, the doyen of the academic psephologists, who has covered every election since 1945, argued 'Experts are no more likely to make accurate predictions than anyone else, they just make them for more sophisticated reasons.'[17] Butler also noted in an article in the *Financial Times* of 1 April in a footnote: '30 days left and every national poll gives Labour a lead of 20 per cent or more. That is a 14 per cent swing from 1992 and, applied nationally, indicates a clear majority of about 200 seats for Labour. No one has yet had the courage to predict that.'[18]

Reuters set up a panel of 20 'experts' across a broad spectrum of political scientists, psephologists, political historians and pundits to track the election, so in a way this became an experiment in the Delphi Technique, in that following each of 11 recalls on the panel they distributed the findings so that each panellist could see how their estimates of the election outcome compared with that of others on the panel, and adjust, or not, their own answers accordingly.

The Reuters expert panel was first polled on 3 October 1996, and collectively forecast the outcome as being likely to be a Labour majority of 36 seats, on a 37 per cent Conservative, 42 per cent Labour, 17 per cent Liberal Democrats, 5 per cent other parties' share of vote. The chart below shows how this changed over time, and how it compared with the eventual outcome. As can be seen, the panel overestimated the Conservatives' share by 2.6 per cent, estimated Labour's correctly, understated the Liberal Democrats' comeback, and underestimated the collective vote of the other parties. On balance, not bad on share, but woefully wrong, by some 87 seats, on turning their share estimates into seats in the House of Commons.

Table 6.4: Average estimates of Reuters' 'Panel of Experts' (%)

Survey dates	3 Oct.	30 Oct.	2 Dec.	8 Jan.	3 Feb.	5 March	2 April	9 April	16 April	23 April	30 April	Result	Difference
Conservative	37	37	37	36	36	36	35	35	35	35	34	31.4	+2.6
Labour	42	42	42	42	43	43	44	45	44	44	44	44.4	+0.4
Liberal Democrat	17	17	16	16	16	16	15	15	15	16	16	17.2	−1.2
Others	5	5	5	5	5	5	6	6	6	6	6	7.0	−1.0
Labour lead	+5	+5	+5	+6	+7	+7	+9	+10	+9	+9	+10	+13	−3.0
Labour majority	36	37	34	41	46	56	77	83	79	82	92	179	−87

Source: Reuters.

Individually, panellists were all over the place, from David Carlton's hung parliament, to 'unattributeds' 153, but none of the panel was close to the eventual 179-seat majority. Sadly, John Curtice had presciently forecast an overall Labour majority of 185 seats right up to the wire, consistently expecting a Labour landslide (believing the polls?), but at the last minute havered, and dropped his forecast to 131, to end up in fourth place behind unattributed's 153, Paul Whiteley's 145 and John Benyon's 143. Just two of this panel of experts guessed Labour would do so much better than average in its marginal seats, and predicted a majority significantly higher than their share predictions would have given on uniform swing: John Curtice (who had explained how his analysis of ICM's poll data led him to expect this on 12 April[19]) and John Benyon both predicted a majority about 30 seats higher than uniform swing – in the event Labour's majority was around 50 higher than uniform swing would have predicted.

Table 6.5: Final forecasts of Reuters' 'Panel of Experts' (30 April 1997)

	Con.	Lab.	Lib. Dems.	Other	Lead	Lab. maj. Seats
	%	%	%	%	%	
Election result	*31.4*	*44.4*	*17.2*	*7*	*13.0*	*179*
Unattributed [a]	30	46	16	8	16	153
Paul Whiteley (Sheffield Univ.)	33	46	16	5	13	145
John Benyon (Leicester Univ.)	32.5	45	17.5	5	12.5	143
John Curtice (Strathclyde Univ.)	34	45	15	6	11	131
Peter Kellner (Independent analyst)	34	45	15	6	11	121
Ivor Crewe (Essex Univ.)	33	45.5	15.5	6	12.5	119
Robert Worcester (MORI)	33	45	17	5	12	101
Ben Pimlott (Birkbeck College London)	33	45	16	6	12	101
Dominic Wring (Nottingham Trent Univ.)	34	44	15	7	10	93
Panel average	*34.2*	*44.4*	*15.7*	*5.8*	*10.3*	*92*
Justin Fisher (London Guildhall Univ.)	34	45	15	6	11	91
Unattributable	35	46	13	6	11	81
Colin Rallings (Plymouth Univ.)	34	43	16	7	9	81
Eric Shaw (Stirling Univ.)	35	44	16	5	9	73
Neil Carter (York Univ.)	35	44	16	5	9	71
David Denver (Lancaster Univ.)	35	44	15	6	9	71
Unattributable	34	43	17	6	9	71
Sydney Elliot (Queen's Univ., Belfast)	34	44	17	5	10	67
Michael Thrasher (Plymouth Univ.)	34.5	43.5	16	6	9	65
David Sanders (Essex Univ.)	37	43	17	3	6	55
David Carlton (Warwick Univ.)	39	41	15	5	2	0

Source: Reuters.
Note: [a] This 'unattributed' was revealed by himself after the election as David Butler (Nuffield College).

To cite the *Economist*'s Political Editor, David Lipsey, who was not one of the panel:

> The Reuters' Panel of 'Experts' predicted Labour's landslide more accurately than politicians, gamblers and most commentators. But that is saying little. In fact, the 'experts' were inaccurate to a degree that, in a closer election, could have led them to predict the wrong result.
> The only pre-election bull's eye on the Labour lead was Whiteley's. But this was thanks to two errors (on the Labour and Tory share of the vote, respectively) that cancelled each other out, both being equally wide of the mark. This is a good example of one of many

reasons that commentators and poll pickers, politicians and pundits and especially headline writers and caption writers should watch the share, not the gap. It not only doubles the margin of error of the polls misleadingly, it confuses the public.

This election also shows that you cannot simply rely on 'experts' to read the polls and their own water and extrapolate from these to the number of seats. Most of the Reuters' 'experts' underestimated the Conservatives' vote, while collectively getting Labour's spot on. Their error was compounded by collectively and individually failing to spot the Liberal Democrats' resurgence and the strength of the combined other parties in this election.

With some of the Reuters panel, it is not clear how they reached their conclusions. Others, however, were writing regular columns. Those who trusted the polls tended to do substantially better than those who did not.

Peter Kellner was one whose reasoning was open for all to see, in a regular pollwatch column in the London *Evening Standard* which ran for months up to the election. He generally considered the polls to be reliable, although he thought that some over-estimated the Labour lead. His final poll article in the *Observer* predicted 'Labour on course for three-figure majority'.[20] Kellner continued in the *Evening Standard* to predict a Labour landslide, with his own estimate of a 121-seat overall majority before the final polls were published,[21] which he upped to 129 on election day.[22] The straight projection of the MORI share figures published on election day in the *Evening Standard* would, however, have forecast a majority of 183.

Kellner also wrote up the MORI poll conducted among voters in London for the *Evening Standard* in the first week of April. It proved remarkably predictive: 'If Labour were indeed to achieve this, the political landscape of the capital would be utterly transformed ... Michael Portillo would be unavailable to stand as the Right's standard-bearer in an early leadership election. His seat in Southgate would fall ... The Tories would lose 33 seats, leaving them with just eight in the capital.'[23] They ended up with 11.

Ben Pimlott was another who upped his final prediction after the Reuters figures were collated. He told the *Daily Telegraph*: 'The temptation is to follow what everyone else is saying. I was saying 101 but I think that's more likely to be too low than too high. I'll say 121.'[24]

And John Curtice, writing in *Scotland on Sunday*, in his 'What the Polls Say' column, was headlined 'Forsyth, Lang and Rifkind heading for defeat'.[25] And my own 'last gasp' was given in a speech to the Carlton Club's political committee on 30 April, when I said 'It could be as much as 120'.

The one Reuters' 'expert' whose predictions stood out from the rest was a lecturer in politics at the University of Warwick, Dr David Carlton, who week in and week out avowed that the best result that Labour could hope for was a hung parliament, and kept his forecast of the seat result at a steady zero overall majority in the weekly Reuters report. As if that weren't enough, he wrote articles in the *Sunday Telegraph* and was quoted in the *Spectator* by Sarah Bloomfield as saying that a hung result was likely.[26]

The final weekend of the election saw the *Sunday Telegraph* feature the hapless Carlton's repeated forecast under the headline 'Get ready for a hung parliament: Don't believe what the opinion polls are reporting.'[27] His continuing bravado in the face of the united opposition of all the other score of Reuters' 'experts', the opinion polls and most commentators other than Bruce Anderson and Woodrow Wyatt was based on his analysis of 'how real voters have behaved on past occasions', pointing out that 'if history is any guide, low turnout is detrimental to Labour'. History wasn't any guide. The turnout in 1997 was the lowest since the war, and yet it was Labour's greatest victory ever. His final paragraph concluded 'a Labour landslide is quite unlikely. Much more probable is a close result, perhaps even a hung parliament'.

Undeterred after all that, Carlton was in the *Spectator* a fortnight after the election, arguing from 'real voters' the same faulty analysis line, and pleading that he be allowed to continue political punditing.[28] Having forecast a hung parliament with a nil seat lead, he criticised one pollster for his forecast of a Labour victory of 101. He described the forecast of the Reuters panel as a 'mere 92-seat overall majority for Labour – a massive 87 seats below the actual result', while neglecting to mention that his own forecast was 179 seats below the actual result, double the average of the panel. He also compounded his error by stating that the 92-seat overall majority for Labour was 'roughly what a majority of opinion polls were then predicting': the headline in *The Times* on the morning of the election was 'MORI points to 180+ majority' and Tony King reported in the *Daily Telegraph* of 29 April, 'An average of the polls over the weekend also suggests a majority of nearly 200.'[29]

Professor David Sanders has, in the past, relied upon economic determinism, producing statistical models of voting behaviour from economic indicators such as unemployment and inflation figures and from economic 'mood' measures such as the Economic Optimism Index (EOI). In 1987, the r^2 coefficient of correlation between MORI's EOI and the Conservatives' lead over Labour was no less than 0.90, that is, 90 per cent of the variation in the electorate's voting intention in the six months leading up to the election could be explained by the 'feel-good factor', leading to Sanders's accurate prediction six months in advance of the election that the Tories would win and by how much. In 1992, however, it was only 6 per cent and in 1997, less than 2 per cent. His economic formulae didn't help him this time.

Like David Sanders, Colin Rallings and Michael Thrasher, of the *Local Government Chronicle* elections centre at Plymouth University, allowed their predictions to be influenced by their belief on the basis of past history that what the polls were implying was effectively impossible (but which turned out on 1 May to be perfectly possible). Under a headline they would probably not have preferred, 'Don't bank on a Labour landslide', they wrote,

> What if, as the Tories' gloomy party political broadcast began last week, the polls are right? A 12 per cent swing away from the Tories … would put Tony Blair in with a majority of more than 150. Labour would win in places like Braintree, where Tony Newton, leader of the House, is defending … and in Thanet South – Jonathan Aitken's seat – which has returned Tories at every general election since 1918 … Labour is more likely to get a comfortable majority than a landslide … There is something very familiar and misleading about polls which show health and education – issues on which Labour scores well – to be of greatest concern to voters. In the polling station, these count for little.[30]

Later in the election, on 25 April, based on votes cast in local government elections (which they reminded readers and viewers so often were a better guide than opinion polls to the outcome in 1992), Rallings and Thrasher reported that 'Our computer projection from these results suggests that Labour support was equivalent to a national share of 44 per cent with the Conservatives on 31 per cent and the Liberal Democrats on 20 per cent', which would have been remarkably accurate had they believed it. Instead they adjusted their published prediction to Labour 43.5 per cent, Conservative 34.5 per cent and Liberal Democrat 16 per cent, and forecast a 65-seat majority for Labour,[31] and their final Reuters predictions a couple of days later were both close to this.

Still, most of the Reuters' 'experts' were more expert than some of the paid commentators such as Stewart Steven, who wrote with a self-important certainty in the *Mail on Sunday* in December that the polls suggested that the next election is going to be a shoo-in for Labour, but that they were wrong. 'People lie something rotten when they speak to the pollsters,' he asserted, saying that the country was in a cautious mood, and that although we wanted more spent on the public services, we were 'all too aware these days that if we spend too much, it is our pocket which will suffer'. In this respect, he concluded, Mr Major is surely a safer bet than Mr Blair.[32] Later he admitted that what one pollster had to say was 'nevertheless compelling', but that he contended still that 'I have nothing against opinion polls, I just don't take them as seriously …'[33] Perhaps now he will.

Or the *Daily Mail*'s Simon Heffer, 'the pundit the politicians dread' as the *Mail* bills him, no doubt to his embarrassment: 'One reason why I have never subscribed to the Labour landslide school of thought is a firm belief that many people are lying to the opinion polls.'[34] I wonder what he thinks now; though we shall no doubt be told, for one thing is certain – even an error more colossal than that of the pollsters in the 1992 election, multiplied by a factor of ten, will not stop the pundits from punditing.

Of course, the disingenuous nonsense that was spoken by politicians on both sides is understandable if not justifiable as a campaigning tactic, even if in the long term the cure is worse than the disease. Less easily excused are the newspaper pundits who took their cues from John Major. Bruce Anderson argued:

> I could not detect any sign of a Labour landslide … A majority of the voters would prefer to see Mr Major as prime minister … I did not, however, come across many former Tory voters who had repudiated their allegiance … A Tory victory is still possible, though unlikely. But an overall Labour majority seems equally unlikely. At the time of writing, I do not believe that Mr Blair is on course to win the 57 seats he would need for an outright win.[35]

And he subsequently elaborated: 'A hung parliament with the Tories the largest party on 315, Labour 304 and Liberal Democrats 12.'[36]

Even further from the mark was Woodrow Wyatt: 'I believe that John Major, who has fought brilliantly, is on course for a majority of around 30–40.'[37]

Even Hugo Young, the *Guardian*'s pundit: 'There will be no electoral melt-down for the Conservatives on May 1. It's hard to imagine them emerging with fewer than 200 seats in the next Parliament.'[38]

By contrast, one perspicacious editor, at the *Independent on Sunday*, Rosie Boycott, headlined her newspaper the Sunday before polling day 'Labour landslide', making her colleagues (and her pollster) exceedingly nervous.

In fantasy land, literally and literarily, was *The Times*'s Philip Howard, whose well-known scepticism of polls and pollsters spilled over into Tolkienery. 'Both hobbits and pollsters are sometimes silly. Both set out to dazzle outsiders with cod scholarship. Both hobbits and opinion polls are branches of fantasy. Both are popular because they are escapes from being grown-ups in the real world.'[39]

Meanwhile, other editors opened their columns to the stargazers. The *Express* noted that 'A Tory victory is written in the stars, according to the leading Asian astrologer Vasudeva. He predicts a Tory win by between 12 and 15 seats. He says Tony Blair is doomed due to the poor positioning of something called the planet Rahu.'[40] Oh well, closer than Woodrow Wyatt! In the *Evening Standard*, Shelley von Strunckel was given a whole page to avoid committing herself to any numerical predictions whatsoever, but giving the general impression that a hung parliament should be expected. 'People are not always honest when polled', she opined. 'John Major's greatest challenge is not political, it is overcoming the shadow caused by the moon in his birthchart ... Now Blair's in for it – on election day, Saturn is next to Blair's Venus ... The results are likely to be as inconclusive as the stars. Which means Labour loses its huge poll lead, Tories gain points, and both the Liberal Democrats and the Referendum Party get more votes than expected.' All this under the headline 'Forget Polls, the Result is in the Stars'.[41]

Those pundits who wanted to disbelieve the polls presumably took encouragement from what I believe to be the worst article, in any election, in memory. Error-ridden and misguided, it was written by a one-time pollster, Conrad Jameson, described as the 'retired managing director of a market research firm', and appeared in the *Independent* on 24 April under the heading 'Polling: It's Broke, but How Do We Fix It?'[42]

'Inadequate methods and unreliable respondents are challenging pollsters, says Conrad Jameson', was the sub-head. The article contained howler after howler. The second paragraph demonstrated that he did not even know how to calculate swing. Using emotive and lurid language, he seemed to be suggesting changes: 'Its gaskets blown, its tyres flat, the clapped-out opinion poll needs an upgraded replacement, featuring long, cross-examining questionnaires, panels for tracking opinion over time and experiments to find out which issues and personalities really do flip voting intentions.'

What did he think we were doing? Had he asked we could have shown him just that, which was being done by several of the pollsters (as it has been in the past). Total fiction replaced reason, colourful similes took the place of factually based argument, ignorance of methodology and of techniques were passed off as understanding and knowledge; he even got the name of the *Independent*'s own pollster wrong. His most serious, and unproven, allegation was: 'All of us, lay and professional alike, know the answer [as to why polls were inaccurate in 1992]: Poll respondents were lying.' They weren't this time – nor is there evidence that they were in 1992.

He went on: 'Pollsters are don't knows, too, in that they don't know which way the "don't knows" will flip. That, no doubt, is why "don't know" scores are so rarely published.' But they are published every month, year in and year out, in Peter Riddell's write-up of MORI's monthly poll in *The Times* and every week during the election; the *Daily Telegraph* is normally just as punctilious in presenting its Gallup poll data. All he needed to have done was look. This was a supposedly quality broadsheet newspaper's most substantial contribution to its readers' understanding of the polls in 1997, narrowly beating a do-it-yourself poll carried out by the paper's own journalists, and not worth the paper it was printed on.

THE MOST BORING ELECTION?

No, not by a mile. The readers, for the most part, remain interested in election news, for all the media conviction that they are bored with it. A week before the election in MORI's panel survey for the *Independent on Sunday* and the *Sunday Mirror*, 16 per cent said they were 'very interested' and a further 42 per cent 'fairly interested' in news about the election, while only 14 per cent were 'not at all interested'; interest was lower than at the end of the shorter 1992 campaign, but only marginally so. The public was evenly divided as to whether there was too much coverage of the election in the newspapers, though a majority thought there was at least a little too much coverage on television; but in both cases, considerably fewer thought there was too much coverage than had done so in 1987 and 1992, though rather more did so than in 1983 (the last election when the gap between the main parties was as wide).[43]

Table 6.6: Degree of media coverage

Q. *How do you feel about the amount of coverage newspapers have been giving to the election campaign. Have they given ...?*

	1983 %	1987 %	1992 %	1997 %
Much too much	18	30	34	20
A little too much	18	22	22	21
About the right amount	46	35	32	41
A little too little	3	2	1	2
Much too little	1	1	–	–
No opinion	13	9	10	16
Too much	36	52	56	41
Too little	4	3	1	2

Q. *And how do you feel about the amount of coverage given to the election campaign on television?*

	1983 %	1987 %	1992 %	1997 %
Much too much	24	49	45	29
A little too much	26	22	23	24
About the right amount	40	24	27	37
A little too little	2	2	2	1
Much too little	1	–	–	1
No opinion	7	3	3	8
Too much	50	71	68	53
Too little	3	2	2	2

Q. *And how do you feel about the amount of coverage given to the election campaign on radio?*

	1983 %	1987 %	1992 %	1997 %
Much too much	4	12	13	8
A little too much	4	6	8	4
About the right amount	25	30	32	33
A little too little	3	3	4	3
Much too little	2	2	2	1
No opinion	61	46	41	51
Too much	8	18	21	12
Too little	5	5	6	4

MORI survey for the *Independent on Sunday* and the *Sunday Mirror*.
Fieldwork: 23–24 April 1997.
Base: 941 British adults aged 18+.

Source: Robert M. Worcester and Roger Mortimore, *British Public Opinion: The British General Election of 1997* (London: MORI, 1997).

EXIT POLLS

The exit polls conducted at the conclusion of the 1997 election did their job creditably, and the BBC's forecast of an overall majority of 'about 200' and ITV's of 159 was commendably close to the final 179, and much closer than the Reuters' 'experts' panel average of 92. However, the media need to revise their expectations of what polls are and what they can do. It is not enough merely to mention margins of error in the introduction to a report on a poll if the report then goes on to treat the figures as if they were accurate to fractions of a percentage point. Nor should the BBC or anybody else take the attitude that because polls cannot be accurate to fractions of a percentage point they are therefore useless.

This is particularly the case with exit polls. The BBC's embarrassment over its 1992 exit poll seems to have been in large measure the cause of the restrictive new *Producers' Guidelines*[44] and of the BBC's excessive suspicion of the polls in 1997. The error in the predicted share of the vote in the exit polls in 1992, though larger than the pollsters would have liked, was considerably smaller than the error in the campaign polls and in any case showed a clear and significant lead for the Conservative Party. Most of the error in the BBC's exit poll 'prediction' arose not from failures in the polling but from failures in the psephology – the design of the poll to enable it to predict numbers of seats won.

- The margin of error allowed on the seat prediction in the 1992 BBC exit poll was far smaller than was realistic: it needs to allow not only for the normal sampling variation margin of error in measuring the overall vote, but also for variance in swing between constituencies which would affect the translation of votes into seats.
- The BBC exit poll was heavily dependent on the assessment of the likely results in 'special seats' where the exit poll itself was not expected to be able to provide a meaningful prediction, such as seats, where there had been an intervening by-election. Most of these assessments were inaccurate, and a considerable proportion of the error in the prediction poll was attributable to this factor rather than to inaccuracy in the polling.
- The BBC put all its eggs in one basket by relying upon its marginals (prediction) poll for seat projection. It made no allowance for use of figures from its national (analysis) poll, and indeed these were not available at an early stage – in fact, somewhat fortuitously, these figures would have given a very accurate indication of the share of seats. Furthermore, the importance of the error in the prediction exit poll was magnified by the way in which it was tied into the ongoing computer projection on a regional basis, so that even after many results had been declared and it was clear that the exit poll was unreliable, it was still being used to predict the results of seats in many parts of the country.

None of these mistakes was the fault of the pollsters. Nevertheless, there followed a policy of not commissioning exit polls. But the only means of experimentation available to test methodologies for national exit polling is to carry out a national exit poll, and national electoral contests are few and far between – the only concrete effect of the broadcasting organisations' failure to commission a national exit poll in the 1994 European elections was to ensure that they went into the 1997 general election as badly off as before, with no chance to test any new methods or procedures. On the other hand, MORI was commissioned to conduct such an exit poll (in London) by the Electoral Reform Society, and we were able to apply lessons learned there to the work for ITN at the 1997 general election. MORI also had the benefit of the consultancy of Dr Robert Waller, who had in 1992 been part of the Harris exit poll team. One can only hope that the BBC's decision to commission an exit poll in 1997 – from the same pollsters as in 1992, NOP – and its comparative success in predicting the result, will herald a more realistic attitude in the future, although to date there seems to be a continuance of the *Guidelines* practice of censorship and ghettoising.

CONCLUSIONS

The election campaign, culminating in the Labour victory on 1 May, gives us insight into the power of public opinion. What lessons can be learned by politicians, by the media and by the pollsters?

For the politicians

Listen, and listen hard to public opinion. The polls during the last parliament and the Wirral South by-election result were warnings to the last Tory government, and they failed to heed the message.

For the media

Put the polls into perspective by all means, but don't kid yourselves that the astrologers, soothsayers, politicians and pundits are going to be better forecasters than those who rely on objective and systematic survey data, leavened with an understanding of politics and political psychology. And remember that polls are more useful as tracking and interpretative devices than horse-race forecasting.

For the polling organisations

Following the election the British pollsters were marginalised, largely ignored in Britain if not abroad, during the search for understanding of the public reaction to the death of Diana, Princess of Wales. For all the acres of newsprint devoted to journalists trying to understand the public mood, few in Britain sought understanding through poll findings; yet the US quality newspapers and news magazines were on, as were the Canadian, to find out really what people were thinking and how they were reacting. Why are the British media so hubristic, or is it self-confident, about their understanding of what people are thinking? Is our role merely to track voting intentions, unlike the media in other democratic countries, who rely on the modern tools of survey research to understand public opinion? And why is the BBC so reluctant to use the tools of survey research to aid its editorial understanding, yet so reliant on them for assessing their own output, listener reaction and staff attitudes?

NOTES

1 Lord Cocks, quoted in the *Independent*, 18 March 1996.
2 'Key Poll Boosts Labour', *Guardian*, 25 March 1997.
3 Eben Black, 'True Blue Basildon Turns on the Tories', *News of the World*, 6 April 1997.
4 'Street of Shame', *Private Eye*, 18 April 1997.
5 'Readers Ring in a New Era', *Daily Record*, 1 May 1997.
6 'New Poll Sensation: Labour "Bloody Miles Ahead"', *Daily Mirror*, 11 April 1997.
7 For example, James Blitz, 'Europe Provides Major with Glimmer of a Silver Lining', *Financial Times*, 18 March 1997.
8 Anthony Bevins, 'Out There, It's Not Over Yet', *Independent*, 21 April 1997.
9 Lucy Kellaway, 'The Long and Short of Executive Pay', *Financial Times*, 28 April 1997.
10 James Blitz, 'Floating Voters Drift Labour's Way', *Financial Times*, 11 April 1997.
11 Lucy Kellaway, 'The Long And Short of Executive Pay', *Financial Times*, 28 April 1997.
12 'In the Tearoom', *Private Eye*, 7 March 1997.
13 Peter Riddell, 'Major's Poll Claims Do Not Fit The Facts', *The Times*, 1 February 1997.
14 David Butler, 'Still Far Off the 38 per cent They Need', *Financial Times*, 21 April 1997.
15 Ewen MacAskill, 'Tories' Turning Point? Or still Trailing Points?', *Guardian*, 22 April 1997.
16 Peter Kellner, 'Landslide: The Word Neither Side Wants to Hear', *Evening Standard*, 22 April 1997.
17 Huw Richards, 'Whether or not Forecasters', *Times Higher Education Supplement*, 27 March 1997.
18 David Butler, 'Marginal Results from Intensive Campaigning', *Financial Times*, 1 April 1997.
19 John Curtice, 'Geography of Poll Swings Maps out a Landslide for Labour', *Guardian*, 12 April 1997.
20 Peter Kellner, 'Labour on Course for Three-Figure Majority', *Observer*, 27 April 1997.
21 Peter Kellner, 'Whatever the Polls' History, it's still Labour by over 100', *Evening Standard*, 28 April 1997.
22 Peter Kellner, 'Labour with 129 Majority', *Evening Standard*, 1 May 1997.
23 Peter Kellner, 'Labour Massing at the Gates of the Tory Citadels in London',

Evening Standard, 4 April 1997.

24 'Were the Experts Right?', *Daily Telegraph*, 2 May 1997.

25 John Curtice, 'Forsyth, Lang and Rifkind Heading for Defeat', *Scotland on Sunday*, 27 April 1997.

26 David Carlton, 'Voters Doubts Begin To Turn Tide for Tories', *Sunday Telegraph*, 13 April 1997.

27 David Carlton, 'Get Ready for a Hung Parliament', *Sunday Telegraph*, 27 April 1997.

28 David Carlton, 'On Getting it Wrong', *Spectator*, 10 May 1997.

29 Anthony King, 'Brutal Truth Facing the Tories', *Daily Telegraph*, April 29, 1997.

30 Colin Rallings and Michael Thrasher, 'Don't Bank on a Labour Landslide', *Sunday Times*, 13 April 1997.

31 Colin Rallings and Michael Thrasher, 'Poll Gurus Predict Labour to Win with 65-seat Majority', *Local Government Chronicle*, 25 April 1997.

32 Stewart Steven, 'Why the Polls Could Be Wildly Wrong', *Mail on Sunday*, reported in *The Week*, 7 December 1996.

33 Stewart Steven, 'Sorry Michael – but the Fat Lady Has Cast Her Vote', *Mail on Sunday*, 13 April 1997.

34 Simon Heffer, 'Battle for those Missing Millions', *Daily Mail*, 5 April 1997.

35 Bruce Anderson, 'The Election Will Be Decided by the Undecided', *Spectator*, 26 April 1997.

36 'Were the Experts Right?', *Daily Telegraph*, 2 May 1997.

37 Woodrow Wyatt, 'Don't Be Duped by the Polls', *The Times*, 29 April 1997.

38 Hugo Young, 'Tories Bloom in their New-Found Freedom', *Guardian*, 16 April 1997.

39 Philip Howard, 'Rogue or Telephone or Greasy – Polls Can Be Hobbit Forming', *The Times*, 11 April 1997.

40 *Daily Express*, 26 April 1997.

41 Shelley von Strunckel, 'Forget Polls, the Result is in the Stars', *London Evening Standard*, 28 April 1997.

42 Conrad Jameson, 'Polling: It's Broke, but How Do We Fix It?', *Independent*, 24 April 1997.

43 Robert M. Worcester and Roger Mortimore, *British Public Opinion: The British General Election of 1997*, MORI 'Green Book' (London: MORI, August 1997).

44 *Producers' Guidelines* (London: BBC, 1994), ch. 16 and, slightly revised, *Producers' Guidelines* (London: BBC, 1996), ch. 20.

7

Constituency Campaigning in the 1997 General Election: Party Effort and Electoral Effect

DAVID DENVER and GORDON HANDS

In the past few years, what used to be the orthodoxy about constituency campaigning – that it was a meaningless ritual, hardly worthy of serious consideration and very rarely having any effect on constituency election results – has come under sustained attack. Using a variety of methods and measures, Johnston and Pattie, Seyd and Whiteley and we ourselves have explored variations in campaign strength and shown that constituency election campaigning can significantly affect election outcomes; parties which mount strong local campaigns achieve better results than those whose campaigns are weaker.[1]

The work of Johnston and Pattie and Seyd and Whiteley is based on indirect or surrogate indicators of campaign strength, but for the 1992 general election we were able to devise a more direct measure of campaign strength based on a nationwide survey of election agents (who are normally in charge of constituency campaigns). The results of our research are reported in detail in *Modern Constituency Electioneering*, but four of our main conclusions may be summarised as follows:

- The central party organisations have greatly increased the extent of their involvement in local campaigning. In all parties 'target' or 'key' seats are selected and party headquarters devote considerable effort to ensuring that campaigns in these constituencies are as strong as possible.
- The strength of campaigning in all parties varies with the electoral status of the constituency. For all three major parties in 1992 campaigns were weakest in hopeless seats. Labour and Liberal Democrat campaigns were strongest – as might be expected – in their marginal and possible seats. By contrast, Conservative campaigns were strongest in their safe and comfortable seats.
- The Conservatives, overall, had the strongest local campaigns in 1992,

Labour the next strongest and the Liberal Democrats the weakest. But Labour was most successful in focusing its campaigning effort where it mattered – the strongest campaigns of all, by some margin, were Labour's in their marginal seats.

• The performance of Labour and Liberal Democrat candidates (measured by change between 1987 and 1992 in the share of the electorate that they gained) was significantly affected by the intensity of their local campaigns. But, surprisingly, Conservative campaigning had no measurable effect on their performance.

In this chapter we present a preliminary report on the results of a further survey of agents carried out immediately following the 1997 election.[2] As we shall see, in the period between 1992 and 1997 there were significant developments in the application of new technology in local campaigning, and there is evidence that all of the major parties became increasingly aware of the importance of their local effort – at least partly as a result of the academic work cited above.[3] The parties expected that in 1997 the constituency campaigns would be a key part of the electoral battle, and they made their plans accordingly. The Liberal Democrats determined to focus ruthlessly on winnable seats; only the campaigns in these seats were co-ordinated and monitored from Cowley Street, the rest being delegated to regional level.[4] Conservative Central Office, conscious of the decline in numbers of their full-time agents – traditionally a source of strength for them – for the first time directly appointed and paid for a large number of agents in key seats. Meanwhile, Labour launched 'Operation victory', a strategy for local campaigns which in many ways rewrote the rules, and involved an immensely detailed and thorough plan of action for implementation in target seats.[5]

Table 7.1: Responses to agents' questionnaires, 1992 and 1997

	1992		1997	
	N	% of possible	N	% of possible
Conservative	266	42.0	433	67.8
Labour	356	56.2	444	69.5
Liberal Democrat	386	60.9	405	63.4
Plaid Cymru	21	55.3	25	62.5
SNP	26	36.1	44	61.1
Total	1,055	53.0	1,351	66.6

1997 SURVEY OF AGENTS

As in 1992, self-completion questionnaires for our survey of agents in the 1997 election were sent out immediately after polling day. Thanks largely to the enthusiastic cooperation of the national officials of the parties, we obtained many more responses than in 1992. Questionnaires were sent to the agents of the major parties in 639 British constituencies and the number of replies received, as compared with 1992, are shown in Table 7.1.[6] As can be seen, the response rate was sharply higher in each case and the rise was especially marked in the case of the Conservatives (+25.8 per cent).

Table 7.2: Response rates according to electoral status of constituency (%)

	Very safe	Comfortable	Marginal	Possible	Hopeless
Conservative	66.5	58.8	74.8	69.7	65.8
	(119)	(47)	(119)	(46)	(102)
Labour	60.0	66.2	66.9	81.0	74.9
	(81)	(47)	(91)	(34)	(191)
Liberal Democrat	50.0	71.4	44.8	48.8	65.4
	(1)	(5)	(13)	(21)	(365)

Since the electoral status of constituencies prior to the election is a key variable in our analysis, we show in Table 7.2, for the three parties on which this paper focuses, the number of responses (in parentheses) and response rates for different categories of seat.[7] Only Liberal Democrat responses in their safe, marginal and possible seats (where the numbers involved are very small) fell significantly below the average.

CAMPAIGN EFFORTS

In our study of the 1992 election we developed an index measuring campaign intensity across parties and constituencies. The index was based on answers to a range of questions covering seven dimensions of campaigning – the degree of advance preparation, the nature and extent of constituency campaign organisation, the number of volunteer workers, the extent of canvassing, the amount of literature distributed, the extent of computer usage and the sophistication of the polling day operation.[8] In the 1997 questionnaire we included a number of new questions designed to tap some of the technological and organisational developments we referred to above, and at a later stage in our analysis we expect to incorporate the responses to some of these questions into a revised version of the index of campaign strength. One of the advantages of having survey results for two consecutive elections, however, is that comparisons can be made, and so the preliminary analysis of the 1997 data presented in this chapter replicates the method used in 1992 in order to produce a comparable index.

Campaign workers, canvassing and computers

Three of the dimensions of campaigning are worth discussing in some detail before we consider the overall index of campaigning – the numbers of campaign workers, the level of canvassing and the use of computers. In each case we are able to make revealing comparisons between 1992 and 1997.

Table 7.3: Mean numbers of party members in different categories of seat, 1992 and 1997

		Very safe	Comfortable	Marginal	Possible	Hopeless	All
Conservative	1992	2,495	1,973	1,086	507	305	1,542
	1997	1,367	1,095	629	291	167	737
Labour	1992	483	558	577	504	348	444
	1997	669	602	765	575	474	592
Liberal Democrat	1992		408		327	128	166
	1997		449		435	127	159

Notes: In this and subsequent tables the numbers are close to those reported in Table 7.2. Fifteen cases have been excluded from all tables since they contained extensive missing data. In individual tables the numbers vary slightly because of missing data on particular questions. Since the numbers are small, Liberal Democrat results for safe, comfortable and marginal seats are combined and reported as a single figure.

To start with, Table 7.3 shows the mean numbers of party members as reported by agents. Although the size of party membership in a constituency is not itself a component of our campaigning index, it is likely to give a good indication of the general health of local party organisations, and Seyd and Whiteley, in some of their work, have taken it as a measure of the likely strength of local campaigning. There has been a good deal of speculation that there has been a dramatic decline in the health of the Conservative Party organisation at the grass-roots in recent years and our figures provide strong evidence that this is indeed the case. Between 1992 and 1997 the average reported Conservative membership has fallen from 1,542 to 737 – a drop of more than 50 per cent – and a large decline has occurred in each category of seat.

Labour membership, on the other hand, has increased somewhat across the board, as has Liberal Democrat membership in seats where they are strongest. Not all party members are active in election campaigns, of course, but they represent a pool of potential workers who can be called upon. The Conservatives on these figures still just about have the largest pool overall – but the gap between them and the other parties is much smaller than it was and in marginal and possible seats the Conservatives now lag some way behind Labour.

Table 7.4: Mean numbers of campaign workers, 1992 and 1997

		Very safe	Comfortable	Marginal	Possible	Hopeless	All
Conservative	1992	134	113	78	30	15	91
	1997	99	77	62	21	13	58
Labour	1992	43	70	78	77	30	50
	1997	55	72	76	73	39	56
Liberal Democrat	1992		110		63	19	31
	1997		131		125	19	30

Tables 7.4 and 7.5 give details of the numbers of volunteers working in the election campaign. Table 7.4 shows the average number of workers helping on an average day towards the end of the campaign. Overall, the figures suggest that fewer people were active in 1997 than in 1992 – possibly due to the length of the campaign – but almost all of the decline is attributable to the Conservatives. There was little change in the Labour numbers, and the Liberal Democrats had substantially more workers in their best seats. As in 1992, the Conservatives had most workers in their safest seats – which may have been no bad thing on this occasion – while the other parties had more workers in constituencies which, on the face of it, were more likely to change hands. Similar patterns are evident in the case of the numbers of workers on polling day, as can be seen from Table 7.5. Here the numbers are larger, as one might expect – polling day work is more exciting than the grind of canvassing and delivering leaflets during the build-up – but, as compared with 1992, the figures again show a sharp decline for the Conservatives. In 1992 we estimated that, overall, about 280,000 people played a part in helping one or other of the major parties on polling day; on the basis of our data that figure fell to about 205,000 in 1997.

Traditional doorstep canvassing has long been a central element in any serious constituency campaign. Its purpose is to identify supporters who can then be mobilised on election day in a 'get out the vote' effort. Two innovations have modified the use of traditional canvassing,

Table 7.5: Mean numbers of polling day workers, 1992 and 1997

		Very safe	Comfortable	Marginal	Possible	Hopeless	All
Conservative	1992	386	356	230	69	34	263
	1997	243	179	138	57	19	135
Labour	1992	114	147	208	194	73	124
	1997	95	123	213	181	87	127
Liberal Democrat	1992		222		159	40	65
	1997		200		247	41	59

however. First, in recent elections canvassing by telephone rather than on the doorstep has become more popular. With telephone ownership now close to universal, telephone canvassing has a number of advantages – it can be done in bad weather, people who might be unwilling to open their doors to strangers or who live in remote areas can be contacted easily, supporters who are elderly or infirm can undertake it, and so on. We commented in our 1992 study that telephone canvassing seemed to be here to stay and our data show that in 1997 it became much more common.[9] 'A substantial amount' of telephone canvassing was undertaken by 25 per cent of Conservative campaigns (15 per cent in 1992) and by 26 per cent of Labour campaigns (8 per cent in 1992). In Labour's marginal and possible seats the figures reached 60 per cent and 59 per cent respectively, the largest proportion for the Conservatives being 40 per cent in their marginals. Although the Liberal Democrats certainly use telephone canvassing in by-elections, only 1 per cent of their agents claimed to have done so in the general election – the same figure as in 1992. In seats where some telephone canvassing was done, the Conservatives canvassed an average of 15 per cent of the electorate in this way, Labour 19 per cent and the Liberal Democrats 7 per cent. It seems likely that in future elections telephone canvassing will increase in popularity, and clearly the Liberal Democrats have some catching up to do in this respect.

A second innovation in canvassing is that in well-organised constituencies much of it is now done before the campaign formally begins. Labour's 'Operation victory' not only renamed the activity 'voter identification' – their *General Election Handbook* proclaimed 'Canvassing is dead. Long live voter i/d' – but also aimed to ensure that in target constituencies 'voter identification' was completed well before the start of the campaign. In addition, this process involved much more than simply noting down whether electors were 'For', 'Against' or 'Doubtful', which was the traditional form of the canvass return. Party workers – carefully vetted, in at least some constituencies, to ensure that they were presentable – were provided with a script and, depending upon the answers to pre-worded questions, voters were classified into one of no less than ten main categories and six sub-categories. These included, for example, 'reliable Labour voter', 'SNP identifiers with Labour as their second preference', 'Undecided voters who voted Conservative in 1992' and so on. The plan was that relevant groups (loyal Conservatives, for example, being ignored) would then be targeted with appropriate direct mail communications and further telephone calls.

In order to explore the extent of pre-campaign work of this kind we asked agents of all three parties how far advanced their preparations were in 'identifying potential supporters through canvassing' when the date of the election was announced. In comfortable, marginal and possible seats 31 per cent of Labour agents said that they were fully prepared. The same was true, however, of 23 per cent of Conservative campaigns, so that the Conservatives too appear to have been preparing the ground in advance. However the corresponding figure for the Liberal Democrats was only 5 per cent.

The more widespread use of telephone canvassing, and the fact that a good deal of canvassing was completed before the campaign started, create some problems for our analysis, since our 1992 index involved a question asking about the proportion of the electorate canvassed in the traditional manner during the campaign itself. A number of respondents answered 'none' to this question in 1997, but took the trouble to point out that all of their canvassing had already been done before the campaign started. In this analysis, in order to allow comparison with 1992, we have not altered the construction of our index using the 1997 data, but in further work we will need to reconstruct the index to take account both of more extensive voter identification in the pre-campaign period and of telephone canvassing.

Table 7.6: Doorstep canvassing in 1992 and 1997; total canvassing in 1997

		% of electorate canvassed					
		Very safe	Comfortable	Marginal	Possible	Hopeless	All
Conservative	1992	51	52	45	31	20	42
	1997	36	37	28	25	14	28
	1997 total	43	46	41	32	18	36
Labour	1992	28	50	56	50	23	35
	1997	21	30	32	27	24	26
	1997 total	23	38	56	52	29	36
Liberal Democrat	1992		29		26	10	13
	1997		28		34	9	12
	1997 total		33		38	10	13

Table 7.6 shows the mean percentages of the electorate canvassed on their doorsteps during the campaign (the variable used as part of the campaigning index) in both 1992 and 1997, but also gives, for 1997, the total percentages canvassed during the campaign, arrived at by simply adding the percentages reported for doorstep and telephone canvassing. (If anything this is likely to exaggerate the amount of canvassing done, since there may have been some overlap between the figures reported for doorstep and telephone canvassing.) The figures show that doorstep canvassing by the Conservatives and Labour declined quite sharply, especially in comfortable, marginal and possible seats. As explained above, this seems likely to have been due to the increase in telephone canvassing and in pre-campaign canvassing. When campaign telephone canvassing is included, however, the Conservatives' overall 1997 figure still falls well short of their doorstep canvassing figure for 1992. For Labour, the total canvassing figure for 1997 is similar to that for 1992 – but it has to be remembered that the 1997 total figure is likely to be an exaggeration. Although both parties contacted just over a third of the electorate in 1997, it can be seen that Labour's canvassing effort was more effectively concentrated in marginal and possible seats. Traditional canvassing is certainly not yet dead and, given a volatile electorate, the parties would surely be unwise to cease seeking to identify supporters in the last few weeks before polling day. But the familiar sight of party activists going from door to door, armed with a canvassing pack, seems likely to become less common in future general election campaigns.

Another important development in recent election campaigning is the use of personal computers. Our results from the 1992 election showed that the use of computers was then already widespread, but it seems clear that there was a further substantial expansion in computer usage in 1997. The major parties provide software packages for campaigning and put considerable efforts into training party workers

Table 7.7: Use of computers (%)

		Very safe	Comfortable	Marginal	Possible	Hopeless	All
Conservative	1992	87	90	93	71	45	79
	1997	99	100	97	82	61	88
Labour	1992	73	73	97	97	67	77
	1997	82	89	99	100	88	90
Liberal Democrat	1992		79		89	65	68
	1997		100		100	74	76

in their use. Computers can take much of the drudgery out of campaign work and greatly facilitate the use of personalised direct mail communications targeted on particular groups of voters. As the ownership and use of personal computers spread it was to be expected that parties would also use them for their own purposes. As Table 7.7 shows, in 1992, 79 per cent of Conservative campaigns already made some use of computers, as did 77 per cent of Labour campaigns and 68 per cent of Liberal Democrat campaigns. In 1997 these figures increased to 88 per cent, 90 per cent and 76 per cent respectively. By the next election, constituency campaigns without computers will be rare. The figures for the number of machines used by campaigns given in Table 7.8 also show sharp increases as compared with 1992. The Conservative increase is more modest than for the other two parties, but Labour and the Liberal Democrats were very well supplied with hardware in their comfortable to possible seats, and even in their hopeless seats averaged more than two PCs per constituency.

Table 7.8: Mean number of computers used

		Very safe	Comfortable	Marginal	Possible	Hopeless	All
Conservative	1992	1.4	1.4	1.5	0.9	0.5	1.2
	1997	2.0	2.0	1.8	1.0	0.9	1.6
Labour	1992	1.5	1.8	4.2	3.5	1.4	2.3
	1997	1.9	3.7	4.8	4.5	2.6	3.2
Liberal Democrat	1992		2.7		3.0	1.4	1.7
	1997		4.3		6.0	2.2	2.5

Overall campaign intensity

In order to analyse campaigning and its effects across a large number of constituencies, it is desirable to have a single 'campaign intensity score' for each party in each constituency. As noted above, for the 1992 campaign we combined the three dimensions of campaigning that have been discussed here with four others in order to create such a score. We have repeated this analysis for 1997, using a principal components analysis of all seven dimensions of campaigning and taking the factor scores that this produces as a standardised campaign strength score.[10] Table 7.9 shows the mean party scores for 1997 according to the status of constituency.

Unsurprisingly, all three parties had weak campaigns in their hopeless seats, as did the Conservatives in their possibles and Labour in very safe seats. The strongest Conservative campaigns were in their very safe seats and their next strongest in seats that they held comfortably. Labour and Liberal Democrat campaigns, in contrast, were strongest in constituencies where the payoff in terms of winning seats seemed likely to be greatest. For the second successive election Labour campaigns in their marginal seats were the strongest of all and their campaigning efforts were much more effectively focused than those of the Conservatives.

Table 7.9: Mean campaign intensity scores, 1997

		Very safe	Comfortable	Marginal	Possible	Hopeless	All
Conservative	1997	0.81	0.72	0.58	−0.25	−0.81	0.24
Labour	1997	0.04	0.53	1.09	1.02	0.04	0.39
Liberal Democrat	1997		0.97		0.90	−0.79	−0.62

The figures in Table 7.10 show that, in regional terms, the Conservatives were relatively weak in Scotland, Wales and the three northern regions but strong in East Anglia, the south-east and south-west. Labour campaigns were above average strength in every region, but weakest in the south-west, Yorkshire and Scotland. The Liberal Democrats were very weak in Wales and in the northern and midlands regions but above average in the south-west and (just) the south-east. It should be noted, however, that these regional variations are affected by, among other things, the distribution of safe, marginal and hopeless seats within them. A fuller account of regional differences requires multivariate analysis, to be reported elsewhere.

Table 7.10: Mean campaign intensity scores by region

	Conservative	Labour	Liberal Democrat
Scotland	−0.08 (47)	0.25 (44)	−0.87 (39)
Wales	−0.64 (22)	0.35 (22)	−1.08 (24)
North	−0.25 (30)	0.27 (21)	−0.97 (28)
North West	0.00 (48)	0.37 (45)	−0.97 (42)
Yorks and Humberside	−0.30 (42)	0.15 (41)	−0.97 (39)
West Midlands	0.05 (40)	0.48 (46)	−0.90 (34)
East Midlands	0.47 (19)	0.63 (26)	−0.92 (28)
East Anglia	0.95 (13)	0.53 (15)	−0.67 (17)
South West	0.77 (36)	0.01 (41)	0.46 (28)
South East	0.91 (83)	0.42 (82)	0.03 (79)
Greater London	0.33 (49)	0.74 (54)	−0.70 (44)
All	0.24	0.39	−0.62

Note: the number of cases is shown in brackets.

We cannot make a direct comparison between the campaign intensity scores we previously reported for 1992 and those calculated for 1997, since each set of scores is standardised for each particular election. In order to compare the two, therefore, we combined the two data sets and conducted a new factor analysis, thus producing standardised intensity scores for all campaigns in the two elections. The new data, shown in Table 7.11, allow a direct comparison to be made of the two elections. Given our discussion of some of the components of the campaigning index, it is not surprising to find that the overall intensity of constituency campaigning by the Conservatives declined sharply in 1997 – the Conservatives could no longer claim the strongest overall organisation. Moreover, the decline was greatest in comfortable and marginal seats and smallest in hopeless seats where, in strictly instrumental terms, efforts are largely wasted. Labour campaigning in 1997, on the other hand, was stronger overall than it had been in 1992 but most of this increase is accounted for by hopeless seats. Labour campaigning in marginal and possible seats apparently declined in intensity on these figures. However, our earlier discussion of the ways in which the pattern of campaigning changed in 1997 needs to be borne in mind. Our index does not take account, for example, of the growth in the use of telephone canvassing and the greater stress on 'pre-campaign campaigning' in 1997. Labour campaigning may, therefore, have been stronger in these sorts of seat in 1997 even though our index, based on 1992 campaigning techniques, shows a decline. The successful effects of the Liberal Democrats' targeting strategy in 1997 can be seen in the fact that the intensity of their campaigns did not change very much in their hopeless seats but increased sharply in others.

Table 7.11: Mean campaign intensity scores: 1992 and 1997 compared

		Very safe	Comfortable	Marginal	Possible	Hopeless	All
Conservative	1992	1.04	1.11	0.91	−0.02	−0.56	0.62
	1997	0.76	0.68	0.55	−0.24	−0.78	0.22
Labour	1992	0.06	0.44	1.24	1.15	−0.22	0.29
	1997	0.03	0.50	1.03	0.96	0.03	0.36
Liberal Democrat	1992		0.63		0.56	−0.84	−0.60
	1997		0.86		0.83	−0.77	−0.61

THE EFFECTS OF LOCAL CAMPAIGNING ON PARTY PERFORMANCE

Despite the huge efforts made by the central party organisations, not to mention thousands of agents, organisers and 'foot soldiers' on the ground, the impact of local campaigning remains controversial. Even among the 'revisionist' academics who argue that there are significant effects, there is no consensus about the appropriate measure of party performance and there are considerable disagreements as to, for example, whether there are differential effects for challenging and incumbent parties.[11] We offer here, however, a preliminary analysis of effects in the 1997 election without getting into these controversial areas.

Our preferred measure of party performance is the change in a party's share of the electorate since the previous election but, unfortunately, we cannot use this measure for 1997 owing to the extensive boundary revisions that were implemented between 1992 and 1997.[12] We concentrate, therefore, on two other measures – change in share of the vote obtained (change from the notional share in 1992 in many instances) and actual share in 1997, controlling for share in 1992.

A priori one might expect that constituency campaigning would have had little if any effect on the performances of the Labour and Conservative parties in the 1997 election. Labour won a landslide victory, gaining not only their target seats where a major campaign effort was made, but also many seats that must previously have been considered hopeless, or at least very long shots. In these sorts of seats the strategy of Labour's campaign managers was to run 'high-profile, high-impact and minimal-resource' campaigns with 'minimal numbers of volunteers'.[13] On the other hand, the Conservatives had, as before, relatively well-resourced campaigns in their safe seats, but analysis of the election results shows that their share of the vote declined most in their safest seats. The data in Table 7.12 challenge these expectations, however.

The first two rows present simple correlation coefficients showing the relationship between score on the campaigning index and change in share of vote in 1992 and 1997. The 1997 coefficient for the Conservatives is negative – where they campaigned hardest they lost most. But this result is not new: exactly the same relationship (although to a lesser extent) was found in 1992. The correlation for Labour is positive and significant and indicates a relationship very similar to that found in 1992. The strength of Liberal Democrat campaigning is also positively associated with their performance, with a slightly stronger correlation than in 1992. The third and fourth rows of Table 7.12 show partial correlation coefficients indicating the strength of association between constituency campaigning and share of vote, controlling for vote share in the previous election. Here we have something of a puzzle. The results for Labour and the Liberal Democrats are very close to those obtained using change in share of the vote, and again suggest clear positive relationships between party performance and campaigning.

But in this case the result for the Conservatives in 1997 – a significant positive coefficient, though smaller than those for the other parties – contrasts with that found in 1992 and with those found for change in share of the vote in both 1992 and 1997. This simple analysis suggests, therefore, that as in 1992 Labour and Liberal Democrat campaigns affected the results that they obtained – more effort and better organisation produced a better performance. In the case of the Conservatives the evidence is inconclusive: the correlation with change in share of the vote suggests that once again in 1997 Conservative campaigns did not have a positive effect; when we use vote share, however, the figures do suggest a positive effect for the Conservatives, though a weaker one than for the other parties.

Table 7.12: Correlations between campaign intensity and party performance

	Conservative	Labour	Liberal Democrat
Change in share of vote 1987–92	−0.20	0.41	0.27
Change in share of vote 1992–97	−0.34	0.40	0.30
% share of vote 1992 (controlling for share 1987)	−0.06[a]	0.44	0.41
% share of vote 1997 (controlling for share 1992)	0.16	0.42	0.40

Note: [a] not significant

Our next step is to seek to take account of other variables that might explain constituency differences in vote changes. Unlike *levels* of party support, *changes* in party support are not consistently or strongly associated with social structural variables, but there is a good deal of evidence that incumbent MPs do better in terms of vote change than new candidates.[14] In addition, in 1997 there were clear regional differences in changes in party support. Labour, for example increased its vote share by 12.5 per cent in Greater London, but by only 6.6 per cent in Scotland. We therefore incorporate dummy variables for personal incumbency and region, together with the campaigning index, into a series of multivariate analyses.[15] These are reported in Table 7.13. The regression equations reported on the left-hand side of the table have change in share of the vote as the dependent variable. The r^2 figures for these equations are not very impressive, but the object of the analysis is not to account for variations in changes in the shares of votes obtained by the parties. Rather the point is to discover whether campaigning remains a significant influence when other factors are taken into account. As can be seen, incumbency made a difference only for the Liberal Democrats and, although there were significant regional variations for all parties, the introduction of these variables does not alter the original conclusions drawn from the simple correlations. The three right-hand columns of the table have share of vote in 1997 as the dependent variable, with share in 1992 as an additional control. In these cases the r^2 statistics are much larger – share in 1992 is a powerful predictor of share in 1997 – but again it is the coefficients for the campaigning index that are important. Although this analysis constitutes a much more stringent test of campaign effects, the coefficients for the campaigning index remain significant and in this case suggest that for all three parties campaigning significantly and positively affected performance.

In both our correlation analysis and more complex multiple regression analyses, then, the results for the Conservatives appear contradictory. When simple change in share of the vote is used to measure party performance Conservative campaigning appears to have had a negative effect – the better the local campaign the worse the performance. On the other hand, when 1997 vote share is taken as the dependent variable, with 1992 share as a control, Conservative campaigning is seen to have a positive impact – the better the constituency campaign the better the party's performance. How is this contradiction to be explained? Analysis of the results of the 1997 election has established that Conservative losses were larger where they had more votes to lose (for all constituencies the correlation between Conservative vote share in 1992 and change in share between 1992 and 1997 was –0.589).[16] We have also seen (Table 7.9) that Conservative campaigns were stronger in their safer seats – hence the apparently negative effect of campaigning. The positive results found when we take account of previous

Table 7.13: Multiple regression analyses (all responses)

Dependent variable:	Change in vote share			Vote share 1997		
	Con.	Lab.	Lib. Dem.	Con.	Lab.	Lib. Dem.
Index of campaigning	−0.27	0.33	0.34	0.05	0.09	0.26
Incumbent MP	*	*	0.17	0.06	*	0.12
Vote share 1992	n/a	n/a	n/a	0.91	0.95	0.68
Greater London	−0.24	0.15	*	−0.07	0.03	*
Scotland	0.26	−0.18	*	*	−0.05	*
South-East	−0.11	0.09	−0.18	*	*	−0.04
South-West	0.10	−0.12	−0.12	0.03	−0.04	*
Wales	*	−0.25	*	*	−0.06	*
Yorkshire	*	−0.11	*	*	−0.03	*
North	*	*	*	−0.03	*	*
r^2	0.27	0.30	0.15	0.96	0.95	0.89

Note: the figures shown are standardised regression coefficients. * = not significant.

strength, by controlling for 1992 vote share, suggest that the broad pattern of changes in the Conservative share of the vote is overlaid by another. At any given level of previous electoral strength, stronger campaigns tended to produce better results and weaker campaigns worse results. Deviations from the expected 1997 vote share (i.e., expected on the basis of 1992 vote share) are at least partly explained by variations in the strength of local campaigns.

Thus far in our analysis of campaign effects we have been dealing with the campaigns of each party separately. It is likely, however, that a party's performance will also be affected by the campaigns of the other competing parties (as well as by whether an opponent was an incumbent), and in order to take account of this we need to incorporate the incumbency variable and campaign intensity scores for all three major parties into our analyses. This is done in Table 7.14, which presents the results of regression analyses for constituencies from which we had a response from all three parties ($N = 183$). As before, the left-hand side focuses on change in share of vote. The change in the Conservative share of the vote was not influenced by incumbency or by Labour or Liberal Democrat campaigning but only by region and (negatively) by Conservative campaign intensity. Conservative campaigning had no effect, however, on Labour or Liberal Democrat performance, whereas the campaigns of these parties affected their own and the other's performance in the expected ways. The same is true when vote share in 1997 is the dependent variable, although in this case Conservative performance also appears to have been improved by Conservative campaigning (coefficient 0.06) and worsened by Labour campaigning (coefficient −0.04).

Table 7.14: Multiple regression analyses (constituencies with responses from all three parties, N=183)

Dependent variable:	Change in vote share			Vote share 1997		
	Con.	Lab.	Lib. Dem.	Con.	Lab.	Lib. Dem.
Con. index	−0.18	*	*	0.06	*	*
Lab. index	*	0.31	−0.19	−0.04	0.11	−0.13
Lib. Dem. index	*	−0.26	0.32	*	−0.14	0.31
Con. incumbent MP	*	0.19	*	*	*	*
Lab. incumbent MP	*	*	*	−0.09	*	*
Lib. Dem. incumbent MP	*	*	*	−0.05	*	0.14
Vote share 1992	n/a	n/a	n/a	0.86	0.85	0.55
Greater London	−0.27	0.23	*	−0.06	0.06	*
Scotland	0.15	*	*	*	*	*
South-East	−0.18	0.28	−0.22	*	0.05	*
North-West	*	0.15	*	*	0.05	*
r^2	0.16	0.34	0.16	0.96	0.96	0.89

Note: the figures shown are standardised regression coefficients. *=not significant.

CONCLUSIONS

Compared with 1992, constituency campaigning in the 1997 election displayed elements of both continuity and change. Although we have not presented detailed evidence on the topic here, it seems clear that all three central party organisations further increased their involvement in local campaigning. Special organisers or centrally appointed agents were placed in key seats and both the 'long' and 'short' campaigns were closely monitored. Again as in 1992, the strength of campaigning in all parties varied with the electoral status of the seat, and while the pattern of variation was 'rational' in the case of Labour and the Liberal Democrats, the fact that the strongest Conservative campaigns were in their safest seats must remain a matter of concern to their strategists. A significant change in 1997 was that the Conservatives – long believed to have had the most powerful grass-roots organisations – did not have the strongest election campaigns, and in the critical 'swing' seats they were clearly outgunned by Labour.

As far as effects go, our analysis suggests that, as before, Labour and Liberal Democrat campaigning clearly affected their performance. Unlike in 1992, however, we find that on this occasion, once previous electoral strength is taken into account, the level of Conservative campaigning did affect the party's performance in the 1997 election, although to a lesser extent than the campaigns of the other two parties. This result is encouraging for the 'revisionist' researchers who have argued that local campaigning matters, and should also provide some comfort to Conservative party professionals who have been attempting to improve the party's campaigning at local level.

NOTES

The work on which this chapter is based is financed by a grant from the Economic and Social Research Council (ref: R000222027).

1 See R. J. Johnston, *Money and Votes* (London: Croom Helm, 1987); R. J. Johnston, C. J. Pattie and L. C. Johnston, 'The Impact of Constituency Spending on the Result of the 1987 British General Election', *Electoral Studies*, 8 (1989), pp. 143–55; R. J. Johnston and C. J. Pattie, 'The Impact of Spending on Party Constituency Campaigns at Recent British General Elections', *Party Politics*, 1 (1995), pp. 261–73; E. A. Fieldhouse, C .J. Pattie and R. J. Johnston, 'Tactical Voting and Party Constituency Campaigning at the 1992 General Election in England', *British Journal of Political Science*, 26 (1996), pp. 403–18; C. J. Pattie, P. Whiteley, R. J. Johnston and P. Seyd (1994) 'Measuring Local Campaign Effects: Labour Party Constituency Campaigning at the 1987 General Election', *Political Studies*, 42 (1994), pp. 469–79; C. J. Pattie, R. J. Johnston and E. A. Fieldhouse, 'Winning the Local Vote: The Effectiveness of Constituency Campaign Spending in Great

Britain, 1983–1992', *American Political Science Review*, 89 (1995), pp. 969–83; P. Seyd and P. Whiteley, *Labour's Grass Roots: the Politics of Party Membership* (Oxford: Clarendon Press, 1992); P. Whiteley and P. Seyd, 'Labour's Vote and Local Activism', *Parliamentary Affairs*, 45 (1992), pp. 582–95; P. Whiteley, P. Seyd and J. Richardson, *True Blues: The Politics of Conservative Party Membership* (Oxford: Clarendon Press, 1994); D. Denver and G. Hands, 'Constituency Campaigning', *Parliamentary Affairs*, 45 (1992), pp. 528–44; D. Denver and G. Hands, 'Measuring the Intensity and Effectiveness of Constituency Campaigning in the 1992 General Election', in D. Denver, P. Norris, D. Broughton and C. Rallings (eds), *British Elections and Parties Yearbook 1993* (Hemel Hempstead: Harvester Wheatsheaf, 1993), pp. 229–42; D. Denver and G. Hands, 'Constituency Campaigning in the 1992 General Election: The Peculiar Case of the Conservatives', in D. Farrell, D. Broughton, D. Denver and J. Fisher (eds), *British Elections and Parties Yearbook 1996* (London: Frank Cass, 1996), pp. 85–105; D. Denver and G. Hands, *Modern Constituency Electioneering* (London: Frank Cass, 1997).

2   The analysis is based on the 1,351 responses that had been received and coded by 1 September 1997.

3   Indeed, the results of our own study of the 1992 election were cited in Labour's 1997 *General Election Handbook* (London: The Labour Party, 1996), pp. 6–8.

4   See Richard Holme and Alison Holmes, '"Sausages or Policeman?" The Role of the Liberal Democrats in the 1997 General Election Campaign', chapter 3 in this volume.

5   See D. Denver, G. Hands and S. Henig, 'The Triumph of Targeting? Party Campaign Strategies in the 1997 General Election', in D. Denver, P. Cowley, J. Fisher and C. Pattie (eds), *British Elections and Parties Review 1998* (London: Frank Cass, 1998).

6   The constituencies of Tatton and West Bromwich West were excluded, since they were not contested by two of the major parties.

7   The constituency of each local party responding to the survey was allocated to one of five categories on the basis of the 1992 election result (or notional result where constituency boundary changes occurred). The categories are *very safe* (seats in which the party had a majority of more than 20 per cent of the votes in 1992); *comfortable* (seats with a majority of between 10 per cent and 20 per cent); *marginal* (seats where the party concerned either came first or second and the gap between the first two parties was less than 10 per cent, or came third but was less than 10 per cent behind the winner); *possible* (seats where the party came second and was between 10 per cent and 20 per cent behind the winner); *hopeless* (seats where the party was either in second place but more than 20 per cent behind the winner, or in third place and more than 10 per cent behind the winner, or in fourth place (in Scotland and Wales)). The same constituency can, then, be classified in different ways – safe for a Conservative respondent, hopeless for Labour, and so on. The landslide result of the 1997 election made something of a mockery of the terminology we use for this categorisation. The Conservatives lost 60 of their 80 'comfortable' seats and 35 of their 180 'very safe' seats. Labour, on the other hand, won 36 of their 256 'hopeless' seats and the Liberal Democrats also took four 'hopeless' seats (out of 560). Nonetheless, we have retained the categorisation to permit comparisons between 1992 and 1997 and because it is perceptions of the electoral status of seats before the election that are important for local campaigning.

8   For further details see Denver and Hands, *Modern Constituency Electioneering*, pp. 246–52.

 9 See Denver and Hands, *Modern Constituency Electioneering*, p. 122.
10 SNP and Plaid Cymru responses were included in this analysis. As in the 1992 analysis only one component was extracted, indicating that all seven indices form a single dimension. The fact that campaign intensity scores are standardised around a mean of zero means that they measure the strength of one campaign relative to all others. Campaigns which score more than zero were stronger than the average for all the campaigns covered in our survey, while negative scores indicate a below-average constituency campaign.
11 See Pattie, Johnston and Fieldhouse, 'Winning the Local Vote'; D. Denver and G. Hands, 'Challengers, Incumbents and the Impact of Constituency Campaigning in Britain', *Electoral Studies*, 16 (1997), pp. 174–93; R. J. Johnston and C. J. Pattie, 'Where's the Difference? Decomposing the Impact of Local Election Campaigns in Great Britain', *Electoral Studies*, 16 (1997), pp. 165–74.
12 The Boundary Commission for England did not use 1992 electorates to define the new constituencies. The 'notional' 1992 results, found in C. Rallings and M. Thrasher, *Media Guide to the New Constituencies* (Plymouth: Local Government Chronicle Election Centre, University of Plymouth, 1995) and used here, as elsewhere, to measure changes in vote shares between 1992 and 1997, are estimates of what the distribution of votes in the new constituencies would have been in 1992. They do not attempt to give estimates of what the electorates of the new constituencies would have been in 1992.
13 *General Election Handbook* (London: The Labour Party, 1996), p. 31.
14 See for example, P. Norton and D. Wood, 'Constituency Service by Members of Parliament: Does it Contribute to a Personal Vote?', *Parliamentary Affairs*, 43 (1990), pp. 196–208.
15 Given the changes in constituency boundaries, defining personal incumbency is not straightforward. We have relied on agents' answers to a question asking whether their candidate was 'the sitting MP for all or part of the constituency'.
16 See John Curtice and Michael Stead, 'Appendix 2: The Results Analysed', in David Butler and Dennis Kavanagh (eds), *The British General Election of 1997* (Basingstoke: Macmillan, 1997), p. 302.

8

The First Internet Election?
United Kingdom Political Parties
and Campaigning in Cyberspace

STEPHEN WARD and RACHEL GIBSON

The momentous outcome of the 1997 United Kingdom general election tended to overshadow potentially important innovations in the conduct of the campaign. From Labour's unleashing of Excalibur (Labour's instant rebuttal computer) to the Tories' pictorial demonisation of Tony Blair, the parties were widely seen as breaking new ground in their tactics to gain popular support. One area in which departure from standard political practice was particularly noted was the movement of party warfare into a new medium – the Internet. The election of 1997 saw 'Britain on-line for the first election on the Internet'.[1] The launch of special election sites on the World Wide Web (WWW) such as Online Magic's GE '97, and those of the BBC, the *Daily Telegraph* and the *Guardian* received extensive coverage on radio and television news and in the print media. Tony Blair and Paddy Ashdown each took to the Internet for an online question and answer session, more than 50 MPs were accessible through electronic mail (e-mail), and the Conservatives and Liberal Democrats transmitted their party political broadcasts on their Internet pages. Drawing analogies with the US presidential election campaign, Michael Martin, the creative director of Online Magic, declared that the Internet would 'provide a significant new forum for debate' in the United Kingdom.[2]

The use of the Internet certainly represented something new for parties, pundits and voters visiting the web-sites. However, based on even the most generous estimates of Internet use in the United Kingdom, no more than about 10 per cent of the electorate could have accessed information from it during the campaign. The impact of the new medium on the election in terms of voter choice, therefore, was minimal. The attention devoted to it in the media was similarly disproportionate.

Why, given the limited number of people who have access to the Internet, did the parties decide to move to this medium in time for the

1997 general election? Further, and perhaps more importantly, what are the implications of this medium for party politics in the future? If Internet usage continues to expand at its current rate, it will clearly not be a marginal medium at the next general election. In this chapter we seek to assess the implications of the Internet for two particular dimensions of party activity: the levels of inter-party competition, and the style of election campaigning. To do so we use content analysis of 12 parties' web-sites during the general election, and qualitative data from interviews with Internet officials from 12 parties.[3]

OVERVIEW OF PARTIES' WEB-SITE DEVELOPMENT

Before examining the specific questions about parties' WWW strategies during the general election, we will provide an overview of the development of party web-sites. Our aim here is to show when, how and why the parties first went on-line and how the sites have evolved.

At the end of 1996 we sent out questionnaires to each party about their web-site strategies. The results are reported in Table 8.1. The first party to go on-line was Labour in October 1994. The majority of parties followed suit over a year later, with the most active period being the 12 months following September 1995. While the table does not provide an exhaustive list of launch dates for all party web-sites, it does provide a reasonable indication of the trends in party activity on the web. Essentially, by the end of 1996 most United Kingdom parties had, during the course of the previous two years, established a presence on the WWW.

Our interviews with a range of party officials responsible for establishing or maintaining the sites revealed that the reasons for

Table 8.1: Date of web-site launch and organisation responsible

Party Name	Order	Date established	Party controlled	External organisation
Labour	1	Oct. 1994	x	x
Plaid Cymru	2	April 1995	x	
Alliance Party (N.I.)	3	August 1995	x	
NDP	4	Sept. 1995	x	
Conservative	5	Oct. 1995		x
UUP	6	Nov. 1995		x
SDLP	7	Jan. 1996		x
SNP	8	Feb. 1996	x	
SLD	9	March 1996	x	
DUP	10	April 1996	Designed	Maintained
SCP	11	May 1996	x	
Referendum	12	Sept. 1996	x	
UKIP	12	Sept. 1996	x	

establishing the sites were neither particularly lofty nor focused. Most party officials reported that their site was set up in response to external factors, namely other parties' activities on the WWW and a perception of the need to be seen as keeping pace with modern technology. The evidence in Table 8.1 supports this notion of a domino effect. In the year following September 1995 a new party web-site was established virtually every month. Only a few parties seemed to have developed their web-sites solely as a result of some internally generated strategy. The National Democratic Party (NDP), for instance, clearly conceived of its web-site as a means to recruit support, whereas the Liberal Democrats saw their web-site as the public equivalent of their internal electronic conferencing system, an information dissemination and feedback service for members, established as early as 1993.[4]

For most parties the WWW did not constitute an integrated feature of their campaign strategy. There was little coordination. For the majority of parties the site was the result of experimentation by a small number of party volunteers or staff members, with the central leadership's approval. The Conservatives and Labour, however, both employed professional organisations to set up their sites, and a number of the Northern Irish parties – the Social Democratic and Labour Party (SDLP), the Ulster Unionist Party (UUP) and the Democratic Unionist Party (DUP) – also reported using an external body.[5]

Once established, the sites require maintenance and updating. This appears to be a hit-and-miss affair to which parties do not, as yet, devote significant resources. None of the parties interviewed reported having a full-time or paid member of staff responsible for maintaining the web-site. Commonly, members of the party's communications and/or computing staff incorporate Internet updates into their other jobs. Thus, with the exception of the major parties, the extent to which the site is remodelled and/or kept current seems at the moment to depend on the presence of skilled enthusiasts within the party. The Scottish Nationalist Party (SNP), for example, has a very committed group of four staff members who form an informal Internet strategy committee that discusses and reviews the site on a regular basis.[6] At the other end of the spectrum, there is the Ulster Democratic Party (UDP), which, having no-one in its ranks with any significant computing abilities, has simply used the template provided by the Internet Service Provider (ISP).[7]

THE NEW MEDIUM, PARTIES AND ELECTORAL POLITICS

In order to understand what the new medium may mean for party politics in the future it is necessary to establish exactly how it differs from the traditional media. Abramson et al. provide a succinct account of the main differences between the Internet and other types of communications technology.[8]

1. It transmits a far greater volume of information from a wider range of sources to a single access point.
2. It transmits the information at a much faster speed.
3. It allows for far greater user control of information received. Consumers can collate and print their own news sources.
4. It allows for greater targeting of audiences by distributors, since the higher volume of media traffic permits 'narrow-casting' in the place of 'broad-casting'.
5. It allows for decentralisation of information control since the number of sources of information has increased and the costs of establishing oneself as a vendor of information (on the Internet particularly) have decreased.
6. It introduces interactivity to media technology, allowing citizens to debate with politicians, or other groups of citizens from considerable distances, or engage in written dialogue via the computer.

The Internet may therefore have significant implications for political institutions and behaviour.[9] Its effects on electoral politics can be placed in two broad categories: the intensity of inter-party competition, and the style of campaigning.

Intensity of inter-party competition

One hypothesis (the 'change hypothesis') is that the intensity of inter-party competition could be increased as a result of the decentralisation of communications control which the Internet promotes. The ability of a minor party to compete with the major parties is enhanced by the Internet, since it is better able to get its message across to voters than by means of the traditional media. Smaller parties such as the Liberal Democrats have long complained about the imbalance of coverage in the traditional media. At election times, when there are strict guidelines concerning the balance of coverage on television, it has been noted that Liberal Democrat support in opinion polls rises with the increased media exposure they receive.[10] On the WWW, anyone can become a vendor of information, at a relatively low cost, and the information read or viewed is determined by the user, not pre-packaged by an external editor. Thus, the capacity for information output from the parties is equalised, and more importantly, so is the voters' access to that information. What has so often been a 'two-horse' race in the traditional media becomes a much more open field.

An alternative hypothesis is that the Internet will not produce any radical redistribution of power between major and minor parties; rather it will simply strengthen existing patterns. This 'reinforcement hypothesis' is supported by evidence in Margolis et al.'s recent research on US parties' and candidates' web-sites during the 1996 presidential election campaign.[11] They suggested that the Internet simply perpetuated the Republican and Democratic parties' dominance because the quality of their web-sites left the minor parties in the dust. Similar research conducted in the United Kingdom found that differences between the major and minor parties' sites were less stark than in the US case.[12] Given that the US parties have a more established presence on the Internet, a very plausible explanation for these different findings is simply time. As the importance of the medium grows to US proportions, and British parties become more familiar with it, a similar process is likely be observed.[13] The reinforcement hypothesis suggests that the quality of the sites may also affect the structure of party competition. The general election campaign represents an ideal time to examine the 'change' and 'reinforcement' hypotheses, since the parties may be more inclined to divert additional resources to their sites during the campaign.

Campaign style

Another area of electoral politics that may be significantly affected by the rise of the Internet is that of campaigning style. The Internet's interactive elements and its enhanced capabilities with regard to the speed and volume of information transferred, have the potential to accelerate and, conversely, halt current trends in political campaigning.

Drawing on the work of Wring and Norris, Farrell has argued that the United Kingdom, since the early 1980s, has witnessed the arrival of new phase in party campaigning – that of 'political marketing' or, as he terms it, the 'postmodern' campaign era.[14] The eras preceding it, the 'pre-modern' and 'modern' (covering the pre- and post-Second World War years) were characterised by a 'one-directional communication process'.[15] Parties, particularly in the pre-modern era, simply 'produced' the message that they considered best met the needs and aspirations of their audience and proceeded to mobilise people in support of it. While the modern campaign involved more centralised planning and co-ordination and relied much more heavily on television media as a means of communication with voters, the belief that the 'product' was 'sacrosanct' and the audience 'malleable', remained.[16] It is argued that the postmodern phase of campaigning, however, marks a significant break from past practice. Now it is the product or the message which is seen as malleable. The parties now employ a plethora of strategists and analysts to investigate voter opinion continuously and tailor their product accordingly. This new emphasis on the voter as consumer has led, Farrell argues, to innovations in campaigning tactics such as the greater targeting of campaign messages and closer attention to feedback in the shape of focus groups. Indeed, in what is perhaps the most radical implication of this new era, the campaign itself has replaced politics, in that image, presentation and packaging have become the sine qua non of party activity.

The Internet, as a means of voter communication, given its unique traits, can serve both to enhance and to mitigate some of these changes. The greater volume of information made available on the Internet also means that parties can devote more time to packaging their message for a particular audience.[17] This 'narrow-casting' as opposed to 'broad-casting' allows parties to direct their appeal to certain groups in the population without the constraints of time, space and external editing that they face in other media. Two groups, in particular, would seem likely targets for parties to focus upon during an election campaign – younger voters and those in marginal constituencies. While most computer owners now tend to be among the more affluent and educated members of society, the current generation of school-leavers and those who are even younger are arguably the most socialised users of computer-mediated communication in the United Kingdom.[18] Parties' web pages could exploit this by leading these potential voters toward specially prepared pages. Indeed, following the election, the Labour Party claimed that it was keen to develop a strong election web-site, precisely because it was a good communication tool for reaching young people.[19] Similarly, voters in marginal constituencies visiting a party's site could be appealed to very easily through pages dealing with their constituencies and specific localised concerns. Parties could also encourage tactical voting by providing electoral statistics on the state of the parties in marginal constituencies and encouraging supporters of supposedly marginal parties to switch their votes.

The unique capacity for two-way communication on the Internet could also advance party campaigners' use of feedback during an election. The 1997 election brought allegations that the major parties in particular, were importing 'Americanised' styles of campaigning such as focus groups and opinion polling to test their message.[20] The interactive dimension of Internet communication means that voters can express their opinions to the party in an immediate way for little cost. Party web-sites could clearly promote such feedback by incorporating surveys for users to complete regarding their views on policy or party performance. However, with Internet usage currently confined to a highly unrepresentative portion of the electorate, there are clearly dangers in trying to use feedback from such a self-selected sample of voters.[21]

Finally, although not specifically mentioned above, the use of rapid-response techniques by parties, (pioneered so successfully by the Clinton campaign team during the 1992 election), to ensure that their message is not distorted through media and opposition attacks is another postmodern technique that the Internet can clearly facilitate.[22]

On a different note, parties' use of the Internet might also work to undermine the elevation of image and presentation characteristic of present-day campaigns. The WWW is predominantly a text-based medium, although its graphics capabilities and audio/visual techniques are advancing apace. The emphasis on written information, and the web's ability to store so much of it and make it available to such a wide audience, it is argued, may promote a more substantive basis to party campaigning. Thus, attention to presentational issues and the 'sound-bite' politics prominent in other mediums may be diminished by parties' use of the Internet.

CAMPAIGNING AND COMPETING IN CYBERSPACE:
THE 1997 GENERAL ELECTION

Intensity of inter-party competition

To assess whether the Internet bolstered the competitive position of smaller parties during the election, party activities on the WWW were examined in four specific areas: presence, access, space devoted to the election and quality of web-site design. The presence of, and access to, party web-sites was assessed by analysis of the major WWW sites' hypertext links to the political parties. The size of general election space and quality of the overall web-site design were assessed through content analysis of 12 selected party web-sites using a survey designed specifically for this study.

Presence and access

The majority of parties competing in the election had established a presence on the WWW. Of the 56 parties who ran candidates at the election, 31 had sites on the web.[23] Among the parliamentary parties only the small United Kingdom Unionist Party did not have a web-site. The more crucial question at issue, however, was how easily one could access the multitude of party sites. Four main indices providing access to United Kingdom political parties were examined: Keele University's, Warwick University's, the Agora index available through Yahoo and

Online Magic's general election site.[24] Each provided extensive links to more than 20 party web-sites. Keele University's site provided the most links with 27 parties listed, the general election site provided links to 25 parties and Warwick and Agora provided 21 links apiece. Thus, while many of the minor parties appeared on all four indices, some, such as the Communist Party, proved more difficult to locate, appearing on only one of the main indices.

While all the indices provided extensive links, it is important to note that they all promoted the Conservative and Labour parties' sites by placing them at, or very near the top of the parties listed. Beyond the ordering of the parties, the Keele site was the most democratic, in that all parties were presented in the same style. The Warwick site provided icons next to the names of the better known parties, and allowed less space for the listing of some of the minor parties. The general election site placed those parties with parliamentary seats first. Only the Agora index placed the Conservative, Labour and Liberal Democrat links clearly ahead of all the other parties, in a separate box at the top of the screen. Overall, therefore, the minor parties gained proportionately greater exposure than in other media, especially the more obscure parties, which voters may not have been aware existed. Yet, despite this increase in exposure for fringe parties, even on the Internet there was a bias towards the major parties.

Quantity and quality
Of the 12 sites surveyed during the election campaign only two (those of the SDLP and Plaid Cymru) did not revise their sites to take account of the election. Indeed, the majority of parties had set up specific election pages or sites in addition to the regular pages (see Table 8.2). There is evidence, however, of a growing divide between the larger and smaller parties in terms of the amount of space devoted to election. The three main parties all created sizable election sites along with their regular pages, while most of the smaller parties tended to incorporate election material, normally only the manifesto, into their established sites, limiting the amount of space used and the costs involved.[25]

The ability of minor parties to compete on the Internet can also be assessed by comparing the quality of their web-site design with those of the major parties. This was assessed by examining the sophistication and visual appeal of party web pages in terms of their use of graphics, moving icons, audio-video and the presence of a search engine.

Very few parties incorporated an extensive range of audio-video features into their sites (see Table 8.3). While nearly all the sites contained some graphics, normally photographs of the party leader, the minor parties, with the exception of the SNP and the Referendum Party,

Table 8.2: Party web-site election coverage

Party name	Web election coverage?	Specific election site/pages	Election information in normal site
Conservative	x	x	
Greens	x	x	
Liberal Democrats	x	x	x
Labour	x	x	x
Plaid Cymru			
NDP	x		x
Referendum Party	x		x
SNP	x	x	x
Sinn Féin	x	x	
SDLP			
UKIP	x		x
UUP	x	x	x

offered fewer original features on their sites compared with the major parties, particularly the Conservative and Labour parties. However, the more sophisticated sites, with a wide range of features, often required extra software in order to realise the full potential of the site. Moreover, sites with graphics, icons and other special features were generally slower to download than those with basic text. Although a site may be more sophisticated, unless the user has adequate computer facilities, the benefits may not be clear-cut. Consequently, the parties with the most sophisticated sites also provided text-only versions of their sites to assist users with more limited computer software.

While the Internet may be allowing minor parties to reduce the advantage that the major parties enjoy in terms of exposure, in terms of election coverage and the ability to convey an eye-catching and appealing message, the major parties appear to be outstripping their rivals. While the SNP's highly attractive and 'prize-winning' site counters this trend, it is evidently the exception proving the rule. The quality of minor parties' web-sites seems to depend very much on the presence of a coterie of highly committed and computer-literate members and/or supporters who offer their services for free. The Conservative and Labour parties clearly do not need to depend on such fortuitous recruitment, their bigger budgets enabling them to employ professional web-site designers.

Campaigning style

The parties' use of the targeting, rapid response, substantive content and interactive capabilities of the Internet during the election campaign was assessed through content analysis of the 12 selected party web-sites.

Table 8.3: Sophistication of party web-sites

Party name	Search engine	Text only supplied	Extra software needed	Graphics	Moving icons	Video	Audio
Conservative		x	x	x	x	x	x
Greens				x			
Liberal Democrats				x	x		
Labour	x	x	x	x	x	x	x
NDP		x	x	x	x		
PC				x			
Referendum Party		x	x		x	x	x
SNP	x	x	x	x	x	x	x
SF				x			x
SDLP				x			
UKIP							
UUP			x	x	x		

Targeting

Despite the possibilities that the Internet offered for targeting specific geographic or demographic constituencies, and press reports that fringe parties were using the Internet to recruit voters, our survey suggests that the potential of the Internet for targeting and recruitment was largely ignored.[26] As Table 8.4 demonstrates, only two of the parties included special sections devoted to the youth vote – Labour and the Conservatives. Both parties offered pages dealing with mock school elections, with advice and information for the candidates. There was little evidence of parties directly attempting to recruit future voters via their web site, however. This is despite the fact that Labour's election web-site team was headed by those in charge of recruiting first-time voters.

In terms of the focus on marginal constituencies, a number of sites provided information about constituencies, including electoral statistics, constituency search facilities and profiles of candidates (see Table 8.4), but no space in the main sites was devoted to specific constituencies, nor were any appeals for tactical voting ever made.[27] This lack of targeting was confirmed in the interviews with party officials. The Internet as a tool of communication was conceived of largely in broadcasting terms appropriate to the traditional electronic media. The web-site was designed to appeal to as wide an audience as possible. Thus, the narrowcasting possibilities offered by digital communication in the form of the WWW were largely left unexplored.

This lack of emphasis on targeting in party web-sites is perhaps a result of parties' views overall of the WWW as a recruitment tool. As

Table 8.4: Targeting in party web-sites

Party name	Youth pages/focus	Candidate profile	Constituency search	Electoral statistics
Conservative	x	x	x	x (but not on election pages)
Greens				
Labour	x	x	x	
Liberal Democrats		x	x	x (only where there was an LD MP)
NDP				
Plaid Cymru			x (only MPs)	x (1994 Euro-Election)
Referendum Party				
SNP			x	x (all Scottish constituencies)
Sinn Féin			x	x (1996 N. Ireland forum elections)
SDLP				
UKIP				
UUP			x	x (but not on election pages)

one party official put it, 'when it comes to getting votes, the web is still very limited'.[28] This perception is underscored by the fact that very few of the parties conduct any systematic analysis of visitors to their sites.[29] One would have expected that had parties been tailoring the content of the pages to their audience, they would have engaged in user research. Yet in the run-up to the election only four parties – the DUP, the NDP, Plaid Cymru and the Scottish Liberal Democrats – used any kind of survey data to monitor web-site usage.[30]

Parties did have a vague idea of the number of 'hits' on their site during the campaign (Labour claimed 4,000,000, the Conservatives 500,000), and many estimated that the number of visitors doubled during the election period.[31] However, this was not out of line with the overall increase in interest from other sources, such as telephone calls or postal mail. Equally, parties seem to have very little idea of the number of members joining via the web-site. While almost all parties offer membership forms to download and send in by post, no parties could provide specific figures on how many individuals had been recruited in this way – though most thought it was minimal.

Hence, on the basis of our evidence, the Internet's potential for postmodern campaigning in the form of more active targeting and recruitment was not developed during the 1997 election.

Interactivity

In terms of structured feedback, the SNP provided the most extensive opportunity for users to comment via survey forms on policy and the importance of particular issues, and on the design of the site more generally (see Table 8.5). Plaid Cymru also offered an opinion poll of sorts, asking users to vote on the single issue of Welsh devolution. However, the on-line devolution vote had been part of the site for a number of months prior to the election. It was not a new feature designed for the campaign. Only the Conservatives and the NDP actively sought comments on policy from voters in a more open-ended and unstructured e-mail format. Finally, Sinn Féin offered an on-line chat facility from their site, where voters could contact and discuss issues with Mitchel McLaughlin (party chairperson). However, this facility was related to the party's conference, held during the campaign, rather than designed specifically for the election.

Most of the feedback opportunities offered by the parties, however, took the form of a direct e-mail link to an unnamed contact address at party headquarters or to the 'web-masters' for comments about the site design. Furthermore, invitations to comment were not necessarily election-specific and in fact often involved users completing on-line forms. The major parties and the SNP offered e-mail access specifically to the party leader, as well as links to candidates or MPs with e-mail facilities, although there were not many of these. For example, only nine Labour candidates could be e-mailed directly from the site. Follow-up interviews revealed that feedback from web-sites, while welcomed, was not dealt with in any specific way. Most of the feedback that parties received tended to be requests for more information and were dealt with through normal routes of party administration. None of the parties

Table 8.5: Feedback requested by parties

Party name	General	Policy (unspecific)	Policy (specific)	Surveys
Conservative	x	x		
Greens				
Labour	x			
Liberal Democrats	x			
NDP	x	x	x	
PC				x (devolution)
Referendum Party				
SNP				x
Sinn Féin	x			
SDLP	x			
UKIP				
UUP	x			

Table 8.6: E-mail links on party web-sites

Party name	Party leader	Party HQ	Party officials	Regions/ constituencies/ international	MPs/ candidates	Other
Conservative	x	x		x	x	
Greens		x	x			x (party newspaper)
Labour	x	x	x	x	x	
Liberal Democrats	x	x	x	x	x	
NDP		x				x (party newspaper)
PC						x (site designers)
Referendum Party		x				
SDLP		x				
SF						x (mailing list)
SNP	x	x	x		x	
UKIP		x				
UUP		x	x	x		

specifically monitored web-site feedback in its own right. In short, the party sites were not really interactive. There was little opportunity for two-way dialogue with politicians. E-mail contacts were used largely as a speedier version of ordinary postal mail.

Rapid response
As Table 8.7 shows, the parties largely failed to exploit the immediacy of the new medium. Only the three main parties and the SNP updated their sites on a daily basis, and half the sites barely changed during the course of the election campaign. Some parties promised to update but simply failed to deliver. The Referendum Party site promised a list of candidates, but even in the last week of the campaign this had failed to materialise. The Labour and Conservative parties did provide coverage of their daily press conferences, but the majority of the updating took the form of adding press releases to the site. The Labour Party did provide a changing issue focus during the campaign, but most sites highlighted certain themes such as constitutional issues or Europe in a set format throughout the course of the campaign. Parties viewed their sites largely as static repositories of information for journalists and the public, rather than a dynamic tool for immediate rebuttal. One minor party official actually claimed that journalists had contacted the party to complain that information was not available via their web site.[32] Such frustration with the stagnation of the party web-sites is best summarised by one journalist's critique of the parties' use of the medium:

The great joy of the Internet is that it is instant, vibrant and up-to-the-minute. The Labour Party site has a page of 'New Information – The Latest News from Labour's Campaign Team'. There are three 'daily news briefs' from before Christmas, and two of those are from Gordon Brown. A nation sleeps.[33]

Table 8.7: Updating of party web-sites

Party Name	Frequency of updating	Daily press conference details	Press releases
Conservatives	Daily	x	x
Greens	Other		x
Labour	Daily	x	x
Liberal Democrats	Daily		x
NDP	Weekly		
Plaid Cymru	Other		x
Referendum Party	Weekly		x
SNP	Daily		x
Sinn Féin	2/3 days		x
SDLP	Other		x
UKIP	Other		
UUP	2/3 days		x

Content

As Table 8.8 indicates, a significant range of substantive policy-based information was made available on the parties' web-sites. Almost all the parties, except the Conservatives, offered a statement of party values and philosophy in their opening pages or through an icon offered on the first page. Most parties supplied their manifestos and six parties provided a special facility for users to download it to read later. However, common issue themes across different sites were difficult to identify. Any policy focus tended to reflect the single-issue concerns of some parties. For example, UKIP and the Referendum Party unsurprisingly devoted the majority of their election coverage to Europe, while the SNP's site displayed a heavy emphasis on constitutional issues. In no sense could it be said that there was a distinct Internet campaign agenda, except that a number of parties felt it necessary to proclaim the importance of new communications technology, a policy area which barely surfaced in the general election campaign.

There was also a significant amount of non-substantive campaigning, particularly by the two major parties. This more trivial aspect to the web-sites no doubt prompted the complaint that 'by and large most of the party sites are nothing more than electronic brochures'.[34] The Conservative, Labour and the Referendum Parties incorporated the negative campaign billboards seen across the country; for example,

Table 8.8: Policy and information content of party web-sites

Party name	Party values	Manifesto	Focus on specific issues
Conservative		x	x (tax, environment, IT, London manifesto)
Greens	x	x	x (environment)
Labour	x	x	x (broad range of issues)
Liberal Democrats	x	x	
NDP	x	x	x (immigration)
Plaid Cymru	x		x (devolution)
Referendum Party	x		x (Europe)
SNP	x	x	x (devolution)
Sinn Féin	x		
SDLP	x		
UKIP	x	x	x (Europe)
UUP	x	x	

'New Labour, New Danger' images were prominent on the Conservative site. The Liberal Democrats, Conservatives, the SNP and the Referendum Party offered the opportunity to watch their party election broadcast on the net. Labour and the Referendum Party also used their sites to promote party merchandise, such as clothing, posters and videos. Otherwise, the majority of parties (especially the smaller parties) were not overtly marketing or selling themselves systematically. There were one or two rather threadbare gimmicks such as the Liberal Democrats' Fantasy General Election game, and on the SNP site you could hear Sean Connery pledging his support for Scottish nationalism, but these were fairly unusual features. Although some of sites were pared down and made more glossy than their pre-election format (notably that of the Liberal Democrats), they were not trivialised to the extent of the US parties' election sites.[35]

Overall, therefore, except for using the Internet as an information repository for voters to access, parties have failed to exploit the rapid-response, targeting and feedback capabilities of the new medium in their campaign efforts. All the party officials expressed a keen interest in establishing a presence on the WWW, but with a few exceptions (SNP, Labour and Liberal Democrats) did not demonstrate any clear strategy on how to harness the new communications technology. Thus the party sites during the election were a pale imitation of the campaign elsewhere.

BARRIERS TO EFFECTIVE PARTY CAMPAIGNING ON THE INTERNET

A number of underlying societal and technological problems will need to be overcome if the Internet is to join the traditional media as a significant outlet for party campaigning. The most important barriers are as follows:

User access

Clearly, with Internet usage limited to a small percentage of the electorate, the parties currently view it as a peripheral campaign tool, of minimal value in the primary task of electioneering – gathering votes. There is still a sense that it consists largely of elites (the parties) talking to, or more accurately at, other elites (journalists, academics) rather than to the electorate as a whole. As one party official commented 'more people probably saw the Internet sites on the *Nine O'clock News* than actually visited them'.[36]

User initiative

By the next election, however, given current trends and the advent of comparatively cheap 'set top' boxes, it is conceivable that between 25 per cent and 33 per cent of the electorate will have access to the Internet.[37] Even then it is debatable how important the parties' sites will be. Given that the Internet requires users actively to seek out sites, those accessing the parties' sites are likely to be the politically interested, rather than ordinary voters. If the recent US experience is anything to go by, it will be the independent election sites, run largely by the established media, where votes will be won and lost.[38] Party sites will probably end up simply preaching to the converted.

Politicians' technophobia

Even with a sizeable increase in Internet usage, the parties themselves would still need to view the Internet as a more mainstream political tool. The relatively small numbers of MPs who had web-sites and the limited number of candidates with e-mail addresses (fewer than 50 candidates could be e-mailed from the party sites) suggest a rather technophobic political class. As one journalist memorably claimed a few months before the election, 'e-mail is still as alien as gas chromatography to most MPs'.[39] Currently, the parties' Internet strategies are largely being pushed by 'net entrepreneurs', usually middle-ranking officials who are trying to sell the benefits of the Internet within the party. Very few senior politicians have played an active role in developing the web-sites. Whilst such politicians are not necessarily hostile, they understandably do not see the Internet as a priority area. If Internet campaigning is to develop, active support from top-level politicians will be necessary to bring it from the fringe to the mainstream. If this does occur, the smaller parties may find that the major parties dominate the Internet, just as they now dominate the other media.

Security and technical problems

To develop the Internet as a campaigning and recruiting device the technology will need to advance and become more secure. Parties are wary of falling prey to hackers, as happened to the Labour Party in the 1997 campaign.[40] Moreover, on a smaller scale, secure on-line membership forms and credit card donation lines need to be established, so that parties can recruit on-line.

Access overload

As access to the Internet increases, one problem already noted by the parties is their ability to respond to the interactive elements of the WWW. As yet parties have developed only ad hoc structures for monitoring and responding to e-mail and Internet enquiries. Fears have been expressed about access overload, in short, the Internet makes politicians and parties too open to the public, with the result that they cannot *effectively* respond to demands from voters. Such unresponsiveness clearly has the potential for stimulating further disillusionment with the political system. Thus although the Internet is currently seen as a labour-saving device, if the number of users increases significantly, there is a danger that party officials and politicians will come to regard e-mail communication as an additional burden.

Although the impact of the Internet on parties was minimal during the 1997 election, it provoked parties to think about their sites. Whether the election proves to be a catalyst for site development is as yet difficult to determine. All the party officials interviewed expressed a desire to develop a more sophisticated approach in future elections and were enthusiastic about the technology. However, in the six months following the election, very few parties radically altered the format of their sites.

CONCLUSION

Establishing when and how United Kingdom political parties went online was a relatively straightforward process. Addressing the question of why they did so, and the consequences of this for party campaigning, have proved to be more complex issues. Part of the explanation for this lies with the parties themselves, since even they seem unsure of their reasons for going on-line. However, a number of tentative conclusions can be drawn about how the Internet will affect party campaigning in the future.

On the whole, the Internet did not appear to have a significant impact on party behaviour in the 1997 general election. On the one hand, its radical implications for the intensity of party competition were borne out in that it equalised the exposure of parties' ideas, and voters' access to them. On the other hand, the evidence regarding the quality of the web-sites' design suggested that a gap was developing between the major and minor parties' sites. These findings would suggest that if visual appeal is a chief criterion for voters perusing a party's site, then the WWW will simply reinforce the dominance of the larger, better-resourced parties.

In terms of campaign style, in general the parties largely did not exploit the dynamic innovations that the Internet offered them. Most parties, in fact, viewed their Internet sites simply as an additional archival resource. Such timidity is probably largely due to the experimental rather than sceptical approach of the parties to the new medium.

Overall, therefore, while the Internet may lead to changes in party campaigning in the future, those changes are more likely to occur in campaign style, rather than the distribution of power between parties.

NOTES

1 *Independent*, 25 January 1997, p. 9.
2 Ibid.
3 Officials of 12 parties who were responsible for Internet management were interviewed in July and August 1997. The parties were Alliance, Conservatives, Scottish Conservatives, Labour, Liberal Democrat, NDP, Plaid Cymru, Scottish Liberal Democrat, SNP, SDLP, UDP, UUP.
4 Interviews with party officials, 1 July 1997 and 28 August 1997.
5 Rachel Gibson and Stephen Ward, *UK Political Parties and the Internet: Prospects for Democracy*, Working Papers in Contemporary History and Politics No. 13 (Salford: University of Salford, European Studies Research Institute, 1997).
6 Interview with SNP official, 31 July 1997.
7 Interview with UDP official, 22 July 1997.
8 Jeffrey Abramson, Christopher Arterton and Garry R. Orren, *The Electronic Commonwealth* (Cambridge, MA: Harvard University Press, 1988).
9 See, for example, Arthur Lipow and Patrick Seyd, 'The Politics of Anti-Partyism', *Parliamentary Affairs*, 49, 2 (1996), pp. 273–84; Geoff Mulgan, 'Lean Democracy', *Demos Quarterly*, 3 (1994); Janie Percy-Smith, *Digital Democracy: Information and Communication Technologies in Local Politics* (London: Commission for Local Democracy, 1995); Mark Wheeler, 'Multi-mediatisation, Techno-Populism, Political Community and the Citizen's Democratic Rights: The Netizen', paper presented to the ECPR joint sessions (Berne, 1997).
10 Dennis Kavanagh, *Election Campaigning: The New Marketing of Politics* (Oxford: Blackwell, 1995), pp. 153–4.
11 Michael Margolis, David Resnick and Chin-chang Tu, 'Campaigning on the Internet: Parties and Candidates on the World Wide Web in the 1996 Primary Season', *Harvard International Journal of Press/Politics*, 2, 1 (1997), pp. 59–78.
12 Gibson and Ward, 'United Kingdom Political Parties and the Internet', pp. 17–18.

13 One estimate suggested that 28 per cent of US voters had accessed the presidential web-sites during the 1996 Campaign. *The Independent*, 25 January 1997, p. 9.

14 David Farrell, 'Campaign Professionalisation and Political Parties', paper presented to the workshop on Change in the Relationship of Parties and Democracy, Texas A&M University, 4 April 1997; Dominic Wring, 'Political Marketing and Party Development in Britain', *European Journal of Marketing*, 30, 10/11 (1996), pp. 100–11; Pippa Norris, *Electoral Change Since 1945* (Oxford: Blackwell, 1997).

15 Wring, 'Political Marketing and Party Development in Britain', p. 102.

16 Farrell, 'Campaign Professionalisation', p. 4.

17 Raymond Kuhn, 'So What's New? The Media and Electoral Politics in Britain', paper presented at ECPR joint sessions (Berne, 1997).

18 A study conducted by Olivetti, the Italian-based computer firm, reported in the *Guardian*, shows that UK schoolchildren have the greatest access to computers in the world; 100 per cent of primary schools are reported to have a computer, and by the time children reach secondary education there is, on average, one computer for every eight students (*Guardian*, 4 September 1997, p. 8).

19 *Guardian*, 2 October 1997, 'Online', p. 11.

20 For a full discussion of 'Americanisation', see Kavanagh, 'Election Campaigning'.

21 See for example, the Motorola Report, *Prepared for the Future? The British and Technology* (London: Motorola, 1996).

22 Bruce I. Newman, *The Marketing of the President: Political Marketing as Campaign Strategy* (Beverly Hills, CA: Sage Publications, 1994).

23 The term 'party' is used broadly to encompass even single-candidate parties, so this figure may understate the degree of 'party use'.

24 The web-site indices addresses were as follows: 'http://ge97.co.uk'; 'http://www.warwick.ac.uk/~suaba/politics/parties.html'; 'http://www.keele.ac.uk/depts/po/psr.htm'; 'http://agora.stm.it/politic/uk.htm'.

25 The costs of setting up and maintaining a site vary enormously. Based on information supplied by a range of Internet Service Providers, it was estimated that a party could establish a small web-site for a year for as little as £150. This would include a web address, 10–15 MB of server space and assistance in uploading the information required.

26 *Guardian*, 20 March 1997, 'Online', p. 13.

27 The constituency search facility assisted users in identifying their own constituency and sometimes then provided candidate details.

28 Interview with party official, 22 July 1997.

29 A number of the smaller parties, especially the SNP, the NDP and the Northern Ireland parties, noted the importance of the US audience. This is perhaps not surprising given the large communities in the United States claiming family ties with Ireland and Scotland, and also England. The Internet has become an international medium and is accessible to expatriate voters to a far greater extent than other media outlets. Indeed, one fringe party estimated that donations via the web (largely from the United States) allowed them to cover the campaign costs of three constituencies.

30 Gibson and Ward, 'UK Parties and the Internet', pp. 10–12.

31 These figures should be regarded with caution, since they were estimates provided by party officials (interviews, 29 July 1997). Many of the parties appeared reluctant to give any figures whatsoever. Moreover, using hits as a measure of the audience is somewhat problematic, since one user may generate multiple hits, thus distorting the overall totals. Charles Arthur in the *Independent*, 18 April

1997, suggested that the real audience was probably between 10 and 20 times lower than the overall hits figures. Similarly, David Butler and Dennis Kavanagh, in *The British General Election 1997* (Basingstoke: Macmillan, 1997) p. 214, quote considerably lower figures (Labour a total of 1.5 million hits, Conservatives 16,000 per week).

32   Interview with party official, 17 July 1997.

33   *New Statesman*, 21 March 1997, p. 26.

34   *Independent*, Network Section, 26 March 1997, pp. 2–3.

35   Brad Stone, 'Politic '96', *Internet World*, November 1996, p. 44.

36   Interview with party official, 28 July 1997.

37   An electronic device allowing Internet access through a television set without need of a computer is already on sale for under £300.

38   Margolis et al., 'Campaigning on the Internet: Parties and Candidates on the World Wide Web'; Brad Stone, 'Politic '96', pp. 44–8.

39   *Observer*, 23 February 1997, p. 13.

40   The Labour Party site was hacked into and images and text were altered, resulting in the site having to be taken off-line for a number of hours.

PART III:

THE CAMPAIGN IN THE PRESS

9

Swingers, Clingers, Waverers, Quaverers: The Tabloid Press in the 1997 General Election

DAVID McKIE

Was it the *Sun* wot won it? The claim of Britain's biggest-selling tabloid to have swung the 1992 election in John Major's favour was still being disputed when the 1997 election came round. The case for believing that newspaper campaigning had significantly influenced the result was most formidably stated by Martin Linton, now Labour MP for Battersea, then a *Guardian* reporter, who used a year's assignment at Nuffield College Oxford to investigate the effects of the press's performance.[1] The case against was made by John Curtice and Holli Semetko, who argued that press advocacy had had no net effect on the outcome.[2]

One group who clearly believed in the tabloid effect, however, were Tony Blair and close colleagues like his press secretary Alastair Campbell, who had come to the job direct from the world of the tabloids; he had previously been political editor of the *Daily Mirror*. To get the *Sun* cheerleading for Labour might be too much to hope for, but at least they saw some chance of a radically altered Labour Party detaching it from the Tories. The success of their operation, a top priority from the moment of Blair's election as Labour leader, would transform the balance of coverage in the 1997 election. As Hugo Young wrote later in the *Guardian*:

> The day before the election I interviewed Tony Blair ... at what must have been the first moment when he was prepared to acknowledge to an outsider that he was going to win. He didn't know what the majority would be – around 40 seemed to be his best bet – but concerning a prime contributor to this majority ... he had no doubt. His tone was admonitory. Nobody, he vigorously insisted, should underestimate the matchless importance to his victory of the endorsement he received on the first day of the campaign from the *Sun* newspaper. (30 October 1997)

The swinging of the *Sun* ensured that Labour, usually the underdog, would this time command substantially more support, in terms of messages delivered to readers, than the Conservatives. While in 1992 the tabloids had all remained faithful to the parties they supported five years before, in 1997 they could be divided into four groups, which, adopting tabloidspeak, may conveniently be labelled the 'clingers', the 'swingers', the 'waverers' and the 'quaverers'.

The clingers were the tabloids who in 1997 never swerved from the largely uncritical allegiance they declared in 1992 – which in each case was to Labour: the *Mirror* (formerly *Daily Mirror*), *Sunday Mirror* and *People*, owned by a Mirror Group itself radically altered since 1992. Having backed the Labour party in bad times, these papers were hardly likely to dump it now. The swingers were the former Tory supporters who switched to Labour: News International's *Sun* and *News of the World*, United News and Media's *Daily Star* and the *Evening Standard*, part of the Rothermere stable but traditionally run on a far looser rein than the *Daily Mail* or the *Mail on Sunday*. (The *Standard* cannot be classed as a national tabloid, but it is avidly read by politicians, and its support was a boost which Labour were happy to get.)

My waverer is the *Daily Mail*, which started Conservative and ended Conservative but as will be seen had adventures in between, reflecting the role of a proprietor, Rothermere, who himself was a swinger and after the election switched his own allegiance to Labour in the House of Lords. The quaverer was the *Daily Express*, with its two proprietors, Lord Stevens, chairman of United News and Media and an unswerving Conservative, and the Labour peer and Blair confidant Lord Hollick, chief executive of the group and its most powerful influence since the merger of United News with his company MAI in February 1996. The *Express* stuck with its old Conservative faith, but its trumpet through the campaign gave forth an uncertain sound.

THE SWINGERS

The presence of Alastair Campbell at the leader's side wasn't the only reason why Labour had better hopes of the *Sun* in 1997 than in 1992, when the paper wound up the election with two classic expressions of contempt for the party: its 'Nightmare on Kinnock Street' headline on the day before polling day, and on polling day itself, the picture of Neil Kinnock with his head encased in a light bulb and the legend: 'If Kinnock wins today will the last person in Britain please turn out the lights.'[3] For a start, Blair wasn't Kinnock, whom Murdoch and his lieutenants thought wholly unequipped for the premiership. Blair's people had good informal contacts with Murdoch journalists, formed not just, like Campbell's, at work, but on social occasions and at football matches. From the early days of Blair's leadership they worked assiduously to break down the old antagonism of the Murdoch Press to the party. The first known tête à tête dinner engagement between Rupert Murdoch and Blair took place in August 1994 – just one month after Blair won the leadership. Articles ostensibly written by Blair, though they read much more like the work of Alastair Campbell, began to appear in the *Sun*: the *Sun's* attitude to the Labour leader, if not to the Labour Party, noticeably mellowed.

The process culminated in a visit by Blair to a Newscorp leadership conference on Hayman Island, Australia, in July 1995, when the Labour leader Blair delivered a paper which seemed designed to suggest, especially in its belabouring of the establishment and the old boy network, that no great difference remained between New Labour's aspirations and Murdoch's own. *'Ich bin Murdocher'*, he seemed almost to be saying.[4]

All this billing and cooing belonged to a species of romantic manoeuvre which might be termed mutual seduction. Blair wanted Murdoch, certainly: but Murdoch had come to want Blair – so much so that some senior Labour politicians thought Blair's busy courtship of Murdoch was never necessary. Murdoch and the people who ran the *Sun* were terminally sick of John Major. As things went badly wrong for the government after its 1992 victory, the *Sun* at first distinguished between 'honest John' and the duffers about him, especially the Chancellor of the Exchequer, Norman Lamont. But when Major at last disposed of Lamont, he put himself in the firing line, and soon he was being shot at. Honest John disappeared from the *Sun's* leader columns, replaced by an arrant bungler. The vituperation reached its peak in the contest for the party leadership between Major – 'Major couldn't lead a cinema queue, let alone a country' they said of him – and John Redwood.

The *Sun's* disillusion with the party for which it had claimed to have 'won it' reflected its readers' feelings. It was useless telling people in Basildon that all was going swimmingly when the boarded up shops in the High Street, as well as the state of their personal finances, were daily signs that it wasn't. In January 1994 the *Sun* published a leader repenting of the support it had given the Tories less than two years before: 'What fools we were to believe this lot,' the paper moaned. 'Today our eyes are open. We can see we have been conned.' Major was showing 'all the leadership of a lemming'. Murdoch's commercial interests were affected here too. When the *Sun* railed against what high interest rates were doing to people in Basildon, when *The Times* more augustly criticised the damage the Tories were doing to the British economy, those comments were tinctured by some consideration of the difficulties high interest rates were creating for Rupert Murdoch. And the testimony of the polls, which after the ERM fiasco put Labour 20 points in the lead and then by and large left them there, had another lesson for Murdoch. Labour were going to win. A Labour victory in defiance of a *Sun* still rooting for the Conservatives was hardly likely to deter the subsequent Labour government from action, on cross-media ownership for example, designed to curb the power of the Murdoch empire – a course for which many in the party were clamouring. But a Labour government in some way beholden to Murdoch newspapers might be another matter.

So clear was this convergence of interests that some suspected a deal had been made: if not explicit, at least implicit. In the revised edition of his book, *Full Disclosure*, the former *Sunday Times* editor Andrew Neil, once a devotee of Murdoch but now disillusioned because of his own experiences at the proprietor's hands, wrote: 'Blair once said to me that "how we treat Rupert Murdoch's media interests when in power will depend on how his newspapers treat the Labour Party in the run-up to the election".'

In the early days of New Labour there seemed to be three possible outcomes. The hostility of the Murdoch press to John Major's government might bring the Conservative Party to its senses, leading to changes of policy on Europe and the economy and ideally to a new leader. Failing that, the *Sun* might be neutral, or mildly partial, between the election contenders, judging each by how close its policies came to the views of the *Sun*, on Europe especially. Or, if Blair fulfilled its expectations, it might just swing to Labour. In any case it made sense to take a friendlier line to New Labour than to Old. Accordingly, the *Sun* now wrote about Blair, if not with ravished adoration, at least with some goodwill and an open mind – though always with the reservation that he brought with him the frightful incubus of the Labour Party. Blair might have changed, but some around him, the paper often lamented, had not.

By voting to keep John Major, Conservative MPs effectively ruined their chances of the kind of all-out endorsement from the *Sun* and its Sunday stablemate the *News of the World*, which they had had five years before. Left to themselves, the editor of the *Sun* and his closest colleagues would have kept their options open to the last, weighing up the pros and cons of the parties and perhaps concluding that, on Europe at least, the Conservatives, even under John Major, must be preferred. In the run-up to the election, the paper repeatedly stressed that Europe was an issue transcending all others. And with Labour distinctly more favourable to closer relations with Europe and to EMU, that seemed to keep some hope alive for the Tories. In the whole top echelon of the paper – editor, deputy editor, political editor, political leader writer – reservations about Labour persisted. Blair was still an unknown quantity; he had the ball and chain of his party attached; the party remained financially dependent on the unions, who as paymasters could continue to call the shots; they were 'soft' on Europe, and still meant to sign up to the disastrous Social Chapter. The country was asked to 'trust Blair': but how could you trust a man who had changed his opinions so often, and apparently so easily? Let us see, they resolved, what case he and his party can make for themselves during the coming campaign.

They were not allowed that luxury. An edict came from above. Against the collective wisdom of the senior journalists, Rupert Murdoch insisted on an outright Labour endorsement without waiting for the campaign. The consummation of the New Labour/Newscorp affair was completed within two days. On 17 March, a piece by Tony Blair appeared on page 2 of the *Sun* under the heading: 'I'm a British Patriot'. New Labour, its leader declared, would have no truck with a British superstate: 'We will fight for Britain's interests and to keep our independence every step of the way. If we are to remain in Europe – and neither main party is saying we should withdraw – it is time to start leading in Europe, getting a Europe on Britain's terms.' Though he stuck by his case that Britain ought to be part of the Social Chapter he saw formidable obstacles to any early entry into EMU. 'I am a British patriot', Blair concluded. 'Anybody who believes I would sell my country short has not listened to a word I have said in the past three years. I didn't change the Labour Party into the party it is today to give it all away to Europe or anyone else.'

The significance of this declaration was signalled on page 1 by the paper's political editor Trevor Kavanagh – much respected by Murdoch and troubled by what Murdoch was doing – under the headline: 'Blair takes new hard line on Europe'. 'In an astonishing article in the *Sun*, the Labour leader emerges as almost as sceptical on Europe as the most outspoken Tories … His pledges will reassure voters that New Labour still has strong reservations about a totally pro-European policy', Kavanagh wrote. 'Privately, Blair has been constantly questioning New Labour's relationship with Europe and recognises the issue is gathering importance in the run-up to the election.' A leader comment commended him, though it added that the test of whether Blair could hammer Europe into the shape Britain wanted would come over the Social Chapter.

Twenty-four hours later even that mild reservation was effectively buried. 'An historic announcement from Britain's number one

newspaper', the *Sun* trumpeted on 18 March. 'The *Sun* backs Blair ...'
A leader commented: 'The Labour Party say they have changed. They
say they are fit to govern. So today the *Sun* says: Let's give them the
chance to prove it.' Next day the *Sun* was full of reaction to this coup.
On page 2, Blair explained to Kavanagh and the paper's chief leader
writer Chris Roycroft-Davis why he deserved to be trusted, though Lord
Archer disagreed in a piece headed: 'Back Blair and you'll let in his leftie
pals.' He was not alone in his indignation. 'Some readers are angry and
sad because they feel we have betrayed them', the *Sun*'s leader said:

> That's a pity – because it shows they have missed the point. No
> newspaper loves this country more than the *Sun*. We shout from the
> rooftops about Britain's achievements in every field. We wear our
> patriotism as a badge of pride. But under John Major and his
> squabbling, tired, incompetent and divided government this country
> is going nowhere ... How can anyone forget the sky-high interest
> rates, the boarded-up shops, the repossessed homes? If some *Sun*
> readers feel let down by us, at least they understand exactly how we
> feel about the Tories.

In the opening weeks of the campaign the *Sun* smote the Conservatives, especially over sleaze, but without suggesting that Labour was
an entirely easy choice. Thus a leader on Saturday 22 March on Tory
MPs under attack for sleaze – 'If they had a shred of honour about them
they would resign. But that's a bit like asking a skunk to use a deodorant'
– was followed on Monday by another declaring that Labour's windfall
tax looked 'dodgier by the moment'. This was not what Rupert Murdoch
wanted and he said so in characteristic terms at the end of the month,
after which the *Sun*'s commitment to Labour hardened. Having dismissed the Conservative manifesto in contemptuous terms, it warmed
to Labour's, declaring on 4 April: 'Tony Blair laid his cards on the table
yesterday. Face up, for all to see. His vision of a New Britain is based on
being honest and open. What you see is what you get. Well, what the
Sun sees is just what we need. An inspiring leader with a clear sense of
direction.'

Blair offered a series of pledges on Europe and the unions tailored
to satisfy the *Sun*. On 17 April he declared that he loved the pound. Five
days later the Labour leader wrote in the *Sun*: 'Tomorrow is St George's
Day, the day when the English celebrate the pride we have in our
nation.' National identity would be protected under New Labour, not
submerged. 'St George did not slay a dragon so that England could
follow the rest. He did it so that we could be strong and ready to lead.
I am determined that New Labour, a party united and strongly led, will
make that happen.'

This was never the full, joyous and uninhibited 'Nightmare on Kinnock Street' works. It lacked the confident verve of the *Sun*'s 1992 campaign. But this campaign had an issue, in sleaze, superbly tailored to tabloid needs, enabling the *Sun* (and others) simultaneously to bash the Tories, talk about sex, and top it all off with the picture of a 17-year-old 'stunna'. And sleaze underlined the *Sun*'s regular message: this lot are old and tired (though not too old and tired, it appeared, for occasional hanky-panky), corrupt and discredited.

The final message was as resolute as the Labour campaign – or Murdoch – could have wished. The paper of 30 April proclaimed: 'Who Blairs Wins'. 'The *Sun*,' said its leader, 'has always had two reservations about the Labour Party: its attitude towards Europe and the unions. Over the past 44 days, Blair has been emphatic on both issues. He pledges he will fight for what's best for Britain – and that means no federal superstate and no return to the bad old days of union anarchy.' On polling days the front page was dominated by a picture of Blair with a lottery-style magic finger pointing towards him and the headline: 'It must be you.' 'Today you have a unique opportunity to join the greatest jackpot syndicate ever,' the paper said. 'The guaranteed prize is a share in our country's future, a brighter tomorrow … All you must do is vote Labour.' The *Sun* didn't claim to have 'won it' this time, but it had done a far better cheerleading job for New Labour than Blair and his colleagues could have realistically hoped for when the courtship began.

Murdoch's *News of the World* never got round to such cheerleading. Its first campaign leader declared that the credibility of the Conservatives was 'stone dead'. The following week there were mild doubts about Blair – was he a breath of fresh air, or was it just wind? – and on 4 April it suggested that Tony Blair's speech appearing to minimise the clout of a Scottish parliament raised doubts as to whether he could be trusted. Blair's 'one-man band', it declared the following week, seemed to be losing some of its serene confidence, while the 'sinister silence' of the union barons, still Labour's biggest paymasters, was 'deafening'. The leader of 20 April had a note not of cheerleading but of elegiac resignation. 'As John Major bravely fights what will most probably be his last battle, Mr Blair, leading his silent followers towards victory, gives us few clues as to what the future might hold under a Labour government – but entreats us to trust him. And it now looks, for better or worse, [as if] we have decided to do just that.' Only its final pronouncement had any ring of conviction: it backed Blair as 'the man for the new millennium'.

Even some of its rivals had made the *Sun*'s conversion to Labour the top story of the day. The swinging of the *Daily Star* was less of an epic event. Strictly speaking this paper had not endorsed the Tories in 1992:

its only specific advice was not to vote for Paddy Ashdown. But the slant of its reporting and comment was clearly towards the Conservatives. This time its main preoccupation seemed to be to reassure readers that the election campaign wouldn't hurt. On 3 April a *Star* leader warned: 'The Tory manifesto has been published. But manifestos don't win elections.' Next day it said: 'John Major describes the Labour manifesto as a con trick. Well, he would, wouldn't he.' The day after that it had a rare word of commendation for Ashdown – 'good on yer, Paddy' – for coming clean on his party's plans for taxation and public spending. But a leader on 7 April, referring to the overwhelming feeling that the time had come for a change, made its likely endorsement clear.

The *Star* was commendably faithful to its pledge not to swamp its readers in politics. A series of daily analyses of campaign issues with *Star* verdicts on each seemed on balance to favour the Tories more often than Labour, but the final assessment was unequivocal. 'There's Tony One Way To Go', the paper stated. Tony Blair might be untried, but he had transformed his party: 'They offer New Labour, new team, new dream. John Major and his team offer only extra time.'

THE CLINGERS

The *Mirror* enjoyed itself in 1997 as it hadn't in 1992, when partly because it commendably tried to treat things more seriously, it lacked the verve and flexibility of the *Sun*. But in 1997 it sometimes seemed a bit envious at the feast Tony Blair had prepared for what it no doubt saw as the prodigal *Sun*. There were sad little devices to remind *Mirror* readers that their paper had always been loyal to Labour, even when times were toughest. The first day of the campaign proper, when the *Sun* declared for New Labour, found the *Mirror* – 'the paper that's always been loyal', as it said on the masthead – featuring a front-page picture of Blair surrounded by children. 'Tony Blair – my election pledge to you – Labour's TRUE supporters: I will win it for Mirror readers', the caption said. Throughout the campaign there were meaty examinations of issues, all strongly favouring Labour, in the old *Mirror* tradition. On 18 April the *Mirror* made the NHS its 'issue of the day'. Next day this produced a classic campaigning front page, with the headline : 'Read this and weep.' The story said: 'A sobbing nurse phoned the *Mirror* last night to give this devastating indictment of how John Major's Conservative government has destroyed the National Health Service.' 'I've just finished an 18-hour shift', the nurse told the paper, 'and I had to call you. Please don't name me because they'll sack me. All the staff are distraught. I've just watched a young man die, but if he had been given treatment earlier, I know he might have been saved. He was only 22 ...!' That night Paddy Ashdown read the whole report to a party meeting in Chard (the nurse, it was later reported, voted Liberal Democrat).

Like the *Sun*, the *Mirror* revelled in stories of sleaze. Its issue of 28 March was the nearest thing in the 1997 campaign to a 'Nightmare on Kinnock Street' epic. On the front page it ran a picture of Anna Cox, the girl involved in the case of the Tory backbencher Piers Merchant, taken when she was 15, juxtaposing it with a picture of John Major with his hand clasped to his mouth. 'Going down – Major sunk by teen temptress', the caption said, perhaps a little ambiguously. On page 2, a story on Merchant was headed: 'He is just a wicked liar and a cheat: teen lover blasts hypocrite Tories'; on page 3, a story on Neil Hamilton carried the headline: 'Rat MP refuses to quit: PM fury at scandal'. Pages 4 and 5 concentrated on Hamilton ('Vintage Liar') but found room for the fall of the Scottish Conservative MP Allan Stewart ('Shamed Tory MP Goes Berserk in Garden'). A leader said of Conservative members: 'They are arrogant, greedy and insensitive, but it is their smugness which is most sickening', while Mary Riddell, 'Britain's most incisive columnist', asked: 'Why do wives of shamed Tory MPs ritually humiliate themselves?'

A run of celebrity endorsements of Labour produced on 11 April a name that few had expected: 'Reggie Kray is urging friends to vote Labour. He has told staff and fellow inmates at the jail where he is serving life for murder that if prisoners were allowed to vote, he would vote for Tony Blair.' The *Mirror* reporter helpfully added: 'Kray, 64, was once an admirer of Margaret Thatcher. He now favours a more caring society.'

The *Mirror* ended the campaign on a note of high jubilation. 'Your country needs him', it said over a big picture of Blair on page 1, while inside the paper promised: 'Tony Blair is going to take this country by the scruff of the neck and shake it – just as he has done to his party ... Tony Blair is an amazing man and an astonishing politician. He will be a great leader for Britain and great for the British people.' Profiles of society's victims – a mugged old lady, children from neglected schools, jobless young people on Tyneside, a girl who struggled to walk – people whose only hope of salvation lay with New Labour – punctuated the paper.

Neither the *People* nor the *Sunday Mirror* banged the Blair drum with such dedication. Perhaps they believed the votes of their readers were safe for Labour already. On 23 March the *People* declared it was 'time for a new beginning ... time for a change', a message reiterated in the final weekend with a double page spread declaiming: 'Britain needs a breath of fresh Blair.' The *Sunday Mirror* finished the campaign much as the *Daily Mirror* would do, with case histories of people whose futures depended on Labour's success.

THE WAVERERS

Much the most absorbing case history after the *Sun* was the true-blue *Daily Mail*. Discreet little dinners had been going on here too, as Blair and his colleagues sought to fend off the traditional *Mail* onslaught on Labour both in comment and in reporting. Lord Rothermere, the proprietor, was known to be taken with Blair; so was Sir David English, the editor-in-chief. Paul Dacre, the *Mail*'s formidable editor, was also impressed – but warier, especially over Europe. In most newspaper circumstances, the combination of proprietor and editor-in-chief would have been expected to outgun a mere editor. Dacre's record of success, and the knowledge that if he were alienated they would lose him to any one of a long queue of suitors, made for a different balance. Lord Rothermere made it plain from the start that he wanted something different from the *Mail*'s usual blanket adherence to Conservative people and Conservative policies. But Rothermere is a less dictatorial owner than Murdoch, so the fact that he openly favoured such an approach was not conclusive. That the *Mail*'s allegiance was ever in question was historically quite astounding, even if in the end it made the recommendation it usually did. It's in this sense that I call it a waverer.

The extent of the internal divisions was plainly revealed in an interview given by Lord Rothermere in Paris, where he lives most of the time, to the *Independent on Sunday* on 23 March. 'The *Daily Mail* is independent', he said. 'It has always embraced the policy of the Tories because the policy of the Labour Party was not acceptable. This is the most original situation, where we have two political parties with policies not terribly different, the difference being the question of credibility. I don't think we will actually endorse anybody. I don't believe in newspapers endorsing or supporting parties.' He hinted, however, that this rule did not apply to the *Standard*, where the editor, Max Hastings, had been showing clear signs of a Labour endorsement. 'I wouldn't be surprised at anything Max Hastings does', Rothermere added.

There was a lot in New Labour which chimed with the *Mail*'s view of life. For the editor, the main source of encouragement was the adoption under Blair's leadership of a family values agenda, spreading through to its policies on law and order and education, far closer to the *Daily Mail*'s own approach than anything heard from Labour before. Dacre had been at university with the likely Labour Home Secretary,

Jack Straw. Straw in those days ran the student union, Dacre the student newspaper, which brought them into close collaboration. Dacre was also a warm admirer of the probable education secretary, David Blunkett. New Labour wooed the *Mail* on these issues in much the same way as it wooed the *Sun*, and the *Mail* made room for features by Blunkett and Straw which appealed to *Daily Mail* instincts more effectively than John Major's Tories usually did. Yet serious reservations persisted. Tony Blair might be saying the things they would wish him to say: but was the conversion genuine, rather than merely tactical? And could they be certain that Blair, under pressure, would deliver? There were other issues, too, where New Labour could not give the *Mail* satisfaction: on Europe in general and the Social Chapter especially, but also on the unions, taxation and education.

That made, for once in the life of the *Daily Mail*, a truly difficult election choice. It was no use pretending after all its disparagement of John Major and his ministers that the *Mail* could look on their handiwork and declare itself well pleased. So the comment would be less supportive of the Tories: and crucially, the paper's reporting would be less vituperative towards Labour than Central Office wanted or had in the past expected.

But it soon became clear that the *Mail* would be sticking more closely to its traditions than Lord Rothermere might have wished. Rothermere was a waverer who would end up in personal terms as a swinger (after the election he announced he would be backing Labour in the Lords). Dacre, though discontented, would still in the end prove to be a clinger of sorts – but very much on his own, not the Tories', terms. The *Mail* remained pro-Conservative in the sense that it championed *Daily Mail*/Conservative values; but it adopted a pragmatic and often strongly sceptical approach to what the party's current leaders were preaching. It began to hammer away at two themes which, for all its doubts about Major, could only drive it towards the conclusion that Conservative and Labour policies were not in fact as close as poor old Rothermere had deluded himself into thinking. The first was the unions – the intransigent, power-hungry unions, apparently tractable now, but planning to have their way once Labour was in. The second, even more crucial, was Britain's future in Europe. Here again, Rothermere and his editor were divided. Rothermere was less hostile to the project than Dacre. He summarised their positions in an interview in the *Financial Times* on 28 April. 'I am quite clearly in favour of a Common Market but I am not in favour of a federal Europe. Nor is the *Daily Mail*', he told Philip Stephens. Could Dacre sometimes go too far? he was asked. 'Well, sometimes I think he would like to tow England out into the middle of the Atlantic. I am not sure that is what I want to do.'

This relatively mild rebuke, by traditional Fleet Street standards, followed weeks of energetic towing by Dacre, who had made the *Mail* a deeply Euro-sceptical paper and had no intention of abandoning his personal preference, and damaging his newspaper's credibility, by ditching that now. He believed the line his paper was taking chimed with the mood of the nation. Having warned John Major to get off the fence on this issue, only to find that he wouldn't, he began printing daily roll calls of election candidates who had declared against a single currency and were therefore 'sound' in *Daily Mail* terms. Nearly all were Conservatives. The implications were clear. Only by electing Conservatives could we set up defences against intransigent, power-hungry Europe. A leader on 18 April condemned 'the damning silence' of Labour on Europe: the party had resorted to 'waffle, evasion, and a sinister conspiracy of silence'.

Europe, the *Mail* ordained as the campaign ended, was the biggest issue before the electorate. The effect of the *Daily Mail* leader challenging candidates to speak out against EMU had, the paper enthused, been 'electrifying'. Of 648 Conservative candidates, 304 opposed the single currency. Of 640 Labour candidates, only 17 did so. That exploded 'the great myth' (encouraged, they may have forgotten, by their own proprietor) that there was nothing between the parties. The *Mail* held no torch for John Major's administration – it had been its sternest critic. 'To be blunt, John Major has been an ineffectual leader.' And yet: 'There is a terrible danger that the British people, drugged by the seductive mantra, it's time for a change, are stumbling, eyes glazed, into an election that could undo 1,000 years of our nation's history.' So after six weeks in which by previous standards expected in Central Office the *Mail* must have sometimes seemed grossly disloyal, the party got its endorsement – just.

The *Mail on Sunday* predictably arrived at the same destination, though by a slightly less scenic route. Though sickened by Tory sleaze, it never seemed likely to ditch its old allegiance. It warned of the union grip on Labour, even under Blair. On 13 April, at the end of what it called 'a week of woe' for Labour, it described the party's commitment to the Social Chapter as a 'time bomb', while a leader declared that Labour, New or Old, remained the unions' friend. Why should Britain trust Tony with the economy? it demanded the following week. To the unions and the Social Chapter it added new reasons for fearing a Labour victory: new taxes on business and an urge to meddle with everything. Even so, its final leader of the campaign (27 April) sounded uncharacteristically uncertain. Many voters, it conceded, would have painful memories of the recession, of repossessed houses, and of broken promises on tax. Not every crisis had been well handled. Tony Blair had transformed his party – though he had not yet come clean on issues like Europe, the minimum wage and devolution. There was a case for trusting Blair – but there must be fears about his followers. The unions remained a menace, and Labour's devolution plans had the potential to break up the United Kingdom. The paper uneasily concluded:

> The *Mail on Sunday* believes there is a better case – on balance – for trusting Mr Major. He has presided over economic prosperity in difficult and turbulent times. For a vast majority of the British people, life has become better. And when we put on our crosses on the ballot paper on Thursday, that is a good enough reason to support him, and to give the Tory Party one last chance.

THE QUAVERERS

At the *Mail*, potential waverers had recovered their old buccaneering touch. Not so the *Express*, whose predicament evoked the favourite question of its one-time proprietor, Beaverbrook: 'Who's in charge of the clattering train?' There seemed to be rival drivers. In a double page spread in the *Express on Sunday* on 20 April, Lord Stevens, the chairman, and Lord Hollick, the chief executive, argued against each other, Stevens for the Conservatives, Hollick for Labour. Lord Hollick, by all reports, had the greater clout, the relationship being symbolised by the removal, apparently at Hollick's behest, of a bust of Lord Stevens which until Hollick's arrival had adorned the paper's front hall. Yet this was the newspaper which alone of the tabloids had maintained its support for the Tories even when times were darkest: and one which had backed John Major to stay on as leader while the *Mail* and *Sun* deserted him. Its readers appeared to endorse that view: a readership poll in March showed 85 per cent naming Major as best prime minister against 10 per cent for Blair and 5 per cent for Ashdown. (The *Express* also achieved the remarkable feat of recruiting a panel of six floating voters not one of whom at the end declared for the Labour Party.) In the light of its history, the *Express*'s endorsement was scarcely in doubt. What it lacked, in the eyes of a party desperate for some cheer-leading, was any sense of conviction. Some of its editorial comment seemed almost to glory in ambivalence. Perhaps the most bizarre comment was that of 15 March. It hoped the coming campaign would be lively. But then it quoted Voltaire: as Candide had said, we must cultivate our garden. This metaphor, the *Express* confided, was well chosen, since literally cultivating one's garden was one of the most satisfying activities given to men and women. 'That is why the *Express* is today giving away a packet of pansy seeds to all its readers to help them cultivate places of calm and beauty.'

It even seemed in two minds about sleaze. On 27 March it saw no reason why Neil Hamilton should not fight Tatton. 'Let the voters decide', it advised. By 7 April, 'we hope that Mr Hamilton will now see reason and step down'.

Like the *Mail* and the *Sun*, the *Express* was convinced that Europe was the crucial issue. On 16 April it challenged John Major to come off the fence: next day it reported that Major had risen to the *Express* challenge – but only, it admitted, to reiterate his 'wait and see' policy. It attacked British membership of the Social Chapter, yet without specifically drawing the moral that Labour were dangerous.

The *Express* had an additional problem in this election. It was now a seven-day operation under a single editor, Richard Addis. The *Express on Sunday* was integrated with the Monday–Saturday papers in a way the *Mail on Sunday* was not. The *Mail on Sunday* had a separate editor with a separate set of editorial policies (in the Conservative leadership contest the *Mail on Sunday* backed Major, the *Mail* John Redwood.) That mean that the *Mail on Sunday* could offer its final endorsement without committing the *Mail*. The *Express on Sunday* needed to address its readers: but what it said would inescapably pre-empt the final judgment on the eve of the election. The leader published on Sunday 27 April was again equivocal. In previous elections there had only been one sensible option: to vote for the Conservative Party. Now, thanks to Tony Blair, the electors had a real choice. But were all his many changes of heart – on privatisation, on Europe, on nuclear disarmament, on taxing and spending – genuine? The Tories had been 'a rabble'. If John Major got back, could they not be more divided than ever? Deciding which party to back was a fine choice. But one issue was clear. One could be certain the Conservatives would not take the federal road in Europe. One could not be so sure about Blair. 'If it is a choice between John Major and Tony Blair's well drilled army, then we believe that John Major's rabble has its heart nearer the right place.' 'Vote for the rabble': this was hardly the kind of endorsement to gladden the heart of Conservative Central Office.

Next day, Monday, the *Express* offered its weekday readers some similarly lukewarm advice. Major and Blair were both decent men who wanted the best for Britain. Neither would deliberately let the nation down. Their hearts were in the right place. The *Express*'s doubts about Major were well known. 'He thinks leadership, discipline and passion can be exercised spasmodically.' Yet this was the right time to remember some Tory successes. The list which followed mixed Major's achievements with Thatcher's: business freed from red tape, privatisation, trade union reform, council house sales, the thriving economy, low inflation and interest rates, falling unemployment, improving profitability and

efficiency, a falling national debt, greater soundness on devolution ...
Recalling these things, the paper concluded, meant a vote for the Tories
on Thursday.

Another tepid tribute followed next day: the state of the NHS was
another achievement 'worth noting'. On Wednesday, a new commendation: the Tories had worked hard for their vote of confidence;
there had been a remarkable recovery since Britain had been 'liberated'
from the ERM. Better than nothing, no doubt; yet 'worth noting' was
hardly the clarion call which had always issued from the *Express* on
these occasions before. On the morning of polling day, it asked which
party was more likely to preserve British sovereignty, to respect institutions which had served Britain well, to back personal responsibility,
enterprise and thrift and concluded: 'Though like many others we feel
let down by the present government we have in the end little doubt
that the Tory Party remains more likely to run Britain on lines of which
we would approve.' The paper conceded, though, that many readers
must have made up their minds already. A less quavering finale, perhaps
– but still a sharp departure from the kind of Beaverbrookian robustness
for which this newspaper used to be famous.

It has to be said that not much of this made any difference. The party
which got the most positive press backing, Labour, fell back during the
campaign, while the Liberal Democrats, who rarely got even a mention,
gained the most ground. This was never going to be the kind of election
which the role of the press could sway. There had been since 1992 a
change in our politics so profound that New Labour would still have
triumphed even had the *Sun* cheered John Major as once it had cheered
Margaret Thatcher. A newspaper pitch is unlikely to move many voters
unless it chimes with their own experience, plays on doubts already
haunting them, celebrates successes they agree are worth celebrating.
This time, the mood of the voters swayed the tabloids, and not the other
way round. A necessary rebuke, perhaps, for those who believed that
the huge advantage in tabloid readership which the Tories enjoyed in
1992 was set to continue indefinitely. As one especially crass assessment
concluded at the 1992 Essex conference after the *Sun* had 'won it': 'The
Conservative advantage among tabloid readers, and the unscrupulous
way in which these papers behave, is one of the many ways in which
British elections are best assessed as contests not fought on our good
old friend the level playing field. ... What can be done about it? Very
little ... Will it help to sustain the longest period of one party dominance
for over a century? Very probably yes.'

That analysis failed to allow for the fact that newspapers cannot
preach to their readers things that they find ridiculous. It severely
underestimated too the extent to which New Labour was destined to

go to neutralise tabloid antagonism, even to purchase tabloid support. In the light of the 1997 result, one has to suspect that New Labour could have got away with a much more resolute and challenging attitude to the Murdoch Press. Even so, those whose predictions go woefully wrong ought to apologise for them. And I do.

NOTES

1 Martin Linton, 'Was It The Sun Wot Won It?', seventh Guardian Lecture, Nuffield College, Oxford (1995).
2 John Curtice and Holli Semetko, 'Does It Matter What The Papers Say?', in Anthony Heath, Roger Jowell and John Curtice (eds), *Labour's Last Chance: The 1992 Election and Beyond* (Aldershot: Dartmouth Publishing Company, 1994), pp. 43–64. See also John Curtice, 'Is The Sun Shining on Tony Blair? – The Electoral Influence of Newspapers in Britain since 1992', *Harvard International Journal of Press and Politics* 2 (1997), pp. 9–26.
3 Martin Harrop and Margaret Scammell, 'A Tabloid War', in David Butler and Dennis Kavanagh (eds), *The British General Election of 1992* (Basingstoke: Macmillan, 1992), pp. 182–4; David McKie, 'Fact is Free and Comment is Sacred, or Was It The Sun Wot Won It?', in Ivor Crewe and Brian Gosschalk (eds), *Political Communications: The General Election Campaign of 1992* (Cambridge: Cambridge University Press, 1995), pp. 124–30.
4 'Security in a World of Change', in Tony Blair, *New Britain: My Vision of a Young Country* (London: Fourth Estate, 1996).

Table 9.1: Allegiance of national daily newspapers, 1997

	Circulation (000)	Readership (000)
For Labour:		
Sun	3,935	10,211
Mirror	2,390	6,389
Star	660	2,089
Guardian	402	1,274
Financial Times	304	717
Independent	256	867
For Conservatives:		
Mail	2,127	5,159
Express	1,208	2,878
Telegraph	1,126	2,542
For Liberal Democrats:		
–		
Other		
The Times[a]	772	1,904

Note: [a] Vote Eurosceptic.
Source: Various articles by Roy Greenslade in the 'Media' *Guardian*, in 1997.

10

Leaders and Leading Articles: Characterisation of John Major and Tony Blair in the Editorials of the National Daily Press

COLIN SEYMOUR-URE

How did the national daily press characterise John Major and Tony Blair in the 1997 election campaign? The question matters for a variety of reasons. First, the leaders dominate their colleagues in the media coverage of the party campaigns. Second, John Major had steadily lost the support of the press from 16 September 1992 – the day ('Black Wednesday') when sterling was forced to leave the European exchange rate mechanism – onwards. When Major put his leadership on the line in July 1995, only the *Daily Express* stayed loyal (as in 1992). So how would the papers, all except one of whom were under new editors since the 1992 election, view him in 1997?[1] If Major was part of the Conservatives' problem, Blair was part of the Labour solution. Whatever his recent successes, however, he was untried as leader in a general election campaign. How would editorialists judge him?

'Editorialists' is the key term. For this chapter discusses editorials, or leading articles, not general newspaper coverage. Often printed in a distinctive type size or placed within a box, and by convention anonymous, the editorial offers the authoritative corporate judgement of the newspaper. In 1997 papers seemed likely to change their party loyalty – or to support the party but not really the leader, in the case of the Conservatives. Editorials would be the place to track these changes.

A further reason for the study is a comparison with 1992. Then, the author compared the characterisation of Major and Kinnock in the *Sun* and the *Daily Mirror*.[2] The *Sun*'s switch of support in 1997 made for an unsubtle comparison between its view of Major then and now. But how did the comparison work in the *Mirror*, and how did the *Mirror* rate Blair against Kinnock?

This chapter looks first at the amount of characterisation of the leaders, second at its distribution between positive and negative features and between personality and professional skills, third at the differences between individual papers, fourth at the topics and policies to which the leaders were linked, and lastly at the comparative performance of the *Sun* and *Mirror* in 1992 and 1997.[3]

HOW MUCH CHARACTERISATION?

Table 10.1 gives a simple measure of the amount of attention editorial writers paid to the party leaders (excepting Paddy Ashdown, who received almost none). The number of editorials making reference to the leaders in some way or other is high.

Table 10.1: Editorials characterising party leaders, 17 March–2 May 1997

Paper	Total election editorials	Major			Blair		
		Total naming Major	No. 'characterising' Major	No. of 'characterisations'	Total naming Blair	No. 'characterising' Blair	No. of 'characterisations'
Conservative							
Daily Telegraph	65	29	3	3	36	18	35
Express	34	16	3	3	17	9	11
Daily Mail	57	21	4	8	40	11	19
Labour							
Guardian	54	28	11	14	24	8	10
Independent	41	24	8	9	26	11	17
Mirror	47	22	14	28	20	12	20
Sun	56	28	17	30	28	15	45
The Times	49	27	5	10	30	12	19

Note: 'Naming' means using the leaders' name. 'Characterising' means describing or evaluating his personality. The latter numbers are *included* in the former.

The lowest number of references, proportionately, are made by the *Daily Mail*, with, out of a total of 57 editorials, 21 (37 per cent) mentioning Major, and the highest by the *Daily Mail* too, with 40 (70 per cent) mentioning Blair. But the number *characterising* the leaders is very much smaller. This distinction must be strongly emphasised. The focus in this chapter is not on everything which editorialists wrote about and with which the leader was associated, for the leader's name is often used as a label for their party. 'Characterisation', rather, is used to refer to specific personality traits and professional skills, where the editorialist was judging not so much the policy or event involved as the leader himself.

Table 10.1 also shows that particular editorials may contain more than one characterisation: throughout this chapter, 'mentions' refers not to single editorials but to single instances of characterisation. The extreme case is the *Sun*, which had a number of editorials extolling Blair somewhat in the manner of an Old Testament psalm, giving an average of three characterisations per editorial (45 characterisations in 15 editorials).

The other point which Table 10.1 straight away illustrates, and which recurs in the analysis, is the reluctance of the three Conservative papers and *The Times* to editorialise at all about John Major the human being, as distinct from Major the party label. In view of the history of the last five years this is no surprise. Labour papers, of course had no such hesitation. But most papers of either persuasion were happier to write about Tony Blair, whether praising him, such as the *Sun*, or slamming him, such as the *Daily Telegraph*.

THE PARTY LEADERS: POSITIVE AND NEGATIVE, PERSONALITY
AND PROFESSIONAL SKILLS

Table 10.2 illustrates how the newspapers characterised John Major and Tony Blair in their editorials. Each characterisation has been coded as representing one of ten personal characteristics. Six refer to the leader's personality and four to his professional governing skills. The categories are grouped into pairs of opposites (tough/weak; determined/indecisive, and so on). The left-hand columns list positive attributes and the right-hand columns list the corresponding negatives. The pungency of news-paper prose is lost in this process. For example, the statement that 'John Major couldn't run a bath' is coded blandly under 'incompetent'. The newspapers are also divided into Conservative and non-Conservative – the latter in order to accommodate *The Times*, which advised its readers to support selected Eurosceptic candidates from no fewer than six different parties.

This coding method enables some generalisations to be made about the ways in which the newspapers characterised the leaders in 1997, although the numbers are too small to allow more than a few tentative inferences. The totals show that papers overall criticised more than they approved (55 per cent to 45 per cent). But this result is due wholly to the weight of criticism of John Major. Aspects of personality received much more attention than professional skills. On both positive and negative sides the ratio was about 70 per cent to 30 per cent. This surely is to be expected. On one hand, there is the familiar problem of abstraction. 'Government' cannot easily be seen; its results are scored in statistics or are visible at the grass-roots level of classrooms and

Table 10.2: Characterisation of party leaders, 17 March–2 May 1997: Positive and negative

	Number of positive mentions					Number of negative mentions					
	Major Newspapers		Blair Newspapers		Total	Major Newspapers		Blair Newspapers		Total	
	Con.	Non-Con.	Con.	Non-Con.		Con.	Non-Con.	Con.	Non-Con.		
Personality:											**Personality:**
Tough, combative, courageous	1	3	1	22	27	1	15	7	2	25	Weak, panicking, cowardly
Determined, confident, ambitious	–	2	1	10	13	4	4	7	1	16	Indecisive, unconfident, inconsistent
Trustworthy, honest, sincere, decent	1	5	2	12	20	2	11	22	6	41	Untrustworthy, dishonest, unprincipled
Relaxed, good-humoured	–	–	–	5	5	–	1	3	1	5	Hot headed, irresponsible
Exciting, passionate, energetic, visionary	–	1	2	24	27	–	9	1	2	12	Boring, uninspiring, pathetic, ridiculous
Man of the people	–	–	–	1	1	1	5	7	1	14	Arrogant, smug, vain, power-hungry
Sub-total	2	11	6	74	93	8	45	47	13	113	Sub-total
Professional Skills:											**Professional Skills:**
Experienced	–	–	–	–	–	–	–	1	–	1	Inexperienced
Competent, outstanding leader	–	–	4	8	12	3	14	1	–	18	Incompetent, blundering
Effective	2	–	3	5	10	2	19	1	1	23	Ineffective, dismal
Pragmatic, reformer	–	2	2	10	14	–	–	–	–	–	
Sub-total	2	2	9	23	36	5	33	3	1	42	Sub-total
Total	4	13	15	97	129	13	78	50	14	155	Total

Note: The Conservative papers include *Daily Telegraph*, *Daily Mail* and *Daily Express*. The non-Conservative papers include *Guardian*, *Mirror*, *Independent*, *Sun* and *The Times*.

NB. There is often more than one 'mention' in a single leading article.

doctors' surgeries. Governing skills are more easily asserted than demonstrated. Besides, Tony Blair had not done any governing yet. Personality, by contrast, is experienced in a leader's voice and face, and it is perhaps at a premium in an election campaign.

The positive features of the leaders mentioned in the press were concentrated principally, and fairly evenly, in three categories: toughness, trust and excitement. There was more variation among the negatives, largely due to criticism of John Major's incompetence and ineffectiveness. The distribution of negative attributes, indeed, looks more like the pattern traditionally expected of a partisan press. That is, the majority of negative mentions of John Major come in the non-Conservative press and of Tony Blair in the Conservative press. But the positive side is gaptoothed for want of Conservative approval of Major to match non-Conservative support for Blair. Although it was generally offered in passing, Major actually got more approval from his opponents than from his own side. His honesty, determination and courage were acknowledged. But the deep disillusion with his leadership is reflected in the fact that almost no one had a good word for his professional skills.

Blair received a smattering of praise from the Conservative press (more than Major, indeed). Among his own supporters, two categories stand out: his passion, energy and vision, and his toughness. Trustworthiness, honesty and so on are not far behind. While opponents recognised the passion and toughness, there was a corollary and outstanding perception of Blair as untrustworthy, unprincipled and evasive.

This last comment raises the question of symmetry – which Table 10.2 is designed to try and elucidate. Symmetry in a partisan press can take two forms. One applies to individual newspapers: a Conservative newspaper, for instance, might see Blair's weaknesses (such as dishonesty) as symmetrical with Major's strengths (honesty). The second extends to competing papers. Here, the weaknesses a Labour newspaper saw in Major would be symmetrical if they were the same as those seen in Blair by a Conservative newspaper.

The arguments for expecting to find such symmetry in press evaluation of the leaders boil down to two. One is that party leaders' personalities are manufactured, and in a non-ideological competition they will tend to be made similar. (This is not to say that they become identikit; toughness, sincerity, good humour, energy and the rest can be expressed in myriad ways.) The second argument is that editorial rhetoric, especially in the mass-market tabloids, is condensed and reductive, and has a ritual quality. In 1997, indeed, with the result a foregone conclusion, the entire editorial campaign had an air of ritual. The election was a six-week moment in an extended shift of national political mood. Normally anti-Labour newspapers' support for Blair, notably the *Sun*'s, was given strictly on approval.[4]

The collapse of positive characterisation of John Major in the Conservative press demolished the possibility of much symmetry in 1997. There were just a few elements. Non-Conservative newspapers found Blair tough and combative: the same newspapers found Major weak and panicky. Conservative newspapers thought Blair untrustworthy and dishonest (to some extent): non-Conservative newspapers thought him trustworthy and honest. (But note that some non-Conservative newspapers thought Blair was untrustworthy too – and also that Major was trustworthy.) However, there were no Conservative newspapers rooting for Major and providing the other side of the balance.

PERSONALITY AND PROFESSIONAL SKILLS: VIEWS OF INDIVIDUAL NEWSPAPERS

Some of the differences between particular newspapers are illustrated in Table 10.3. The totals are skewed by the large numbers for a few newspapers. Nearly half (27 out of 60) of the criticisms of Blair's personality, for instance, were in the *Daily Telegraph*. Exactly half (33 out of 66) of the positive references to his personality in the Labour press, correspondingly, were in the *Sun*. Disapproval of John Major cropped up everywhere, but notably in the *Mirror* and the *Sun*. The *Sun* was alone in criticising Major's professional skills as much as his personality. The two mass-market tabloids were substantially more concerned than any other papers with characterisation of the party leaders.

The Labour newspapers were almost uniformly uncritical of Tony Blair. With the exception of the *Mirror* they were more positive about Blair than critical of Major. The *Mirror*, again, was relatively more impressed by Blair's professional skills than were the other papers. This was the first election in which the *Independent* committed itself to a party; however, it still achieved a comparatively broad and balanced consideration of the two leaders. In the pitiful level of overall support for Major, the *Express* stands out, as befits the newspaper which was his most faithful supporter during the years after 1992.

Table 10.3 confirms, then, that all the Labour newspapers behaved in a traditional partisan way, offering unstinting approval for Blair, both as person and professional, and varying criticism both of Major's personality and the skills implicit in his record. The *Daily Telegraph* and the *Daily Mail* played the same role in criticising Blair. But the missing part of the quadrant, so to speak, is their comparative silence on the subject of John Major's positive qualities.

Table 10.3: Party leaders: personality and professional skills
(number of mentions, 17 March–2 May 1977)

	Major				Blair			
	Positive		Negative		Positive		Negative	
Newspaper and party support	Personal	Professional skills	Personal	Professional skills	Personal	Professional skills	Personal	Professional skills
Conservative								
Daily Telegraph	–	–	3	–	4	2	27	2
Daily Express	2	1	3	–	2	3	5	1
Daily Mail	–	1	2	5	3	1	15	–
Sub-total	2	2	8	5	9	6	47	3
Labour								
Guardian	5	–	4	5	9	1	–	–
Independent	–	1	5	3	10	2	4	1
Mirror	2	–	19	7	14	6	–	–
Sun	3	–	13	14	33	12	–	–
Sub-total	10	1	41	29	66	21	4	1
The Times	2	–	4	4	8	2	9	–
Total	14	3	53	38	83	29	60	4

SUBJECTS LINKED TO CHARACTERISATION

At some stage of the campaign most newspapers had editorials specifically about the party leaders, and characterisations were made also during discussion of the course of events and of such issues as the television (non)-debates and sleaze. But the leaders were linked to a number of substantive policy issues too, such as education and taxation. These are illustrated in Table 10.4 and Table 10.5. For each leader, Table 10.4 shows 'policy topics' alongside total topics; and for each newspaper, it shows the number of topics and the number of comments linking the leaders with them. Overall, there were fewer concerning Major than Blair. Once again, the chief reason was the dearth of Conservative discussion of Major. In the Labour papers, the number of topics linked to Major was much the same as for Blair, although the number of mentions was less. Within these totals there is quite a range. The *Daily Telegraph* linked Blair to 13 (half being policy topics), while the average was about seven. At the other extreme, the *Daily Telegraph* and *The Times* linked Major to only three.

Table 10.4: Party leaders and editorial topics, by newspaper
(17 March–2 May 1997)

	Major				Blair			
	Policy topics		All topics		Policy topics		All topics	
Paper	No.	Mentions	No.	Mentions	No.	Mentions	No.	Mentions
Conservative								
Daily Telegraph	1	1	3	3	9	18	13	35
Daily Express	2	2	4	6	1	1	5	11
Daily Mail	2	8	5	9	5	9	8	19
Sub-total	5	11	12	18	15	28	26	65
Labour								
Guardian	4	6	6	14	4	6	8	10
Independent	3	4	6	9	3	4	6	17
Mirror	5	5	9	28	3	3	7	20
Sun	3	5	6	30	6	10	8	45
Sub-total	15	20	27	81	16	23	29	92
The Times	1	4	3	10	6	10	10	19
Total	21	35	42	109	37	61	65	176

Note: 'Policy topics' include such substantive topics as education, health, Europe, etc. Others are the campaign, television debates, the candidates themselves, etc.

Rather more than half the topics (21 out of 42 for Major; 37 out of 65 for Blair) were substantive policy areas. These attracted proportionately fewer of the characterisations. The topics are listed in Table 10.5, with the number of newspapers mentioning them. Apart from comment on the course of the campaign itself, the importance of Europe and sleaze as campaign issues stands out. (Sleaze is not defined as a policy topic for present purposes.) Otherwise, the number of topics to which Major is linked at all is only a handful. With Blair the list is longer, but education, trade unions and privatisation were the only ones to attract comment from more than a few newspapers.

THE *SUN* AND THE *MIRROR*: 1992 AND 1997

The *Sun*'s love affair with Tony Blair started long before the election campaign. Courtship in the columns was paralleled by meetings with Rupert Murdoch and between members of their respective entourages. The most publicised of these was Blair's trip to Australia, to the Great Barrier Reef, in 1995, to address Murdoch executives. All this was the

Table 10.5: Party leaders and editorial topics, by topic (17 March–2 May 1997)

	Major			Blair	
	Papers mentioning	*No. of mentions*		*Papers mentioning*	*No. of mentions*
Policy topics			Policy topics		
Europe	8	19	Europe	8	17
Con. manifesto	4	6	Lab. manifesto	5	7
Education	2	2	Education	5	5
Taxation	2	2	Trade unions	4	10
3 others	3	3	Privatisation	4	7
			N. Ireland	2	4
			Lottery	2	4
			9 others	9	12
Sub-total	*19*	*32*		*39*	*66*
Other topics			Other topics		
Sleaze	7	21	Blair	8	51
Campaign	6	20	Campaign	7	36
Major	5	28	Lab. Party	4	8
TV debates	2	3	Sleaze	3	6
			TV debates	3	5
Sub-total	*20*	*72*		*25*	*106*
Total	39	104		64	172

Note: Eight papers were included in the analysis. The *Daily Star* and *Financial Times* were omitted.

corollary of the *Sun*'s disillusionment with John Major.[5] 'NOW WE'VE ALL BEEN SCREWED BY THE GOVERNMENT' was its headline the day after 'Black Wednesday' in 1992, and the tone was set for the next four-and-a-half years.

By declaring for Labour on the day after the election was announced, the *Sun* won maximum publicity. For the first two weeks of the campaign, indeed – up till the time when one of the usual length would have started – the coming role of the media was a major item in the media's election agenda (sleaze, the main headline-winner, being a media-generated story). But the *Sun* actually declared not for Labour but for Tony Blair. Its headline on 18 March was 'THE SUN BACKS BLAIR'. Underneath were the words, 'Give change a chance'. Those two sentences summed it up: Blair, not Labour, and time for a change.

The *Sun*'s whole position rested, then, on its beliefs about (in the present context) Blair's personality and professional skills. Of the 115 square inches of the paper's editorial, 60 per cent were about Labour in general, and 60 per cent of these were about Blair. Only a small part (13 per cent) of the Conservative share was about Major. The Tories had 'all the right policies but all the wrong faces'. In Blair, 'Labour has the face that fits – and many of the Tories' policies. If it works, Clony Blair has hijacked it'. Major was 'a decent man who does his best' but he was no leader. Labour must be given a chance to prove they were trustworthy. If they were not, 'our attack on them will be ferocious'. The paper was especially worried about Europe and would watch with care to see if Blair withstood the pressures to conform on the single currency and kept his promise to have 'no truck with a federal superstate'.

Having declared itself so early rather than play a guessing game, the *Sun* had really nowhere to go. Since it was rooting for the man, not the party, and the man was untried, it could do little more than produce a stream of happy talk (measured roughly in Table 10.3 above) about the wonders to come. Just as paradise taxes poets and preachers more than the depiction of hell, so this happy talk became more vacuous as its range widened and it reached a climax in the week up to polling day. Fittingly, on polling day itself the *Sun* borrowed from the ultimate popular fantasy of the mid-1990s, the National Lottery. The star-spangled finger of fortune – a Lottery advertising device – pointed at a smiley Blair, with the headline 'IT MUST BE YOU'. The prospect of Blair fulfilling all the *Sun*'s dreams might be better than the reported 14 million-to-1 chance of winning the weekly jackpot, but there was surely a large measure of wishful thinking. The attached list (Figure 10.1) gives something of the flavour, although the language is yanked out of context. By comparison the *Mirror*, lacking the zeal of the convert, was restrained.

Both papers, however, took equal pleasure in criticising John Major, though the *Mirror* did so mainly in the first part of the campaign and the *Sun* in the second. Here the characterisation need not be vacuous. To say that Major was so weak that he could not run a bath is good, punchy stuff. To turn the image round ('so efficient he could run a bath') is not an option.

In talking John Major down, therefore, the use of imagery was arguably a key technique which was not readily available when talking Blair up. It has already been suggested above that, in mass market tabloid editorials, it is difficult to produce evidence in support of claims about abstractions such as competence and effectiveness – or even vision, decency and honesty. Instead, evidence gives way to imagery . Argument becomes a process of assertion, buttressed by metaphor. (Compare the crude mode of argument consisting of assertion followed by abuse.) The originality or exuberance of the image, and the inclusion of pun, humour or obscenity, such as the celebrated 'UP YOURS, DELORS!' (the *Sun* headline from 1 November 1990), are signals of the

Figure 10.1: Tony Blair: 'Happy Talk' in *Sun* Editorials, 17 March–2 May 1997

Tony Blair is:
- the breath of fresh air this great country needs;
- the face that fits;
- an inspiring leader with a clear sense of direction; and the guts to admit that the most important commodity in this election is TRUST;
- a man with vision and courage – with the makings of a great Prime Minister;
- hungry to succeed;
- a dynamic new leader who can make us all feel a lot better about ourselves and our country;
- a man of principle;
- the strong, dynamic, purposeful leader this country has been crying out for;
- the best man for the job.

and Tony Blair:
- looks good and he sounds good;
- knows where he is going;
- has dragged his party forwards into the real world;
- offers a fresh start;
- will prove his love for his country by always putting Britain's interests first;
- doesn't promise overnight miracles; but he does promise a REAL difference;
- looks to the future and promises: 'Together we can do better';
- showed great courage, even at the risk of his own downfall;
- promised honest politics;
- won't budge an inch for lunatic [trade union] lefties;
- spells out his determination to make a rapid, 'indelible imprint' on society;
- has shown enormous enthusiasm, energy and good humour;
- pledges he will fight for what's best for Britain;
- will step boldly onto the world stage;
- will not let Britain down;
- has promised to slay the dragon of Europe;
- has fire in his eyes;
- will give us purpose and a sense of direction;
- will herald a new dawn: the Blair Revolution;
- will make us feel good about ourselves and our society again;
- has a passion burning in [him] that can set this nation alight;
- … his vision, his determination and his political strength;
- … his boldness versus the will of Brussels;
- … his crusade to raise the standards in our schools;
- trust him to keep his promises and do his best for the country;
- the nation can move forward under Blair's leadership and achieve so much for its children.

strength of the argument, the confidence with which it is put forward and perhaps the significance of the issue. An election in which the character of one of the leaders was so derided by editorialists was therefore sure to be rich in imagery. A list of examples is attached (Figure 10.2).

Figure 10.2: John Major: editorial imagery in the *Sun* and *Mirror*
17 March–2 May 1997

John Major:
- couldn't run a bath;
- can't see a hole without tumbling into it;
- huffed and puffed and smiled his sickly grin;
- is in danger of fighting for his survival like King Canute – merely wishing and hoping that things go away;
- is as weak as a codfish;
- faced with problems, pulls a blanket over his head;
- is so weak he couldn't stand up in a light breeze;
- lacks backbone;
- is such a poor leader that his troops have decided to fight a different battle [about Europe];
- has got more chance of making it rain;
- hasn't had the stomach for a fight;
- is Johnocchio – like the puppet who couldn't stop telling lies;
- is the spineless leader of a rudderless ship;
- like King Midas in reverse, he turned a golden opportunity into a tarnished bauble;
- dump John Major in the wheelie bin of history;
- don't bother walking out, John; wait for the Pickfords van to give you a lift;
- a nasty streak runs through him like the words in a stick of rock;
- the Fat Lady's singing, John.

In 1992 the *Sun* conducted a memorable campaign of imagery against Neil Kinnock. The whole running feature, 'Nightmare on Kinnock Street', was an elaborate fantasy, including the famous front page Kinnock head-in-a-lightbulb (to switch off), the Page Three flab-o-gram lady (warning against spoilsport legislation) and the double-page spread of 'Kinnock-flee zones' such as Timbuktu and a Japanese space station. The campaign used verbal images and plenty of puns, but it was driven by graphics, and the traditional editorial played a comparatively small part in it.[6]

The *Sun* attempted nothing similar in 1997. Its attitudes to the various leaders in the two elections are set beside those of the *Mirror* in Table 10.6, designed along the same lines as Table 10.2.[7] What comes out is disproportionately slight in relation to the size of the table. In 1992 negative outnumbered positive characterisations in both papers, and again in 1997 in the *Mirror*. But enthusiasm for Blair turned the *Sun*'s figures round in 1997. Given that in 1997 the campaign was half as long again as in 1992, the positive references in the *Mirror* to Blair were not greatly out of line with those for Kinnock. The paper was more willing to credit him than Kinnock with professional skills but saw Kinnock as more determined and relaxed (insofar as the small numbers justify such an inference).

On the positive side the *Sun*, supporting Major in 1992 and Blair in

Table 10.6: The Mirror and the Sun, 1992 and 1997: Kinnock, Major and Blair

	Number of positive mentions				Number of negative mentions			
	Mirror		Sun		Mirror		Sun	
	1992 Kinnock	1997 Blair	1992 Major	1997 Blair	1992 Major	1997 Major	1992 Kinnock	1997 Major
Personality:								
Tough, combative, courageous	4	6	3	10				
Determined, confident, ambitious	4	3	–	4				
Trustworthy, honest, sincere, decent	1	2	5	6				
Relaxed, good-humoured	2	–	2	–				
Exciting, passionate, energetic, visionary	1	3	3	12				
Man of the people	–	–	3	1				
Personality:								
Weak, panicking, cowardly					2	7	5	4
Indecisive, unconfident, inconsistent					1	2	2	1
Untrustworthy, dishonest, unprincipled					2	3	8	4
Hot headed, irresponsible					1	–	4	–
Boring, uninspiring, pathetic, ridiculous					9	3	3	3
Arrogant, smug, vain, power-hungry					1	4	3	1
Sub-total	12	14	16	33	15	19	25	13
Professional Skills:								
Experienced	–	–	1	–				
Competent, outstanding leader	1	4	3	3				
Effective	1	1	2	2				
Pragmatic, reformer	–	1	–	7				
Professional Skills:								
Inexperienced					–	–	5	–
Incompetent, blundering					–	2	5	5
Ineffective, dismal					5	5	3	9
Sub-total	2	6	6	12	5	7	13	14
Total	14	20	22	45	20	26	38	27

Note: The dates are 12 March–9 April 1992 and 17 March–2 May 1997. There is often more than one 'mention' in a single editorial.

1997, saw Blair as tough and exciting much more often than Major, and also as more determined and confident – indeed, it did not spot these last characteristics in Major at all in 1992. It also perceived Blair as a pragmatist and reformer – characteristics which were not discerned in either leader in 1992.

On the negative side, the *Mirror's* view of Major had shifted by 1997. There was more emphasis on his weakness and arrogance and a new criticism of indecisiveness and incompetence. In 1992 the main complaints had been that he was simply boring and ineffective. In the *Sun*, Major certainly was not criticised in 1997 in the same proportions as Kinnock in 1992 (especially taking into account the long 1997 campaign). Criticism of Kinnock had been more frequent and wide-ranging. In particular, and in comparison, he was seen as hotheaded, untrustworthy and arrogant. Obviously, too, Kinnock was also considered inexperienced, whereas Major was incompetent and ineffective – the criticism to which the *Sun* returned most often.

None of this is surprising – and it should be treated, of course, as impressionistic. Nor does it do much to support a thesis about tabloid symmetry in the characterisation of leaders. Clearly, the *Sun* did attribute to Kinnock in 1992 most of the weaknesses seen in Major in 1997, and both papers attributed much the same *range* of characteristics to both their preferred leaders in both elections. That seems the most that may be said.

CONCLUSIONS

None of these findings can be described as 'strong', in the sense either of astonishment or of arriving like a force ten gale. The numbers are small and there may be some coding error. But at least three aspects do seem worth more prolonged thought and study. The first is simply the nature of argument in a mass-market tabloid. This newspaper suggests that its characteristic mode is a kind of higher form of 'assertion followed by abuse' – the street-market or road-rage form. Is this unfair? Moreover, it is more suited to negative than to positive argument – a claim which has discouraging implications.

Second, and more important, is the very topic of the characterisation of leaders. Have perceptions of leaders' personalities ever been more central to party competition in Britain? The question goes to the heart of leadership in a non-ideological, media-driven political age, when pragmatism and no doubt expediency rule. Leaders' entourages have never been more active in seeking to manage the leader's appearance. How papers perceive and portray the leaders should surely be a prime subject of analysis.

Last, and following from this, is the question whether a corollary of the emphasis on personalities is that if and when things went wrong for the Blair government, Blair himself could suffer strong personal criticism. A whiff of what might in those circumstances become a stench was certainly felt during the first test of the government's integrity late in 1997. Early in November the government announced its decision, in seeming contradiction of a manifesto commitment, to exempt Formula One motor racing from a ban on tobacco sponsorship of sport. At the same time, the media disclosed that the Labour Party had received an election campaign contribution of £1 million from the Formula One entrepreneur Bernie Ecclestone. As fuller details emerged, Tony Blair sought to dispose of the matter on 16 November by giving a television interview, followed up by an article in *The Times* next day. He began with an apology but continued with robust protestations of good faith. The issue was hardly substantial, but this fact simply underlined its symbolic importance. For it was Blair's *personal* character – his trustworthiness and openness, and the precious contrast with Tory 'sleaze' – which was in jeopardy and which made this, in the view of *The Times* (17 November), 'the worst crisis of his premiership'. Could this be the shape of image problems to come?

NOTES

1 The survivor was Richard Lambert of the *Financial Times*. Half the editors had been in post for two years or less in March 1997.

2 Colin Seymour-Ure, 'Characters and Assassinations: Portrayals of John Major and Neil Kinnock in the *Daily Mirror* and the *Sun*', in Ivor Crewe and Brian Gosschalk (eds), *Political Communications: the General Election Campaign of 1992* (Cambridge: Cambridge University Press, 1995).

3 The analysis excludes the *Daily Star* and *Financial Times*, both of which had comparatively few editorials about the election. Editorials for the whole campaign were coded for implicit and explicit attributions of character and were allocated to summary categories of personality and professional skills. The subjectivity of the process is acknowledged, but the results are intended to be illustrative and not as a basis of statistical proofs. Thanks are due to Grant Blowers for his help with the coding, and to the University of Kent Social Sciences Research Fund and the Goldsmith Awards Program of the Joan Shorenstein Center, Harvard University, for financial support.

4 See Colin Seymour-Ure, 'Newspapers: Editorial Opinion in the National Press', in Pippa Norris and Neil T. Gavin (eds), *Britain Votes 1997* (Oxford: Oxford University Press, 1997).

5 See Roy Greenslade, 'How Major Lost His Place in the Tory *Sun*', *Guardian*, 19 March 1997.

6 See Seymour-Ure, 'Characters and Assassinations'.

7 The 1992 figures are derived from Seymour-Ure, 'Characters and Assassinations', p. 151.

PART IV:

THE CAMPAIGN ON TELEVISION

11

Too Much of a Good Thing? Television in the 1997 Election Campaign

PETER GODDARD, MARGARET SCAMMELL
and HOLLI A. SEMETKO

For all the significance of its sensational result, it is hard to remember an election in which both the political campaign and its coverage on television were so severely criticised. Most press commentators agreed that this was a 'dispiriting' campaign, dominated by slogans, evasions and negative yah-boo politics.[1] It seemed to offer evidence of the so-called 'dumbing down' of British public life, and television stood accused of contributing to or at best conniving at this dismal process.[2] Turnout was the lowest since the war while audiences complained of too much politics on television. Tony Blair also blamed television, detecting a 'conspiracy against understanding' to set against BBC Director-General John Birt's 'mission to explain'.[3]

The specific charges against television were often self-contradictory:

- that it *failed* to provide sufficient serious debate about public policy;[4]
- that it turned off viewers with *too much* political coverage;[5]
- that it was *too fair*, placing commitment to balance between party spokesmen above rigorous analysis of party proposals;[6]
- that the campaign and its TV coverage were *too negative*.[7]

Although television always offers an easy target for the world's ills, it is legitimate to question whether television reporting, through 'overkill', structure and style, increased voter turn-off or exacerbated campaign defects. This chapter, originating in an on-going research project providing a detailed content analysis of television and newspaper coverage of the 1997 campaign, examines two broad dimensions of television coverage.[8]

First, the *public service aspects*. How visible was the election in overall news coverage? Was reporting generally balanced and fair as between the parties? Was there sufficient emphasis on the substance of parties' policy proposals as opposed to the rough and tumble of the campaign, personality and the 'horserace' aspects?[9] How, so far as we can tell, was coverage received by viewers?

Second, the *style and tone* of reporting. How much evidence is there of a trend towards a 'game' or strategy approach in reporting the election, with journalists playing an increasingly interpretative role marked by growing cynicism towards politicians? Two recent US studies, by Cappella and Jamieson and by Thomas Patterson, have suggested that developments in the *type* of electoral reporting among the US media may have had damaging effects on voter interest and involvement.[10] Patterson differentiates between 'descriptive' and 'interpretive' models of reporting. The former, dominant in the United States until the 1980s, separated facts from interpretation and was marked by relatively straight reporting of newsworthy events without any great depth of explanation. The latter, which Patterson claims has now become predominant in the United States, freely mixes fact with interpretation, with the effect that interpretation provides the theme which the facts are used to illuminate. This approach gives journalists more power, casts them as analysts and enables them to shape the news in a way that the descriptive style does not.[11] The claims for electoral reporting are that politicians' voices are becoming overwhelmed by those of the journalists appraising them and that it has unleashed journalists' cynicism about politicians' motivations and the political process as a whole. Cappella and Jamieson identify a trend towards 'strategy-oriented' coverage, whose most notable effects are to emphasise opinion polls and horserace aspects of coverage, to focus on candidates as performers, accompanied by evaluation of their performance style and of public perceptions of them, and to engender a preference for the language of warfare, sport and competition.

These and other, similar, studies suggest an increasingly autonomous role for the media in US elections, marked by an unwillingness to accept parties' agendas and a growth of negatively evaluative reporting.[12] As a consequence, the media are charged with undermining confidence in the US political system and fostering public cynicism. The ultimate fear, as Jamieson and Cappella see it, is of a 'spiral of delegitimation' in which media scepticism feeds voter disengagement which in turn is reflected in a further reduction in straightforward reporting.[13] If evidence were to emerge for a comparable strategy-oriented approach, this would be a highly significant development in Britain, where television election coverage is traditionally dominated by 'descriptive' reporting, or what has elsewhere been called 'conventional journalism',[14] and where media and political systems differ markedly from those in the United States.

CONTEXT: CAMPAIGN COVERAGE AND THE BRITISH MEDIA
ENVIRONMENT

British television is subject to particularly rigid constraints during the official campaign. Paid political advertising is prohibited and, under Section 93 of the 1983 Representation of the People Act (RPA), it is illegal for any constituency candidate to take part in a broadcast about that constituency unless all other candidates consent or take part themselves.[15] Senior party figures may be broadcast and interviewed freely, provided it is in their capacity as leaders rather than as constituency candidates. This constraint, designed to ensure equal television treatment of all candidates, in practice encourages television news to focus on leaders and national campaigns. Television news is banned from partisan editorialising, and is required to be fair, accurate and balanced in its reporting. By convention, the general requirement for balance is interpreted in a uniquely strict way at election times to include airtime allocated to each party in the news. The convention has been weakened in recent years by the commercial channels' reluctance to accept the stopwatch as a vital statistic of balance. Nonetheless, the main evening news programmes continue to allocate a roughly equal balance of newstime to the two major parties, and roughly two-thirds by proportion to the Liberal Democrats.[16]

In Britain, the BBC and ITV continue to dominate television, and the growth of subscription cable and satellite services has been relatively slow compared with North America and some European countries, such as the Netherlands. This has significant consequences for the coverage of politics. The BBC and ITV developed amid an ethos of public service, with a commitment to 'inform, educate and entertain'. The important point to note is that Britain developed a public service *system*, where the burdens of public service were carried across all terrestrial channels and not simply the public broadcaster. The Thatcher government's broadcasting legislation of 1990 was intended, in part, to lighten significantly the public service obligations of the commercial sector. However, in practice, ITV is still monitored closely by the statutory broadcasting authority (the Independent Television Commission (ITC)), which has so far insisted that ITV retains its flagship evening news programme, *News at Ten*, together with a certain amount of serious factual and current affairs programming in prime time. Consequently, ITV is much less free to pursue ratings at all costs than its relatively unregulated cable and satellite rivals. The expansion of the British television market and the intensified battle for ratings seem to have made little substantial difference to the effort which the election was deemed to warrant among the major broadcasters. With the opening of another terrestrial channel (Channel 5), there was probably more coverage than ever before.

Both in the close attention paid to election campaigns and in the quantity of coverage, British television is remarkable in international terms, and in 1997 it remained true to form, despite the experience of 1992 which gave broadcasters the near-certain knowledge that election overkill would drive away many viewers.[17] Predictably, the BBC's coverage was the most extensive. It once again extended its flagship *Nine O'Clock News* by 15–20 minutes (to 50 minutes maximum), it ran daily phone-in question-and-answer programmes with leading party representatives, turned over its main regular current affairs programmes to leader interviews, and conducted daily discussion programmes featuring party spokespersons and pundits to dissect the state of the campaign. While the commercial terrestrial channels did not extend their news bulletins, they too aired special programmes devoted to leader interviews and audience participation, as well as a few more innovatory formats. In sheer quantity alone, television coverage of the election campaign represented an impressive effort. Our analysis of the content of election coverage shows that 44.1 per cent of news stories in our three flagship news programmes were political and that these tended to be longer than non-political stories, occupying 59.6 per cent of story time.[18]

However, in the post-mortem and even in the midst of the campaign, there were unsettling signs that viewers were unhappy with the quantity of coverage, with disturbing reports of declining viewing figures for news programmes and fears of 'overkill'.[19] It is normal for television news audiences to decline slightly during election times. There was a slight decline for the ITV's flagship *News at Ten*, down from 6 million in the first week of the campaign to 5.6 million in the last.[20] The BBC's flagship, the *Nine O'Clock News*, however, suffered a steep slump, losing nearly one-third of its audience, from 5.8 million in the first week to 4 million thereafter. Most other BBC news and current affairs programmes held their audiences fairly steadily as did *Channel Four News*, although, at 0.6 million, it has never claimed a mass audience. However, the *Nine O'Clock News* remains by comparison with performances elsewhere on television a spectacular ratings failure which has not received a satisfactory public explanation from the BBC.

A degree of viewer dissatisfaction was confirmed in an opinion survey conducted by the ITC, with about 60 per cent saying that there was too much coverage, compared with 29 per cent who said there was too little.[21] There was also some suggestion that the BBC fared rather less well than the other channels on questions of balance and interest (though not on accuracy and information content).[22] Complaints common to all channels suggested too much emphasis on opinion polls (despite a substantial reduction compared with 1992), too many 'outside experts', and too little coverage of issues such as the environment, energy and transport. Television, however, continued to be easily the most trusted source of election news for viewers and seems, from the viewers' perspective, to have been thought of as doing a generally good job overall.

The particular type of public service system operated in Britain might be expected to produce a particular style of news coverage. In the past, comparative international research has found a clear correlation between media systems and the construction of election news, with more commercial competition associated with greater concern with audience ratings and less concern with politicians' agendas.[23] The same research also found a relationship between the extent to which a media system was regulated and types of reporting: closer political oversight of the broadcasters was associated with a tendency to neutral reporting, while less regulation increased the likelihood of evaluative, and often negative, reporting.

The general pattern held true *within* countries too. Thus, in the 1992 British general election, *News at Ten* paid significantly more attention to horse-race aspects, less to substantive issues and was more evaluative than the BBC,[24] a tendency we would have expected to be repeated in 1997. We were able to test the theory further through analysis of Sky News, which, as a satellite broadcaster, is significantly less regulated than ITV, although general fairness rules apply. In designing our study, we would have expected Sky News to be driven more markedly by news values and the need to attract audiences than BBC or ITV and that, of the three British news programmes analysed, it would prove closest to the American model.[25]

CAMPAIGN COVERAGE: THE BROADCASTERS' INTENTIONS

In line with their public service ethos, the BBC and ITN gave guidance to their staff setting out the objectives which their election coverage should seek to meet. In general terms, broadcasters seemed to be very conscious of their role in providing public information to enable the democratic process to function smoothly. A memo planning ITV's 1997 election coverage from Michael Jermey, deputy editor of ITN, concluded: 'the end result of our coverage should be that ITV viewers feel well informed and able to cast a considered vote'.[26] According to Jermey, six principles guided election news on all ITV news programmes, and they resembled closely the intentions of broadcasters from other channels as they were expressed to us in the course of the campaign. Our content analysis provides an opportunity for us to comment on the extent to which they lived up to these intentions.

The *first* was that policies and policy differences matter. In planning campaign coverage, ITV's Jermey noted:

> Our observation of the last election is that on television generally there was probably too much of what I'd call insiders' politics – coverage of campaign strategies and the activities of spin doctors – and probably not enough of the real meat of political debate. We want to focus on how a government will affect people's lives and what difference the parties' policies will make to the viewers.

Second, the election was to be considered both a national and regional event. *Channel Four News*, for example, organised a number of its entire programmes to be broadcast from different regions of the country. This view also prevailed at the BBC. According to Director-General John Birt's post-election memo congratulating all BBC journalists:

> We have avoided a metropolitan bias, reporting on the election from every part of the UK. The unique politics of Scotland, Wales and Northern Ireland have received appropriate and prominent coverage. We have reported with distinction at every level – national, regional and local.[27]

Third, viewers and voters, not just the politicians, were to be featured on the air. According to Jermey:

> We will inject into our coverage the voices of people from across the country and hear how they're addressing key election issues. We'll include voters' voices in a lot of our news packages and will also have special slots that will be concentrated on the views of voters rather than politicians.

Channel Four News' deputy editor Sue Inglish emphasised:

> We want real people to inform all our coverage. We've also called in four or five specific people to make their own films for us during the campaign – an elderly Scottish pensioner, on what old people want … for example, … an environmental campaigner, about the areas the political parties don't touch, an Italian journalist who came back for a week, as to how he sees the campaign going from an Italian perspective.

Fourth, opinion polls were to be reported with due caution following their failures in 1992 and subsequent opinion surveys in which viewers were highly critical of what they saw as television's over-reliance on them.[28] One notable consequence was that ITN declined to commission campaign opinion polls as it had in 1992. Like the BBC, it did run an exit poll on polling day, and it also retained the 'ITV 500' of representative voters who were polled on various specific issues for *News At Ten* in the course of the campaign and involved in special programmes where they quizzed the party leaders, but these were the only television polls. An emphasis on other published polls was also avoided in all three of the main evening news programmes in 1997. Poll stories never led the bulletins, nor, with one exception where the BBC used a *Guardian/ ICM* poll as a baseline marker as it began its own extended campaign coverage on 1 April, were they ever the main subject of the first three stories.

Fifth, ITN planned to avoid over-emphasis on political leaders to the disadvantage of other party spokesmen. In Jermey's words: 'We won't portray it as a completely presidential contest and will ensure that other leading political figures are heard.'

Sixth, reporters' voices were to be heard and television was to help 'make the news' as well as to report it. According to Jermey, 'In the best traditions of ITV, our correspondents will be seen to be out in the field and heard to be putting tough questions to the politicians.'[29] As early as March, Nigel Dacre, editor of ITN, was issuing memos stressing the importance of 'RI' (reporter involvement).[30] And the broadcasters were delighted when it paid off. BBC2 *Newsnight*'s editor Peter Horrocks, for example, was very pleased that its interviews with Conservative rebels had been a significant trigger to the dominant election story of Tory disunity over the European Union. 'Actually,' he claimed proudly, 'we got the whole story going.'

CAMPAIGN COVERAGE: THE EVIDENCE

Policy and substantive issues

As usual, the BBC offered the most substantive coverage (see Table 11.1). It devoted a slightly smaller proportion of stories than did ITV to campaign conduct, and also to party internal politics and party leaders as subjects, though, oddly, slightly more to opinion poll stories. Sky News had a higher proportion again in each of these categories. However, although we expected that Sky might place more emphasis on news values given its lighter regulatory regime, the difference was not so marked as to suggest that news values entirely dominated a public service approach. In coverage of policy areas, the BBC's coverage

Table 11.1: Subjects of political stories[a] – BBC, ITV and Sky News 1997

Heading	BBC		ITV		Sky		BBC & ITV	All
	no.	%	no.	%	no.	%	%	%
Campaign of terrorism	4	0.34	4	0.53	6	0.72	0.44	0.53
Conduct of campaign	280	23.95	200	26.70	235	28.31	25.32	26.32
Defence	1	0.09	2	0.27	0	0.00	0.18	0.12
Economy	173	14.80	89	11.88	110	13.25	13.34	13.31
Education	59	5.05	52	6.94	43	5.18	6.00	5.72
Environment/ energy	5	0.43	5	0.67	0	0.00	0.55	0.37
Europe/ foreign affairs	105	8.98	62	8.28	51	6.14	8.63	7.80
Health	31	2.65	14	1.87	14	1.69	2.26	2.07
Infrastructure	22	1.88	6	0.80	5	0.60	1.34	1.09
Minor parties	33	2.82	15	2.00	19	2.29	2.41	2.37
Non-political	7	0.60	4	0.53	10	1.20	0.57	0.78
Northern Ireland	35	2.99	10	1.34	27	3.25	2.17	2.53
Opinion polls	77	6.59	42	5.61	43	5.18	6.10	5.79
Party internal politics	47	4.02	36	4.81	57	6.87	4.41	5.23
Party leaders	65	5.56	48	6.41	57	6.87	5.99	6.28
Party records/ manifestos	48	4.11	36	4.81	53	6.39	4.46	5.10
Political system	24	2.05	18	2.40	10	1.20	2.23	1.88
Regions/ devolution	60	5.13	42	5.61	22	2.65	5.37	4.46
Sleaze	17	1.45	15	2.00	32	3.86	1.73	2.44
Social welfare	76	6.50	49	6.54	36	4.34	6.52	5.79
Total	1,169	99.99	749	100.00	830	99.99	100.02	99.98

Note: [a] Up to six subjects were coded per story, each to one of 240 variables. After coding, groups of related variables were assigned to one of the headings given above. 'Conduct of campaign' includes parties' campaign organisation, strategy and tactics, advertising and general campaign trail activity. 'Opinion polls' include media and private party polls, predictions of and speculation on the election result and horse-race. 'Party leaders' refers narrowly to leaders of the three main parties and their political and personal qualities.

displayed slightly different priorities from those of ITV, with the latter giving proportionately more coverage to education, the regions and devolution.

For all the broadcasters' intentions, however, a comparison with 1992 shows that the proportion of coverage devoted to campaign conduct increased substantially in 1997 – BBC's *Nine O'Clock News* from 13 to 26 per cent; ITV's *News at Ten* from 24 to 30 per cent, based on the categories adopted to analyse the 1992 election (see Figure 11.1). There was no such

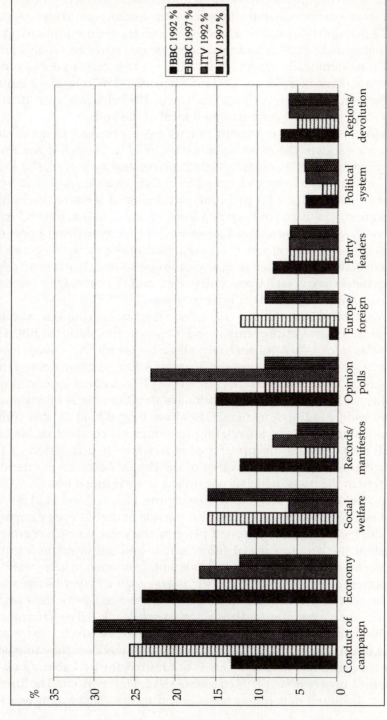

Figure 11.1: Subjects of television news: 1992 and 1997 compared

Note: 1997 categories adjusted to correspond with 1992 data. Numbers have been rounded upwards.

increase in coverage of party leaders and a marked reduction in opinion poll coverage, though in the latter case our findings are likely to reflect ITN's decision not to commission them and the reduced newsworthiness of opinion polls in a campaign where one party had such a large and consistent lead. Significantly, a sizeable reduction in opinion poll coverage (from first place in 1992 to fifth place in 1997) was *also* a feature of the newspapers' front page agenda in 1997 election, even though newspapers actually commissioned most of the polls.[31]

More generally, there seems to have been a broader range of substantive issues in the news agenda than in 1992. Though it remained the most frequently occurring substantive category overall, the focus on the economy was much reduced in 1997 (from an average of 20.5 per cent to just under 13.5 per cent), while social welfare (including education, health and old-age pensions) nearly doubled (from 8.5 to 16 per cent) and Europe showed an astonishing increase (from 1 per cent in 1992 to 10.5 per cent in 1997). Analysed under these categories by length of time rather than frequency, Europe (at over 10 per cent) overtakes the economy (at 6.9 per cent) in BBC and ITV coverage to become the most time-consuming substantive issue.

A notable absence is sleaze. Sleaze was dominant in the March period of the campaign, yet it appears at under 2 per cent overall in the BBC/ITV agendas from 1–30 April and only a little higher for Sky – much lower than the 4.6 per cent figure for 'Jennifer's Ear', a comparable cause célèbre, in 1992.[32] Of course, this downplays its electoral significance: it is likely to have informed perceptions of the Conservative Party much more widely in the campaign and to have been a kind of 'structuring absence' in many stories relating to campaign conduct or Major's leadership. But its disappearance is not merely a function of the restrictions of the Representation of the People Act: a similar trend is evident in the press, which is not subject to such constraints.

A week-by-week breakdown (see Figures 11.2, 11.3 and 11.4) reveals that no single subject dominated the agenda entirely – even campaign conduct was beaten into second place in one week on each channel – but that the prominence of subjects rose and fell in relation to the particular preoccupations of the moment. Economic policies were an important component of the party manifestos launched in the first week and economic issues were important in week two, as Labour came under attack over its spending and privatisation policies. Social welfare, mostly in the shape of education and health, were issues which Labour and the Liberal Democrats focused on in the early weeks of the campaign, but the large rise in week four is accounted for by Labour's claim that the Conservatives planned to abolish the state pension. The 'threat' which Labour's devolution plans posed to the constitution was the

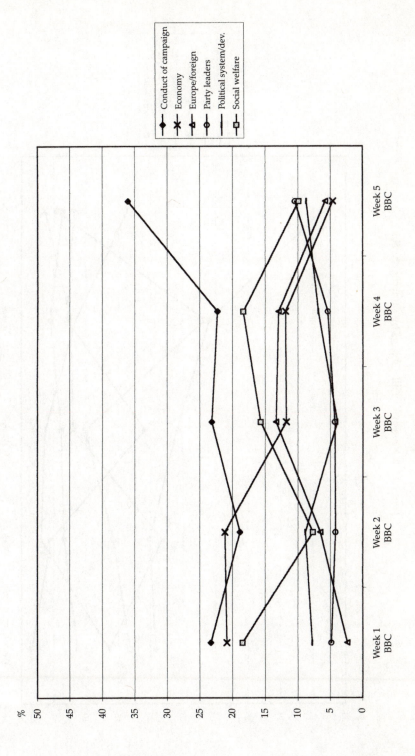

Figure 11.2: BBC Nine O'Clock News: all subjects by campaign week

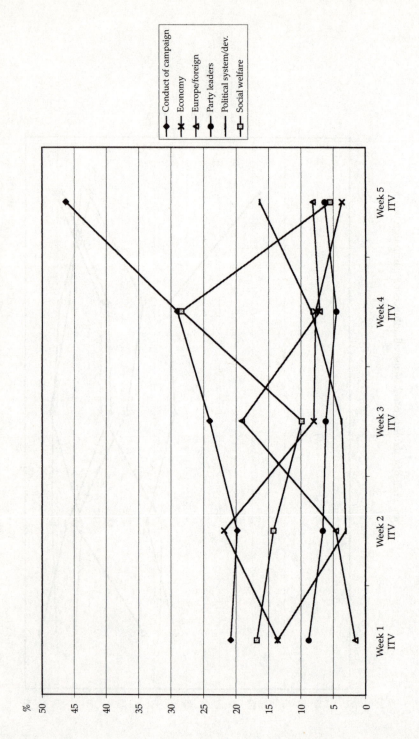

Figure 11.3: News at Ten: all subjects by campaign week

Conduct of campaign
Economy
Europe/foreign
Party leaders
Political system/dev.
Social welfare

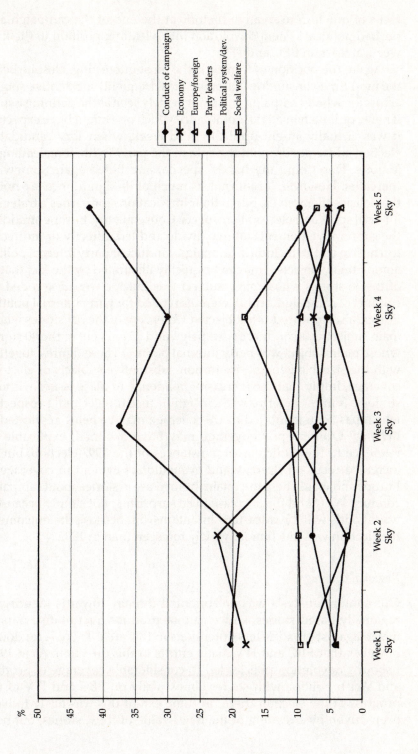

Figure 11.4: Sky News: all subjects by campaign week

focus of much Conservative rhetoric at the end of the campaign and pushed political system/devolution into a leading position in the final week, at least on BBC and ITV.

Again, the position of Europe is the most interesting. Despite being the most time-consuming (if not the most frequent) substantive subject across the whole campaign and being widely seen as the defining issue,[33] it never quite achieved the dominance which one might have expected. It was virtually absent until the third week, when Tory candidates' election addresses brought the split in the party to the fore, leading to Major's 'Don't bind my hands' speech, and faded again somewhat thereafter. However, for journalists much of its significance lay not in the policies themselves, but in their implications for parties' strategies, internal splits and electoral prospects. Consequently, Europe straddled the substantive/non-substantive divide and led, directly or indirectly, to a host of stories including campaign conduct or party internal politics among their subjects. This can be quickly illustrated by the fact that 20 of the 36 stories whose main subject was Europe were *also* coded for conduct of campaign, and 17 were *also* coded for party internal politics. Europe also appeared as a subject in 17 per cent of the 201 stories whose main subject was conduct of campaign and 25 per cent of the 40 stories whose main subject was party internal politics. These figures, together with the sizeable general rise in non-substantive subjects of electoral coverage, imply that the increasing tendency to place issues within a strategic frame – in terms of their significance for electoral prospects – which has been identified in US coverage may be being replicated in Britain.[34] Opinion poll coverage may have declined, explicable by reference to the particular circumstances of the 1997 election, but an increased focus on strategy and evaluation is evident in coverage of Europe and would help to explain the increase in stories about campaign conduct. We found this increase to be surprising, not simply because it was at odds with broadcasters' intentions, but because the outcome of the election was much more widely foreseen than in 1992.

Regional coverage

Our content analysis was not oriented directly towards identifying regionally based stories, so we cannot produce quantitative data to match against broadcasters' intentions in this area. There is no doubt, however, that BBC and ITV made efforts in this direction. As in 1992, Labour's devolution policies led to considerable coverage of Scottish and Welsh politics, with stories almost daily on BBC and ITV of the progress of the election there. To some extent this was likely to have been driven by a reading of the news value of these stories, but both

BBC and ITV also profiled the election issues affecting Scotland and Wales in extended issue-driven coverage on more than one occasion. The requirements for balanced coverage between the parties helped to ensure that the activities of the Scottish Nationalist Party and of Plaid Cymru were always given due attention in stories about the two countries.

There was also a determined effort, especially within the BBC, to investigate the particular issues at stake in the regions of England. To this end, the *Nine O'Clock News* ran a series of news features in which leading reporters visited the various regions and key constituencies around the country. In the constituency of Tatton, however, where the challenge to former Conservative minister Neil Hamilton from a cross-party 'anti-corruption' candidate in the shape of former war correspondent Martin Bell made for one of the best 'stories' of the election, television was virtually absent in the latter part of the campaign. Despite considerable public (and press) interest in the candidates and the relevance of this contest to allegations of 'Tory sleaze', the Representation of the People Act effectively ruled out any but the most generalised reporting of the constituency – a constraint which no amount of good intentions on the part of the broadcasters could overcome.[35]

Regional coverage was one area where there was a considerable divergence between Sky News and the main terrestrial broadcasters. Across our survey period, the proportion of Sky's coverage devoted to devolution and the regions amounted to less than half the average for BBC and ITV (see Table 11.1) and it consistently under-performed both competitors week on week. Sky's independence from the more rigorous obligations of the public service ethos provides the most obvious explanation for this discrepancy, but it was also operating under much tighter budgetary constraints than BBC or ITV.[36] In such circumstances it would be easy to understand why the benefits of extensive regional coverage might not have been thought to justify its considerable cost.

The voice of the people

It would appear that the broadcasters acquitted themselves well in their commitment to air the voices of ordinary people, although our analysis of news coverage may not be the most appropriate place to test it. All channels continued enthusiastically to facilitate phone-ins and audience participation programmes as part of their broader election coverage. Within the news itself, vox pop-type street interviews were a common occurrence and more imaginative formats were also used. Several of the BBC's extended profiles of regional issues were predicated on the economic wellbeing and political priorities of samples of ordinary voters, including a return to the 'barometer' constituency of Basildon to re-interview those who had participated in a similar feature in 1992. As we have mentioned, ITV once again assembled the 'ITV 500' of representative voters. Sky News memorably interviewed a group of London taxi-drivers on their voting intentions and policy priorities, although fortunately no claim was made for the representativeness of their responses.

The presidential race

Television news coverage of recent British elections has reflected both the leader-oriented strategies of the parties' campaigns and the strengths of the medium itself. As usual, each party made its leader the focal point of its campaign in 1997 and Labour, employing arguably the most disciplined communications campaign ever waged in a British election, focused unwaveringly on the person of Tony Blair, while several leading party figures (including Jack Straw, Harriet Harman and David Blunkett) were virtually absent. Television's propensity for reporting personality is well known, with the result that leader and personality-focused campaigns seem to be as much an effect of television itself as of any other factors.[37] And, as we have noted already, the legal restrictions in Britain on the broadcast of (non-leader) candidates can have the effect of increasing still further the extent to which electoral coverage is focused upon leaders – a factor which public service broadcasters themselves consider a hindrance.[38]

In terms of the number of times politicians appeared speaking, coverage of the 1997 campaign was more leader-focused even than in 1992 (the aggregate for the three leaders was 42.67 per cent as against 39.38 per cent – see Table 11.2). Harder to explain, though, is why that the increase is wholly accounted for by the greater prominence of the Liberal Democrat leader, Paddy Ashdown (up 3.39 per cent), though his party also appeared more often. Indeed, in 1997, Ashdown made more appearances on BBC and ITV than did Blair, who, despite his party's 'presidential' campaign, appeared least frequently of the three. Several factors explain Major's greater prominence in comparison with Blair: incumbent prime ministers almost always get more coverage than other leaders, and the troubles which his party faced in the course of the campaign probably exacerbated this. Major was frequently forced to defend his party against attacks by journalists and political opponents, initially over sleaze and latterly over his party's divisions over Europe. Labour also attempted to put his leadership under scrutiny. Blair, by contrast, had a comparatively trouble-free (if unexciting) campaign, choreographed with care to avoid controversy. Not only did this give

Table 11.2: Main political actors appearing as speakers in campaign coverage by frequency[a] – BBC/ITV 1992–97; Sky News 1997

| | BBC | | | | ITV | | | | Sky News | | BBC/ITV | |
| | 1992 | | 1997 | | 1992 | | 1997 | | 1997 | | 1992 | 1997 |
	Freq.	%	Freq.	%	Freq.	%	Freq.	%	Freq.	%	%	%
Major	27	13.57	34	12.59	25	16.23	34	18.18	37	20.56	14.73	14.88
Blair (Kinnock)	24	12.06	33	12.22	24	15.58	28	14.97	27	15.00	13.60	13.35
Ashdown	19	9.55	34	12.59	20	12.99	32	17.11	26	14.44	11.05	14.44
Other Con.	28	14.07	35	12.96	21	13.64	24	12.83	28	15.56	13.88	12.91
Other Lab.	33	16.58	36	13.33	14	9.09	19	10.16	20	11.11	13.31	12.04
Other Lib. Dem.	13	6.53	22	8.15	8	5.19	14	7.49	13	7.22	5.95	7.88
SNP	4	2.01	4	1.48	5	3.25	5	2.67	1	0.56	2.55	1.97
PC	4	2.01	4	1.48	0	0.00	1	0.53	0	0.00	1.13	1.09
Other minor	12	6.03	23	8.52	8	5.19	10	5.35	13	7.22	5.67	7.22
Other[b]	35	17.59	45	16.67	29	18.83	20	10.70	15	8.33	18.13	14.22
Total	199	100.00	270	99.99	154	99.99	187	99.99	180	100.00	100.00	100.00

Note: [a] Actors appearing in stories were logged and timed in order of appearance. This table is based on the first three political actors appearing in each story. Non-political actors (those unaffiliated to political parties) are excluded.
[b] Other includes party supporters and activists, spouses of leaders, MPs or candidates, Baroness Thatcher and, in 1997, Neil Kinnock.

journalists less to report, but it left less scope for them to read the runes for him and to dwell on strategies he might adopt. The elevation of Ashdown and the Liberal Democrats is more baffling. In 1992, a hung parliament with Liberal Democrats holding the balance of power was considered a serious possibility. In 1997, although they were the only major party to see an increased poll rating as the campaign wore on, power for the party was never a likelihood.[39] The most obvious explanation lies in the requirement for balanced coverage and a public-spirited attention to fairness. However, we also suspect that the media may have seen Ashdown as the only leader prepared to tell unpalatable truths about tax and spending.

These figures also suggest considerable discrepancies between channels, with ITV and Sky (50.26 per cent and 50 per cent respectively) offering a much stronger focus on leaders than did the BBC (37.4 per cent). This finding follows a trend identified in 1992 and may reflect a more public service-oriented approach at the BBC, where the three leaders appeared with almost equal frequency, and an approach driven more by news values or ratings at the commercial stations, where a greater discrepancy between leader appearances is apparent.

Table 11.3: Main political actors appearing as speakers in campaign coverage by length[a] – BBC/ITV/Sky News 1997

	BBC		ITV		Sky News		BBC/ITV
	(secs)	%	(secs)	%	(secs)	%	%
Major	1,352	20.34	1,021	26.21	1,142	23.07	22.51
Blair	1,369	20.59	892	22.90	788	15.92	21.44
Ashdown	1,218	18.32	819	21.02	722	14.59	19.32
Other Con.	580	8.72	362	9.29	1,110	22.42	8.93
Other Lab.	543	8.17	279	7.16	318	6.42	7.80
Other Lib. Dem.	314	4.72	192	4.93	507	10.24	4.80
SNP	170	2.56	60	1.54	17	0.34	2.18
PC	139	2.09	12	0.31	0	0.00	1.43
Other minor	412	6.20	122	3.13	184	3.72	5.06
Other[b]	551	8.29	137	3.52	162	3.27	6.53
Total	6,648	100.00	3,896	100.01	4,950	99.99	100.00

Note: [a] Actors appearing in stories were logged and timed in order of appearance. This table is based on the first three political actors appearing in each story. Non-political actors (those affiliated to political parties) are excluded.
[b] Other includes party supporters and activists, spouses of leaders, MPs or candidates, Baroness Thatcher and Neil Kinnock.

However, when we look at leader appearances by length, instead of by frequency, a rather different pattern emerges (see Table 11.3).

Coverage in these terms appears to be even more leader-oriented (BBC 59.25 per cent, ITV 70.13 per cent and Sky 53.58 per cent). The figures for Blair's appearances now exceed those for Ashdown across all three programmes, still lagging well behind Major on ITV but actually overhauling him on BBC. This demonstrates that while Blair made fewer appearances, he tended to appear at greater length, whereas Ashdown's, perhaps reflecting his frequent inclusion for the purposes of balance, were briefer. These figures also offer a different view of the variation between channels, with ITV offering easily the most leader-focused coverage, but with Sky News, rather than the BBC, appearing to offer the least. The clue to this discrepancy lies in Sky's colossal figure for appearances by 'other Conservatives' – more than double that for either of the other channels and largely the product of four extended interviews with Conservative politicians – which have the effect of reducing the proportion of time devoted by Sky to leader appearances by comparison.[40] Oddly, no equivalent interviews with Labour politicians were shown and it is unclear what motivated Sky's choice of interview subjects.

Overall then, these findings confirm an apparent movement between 1992 and 1997 towards more 'presidential' coverage even if it is a relatively small one across all the channels. This is in line with US developments towards more strategy-oriented coverage and distinctly at odds with the expressed intentions of British broadcasters. Although it may be partly the result of more professional campaign techniques, it may also be a response to them, with a more interpretive approach arising out of journalists' attempts to avoid running 'packaged' stories composed almost entirely from party-originated themes, messages and visuals. Interestingly, the differences between the channels – clear in the 1992 data – appear to have increased further. Measured both by time and frequency, ITV offered a much more presidential race than the BBC. In the comparative measure, ITV's leader-focus showed an increase on 1992 double that of the BBC (5.46 per cent as against 2.22 per cent).

The voice of the reporter

By all appearances, this was an unusually self-referential election in the news, giving rise to a distinct sense that the media coverage, as much as the actions of the politicians, *was* the election story. TV interviews frequently provided material for newspaper stories the following day, while broadsheets delighted in monitoring and evaluating television coverage in signed columns and regular 'media-watch' reports.

The emphasis on the contributions of political correspondents across all channels was also part of this self-referential news making. The chief political correspondents were profoundly important to the construction of the story of the day, beginning at the morning press conferences, where they were invariably the first to be called on by their first name – 'Robin' Oakley or 'John' Sargeant (BBC), 'Michael' Brunson (ITN), 'Adam' Boulton (Sky News), 'Elinor' Goodman or 'Jon' Snow (Channel Four) – a reflection of the weight accorded to them by the parties. In the nightly news coverage, they were often to be seen asking their press conference questions – journalists as actors in the news story – as a preface to the politicians' responses.[41] Besides also fronting the main campaign reports of the day, the chief political correspondents were given yet another significant 'framing' role in a marked development from previous campaigns. Cast as experts, Oakley, Brunson and, in the early part of the campaign, Boulton, were interviewed at length in the main nightly news programmes and encouraged by the anchor's questions to interpret the day's events. This inevitably led to the impression of a more openly evaluative role for these correspondents.

We attempted to determine whether this interpretive approach was incorporated routinely into reporting. First, we recorded the initiator of the main subject of each story and compared this with equivalent figures from 1992 (see Table 11.4). While not in themselves a measure of reporting style, these figures do indicate how autonomous the television agenda was from that of the parties.

Table 11.4: Initiation of main subjects in political stories –
BBC/ITV 1992/97; Sky News 1997

Initiator	BBC		ITV		Sky	BBC/ITV	BBC/ITV
	1992	1997	1992	1997	1997	1992	1997
	%	%	%	%	%	%	%
Conservative Party	6.9	10.2	6.6	17.5	16.1	6.7	13.8
Labour Party	13.8	8.9	7.4	13.8	14.4	10.6	11.3
Lib. Dem.	9.5	7.7	5.1	11.7	13.2	7.3	9.7
Media	48.1	46.8	57.4	27.7	31.6	52.7	37.2
Mixture/other	21.7	26.4	23.5	29.2	24.7	22.6	27.8
Total	100.0	100.0	100.0	99.9	100.0	99.9	99.8

The picture here is of an overall increase in party-initiated subjects (from 24.6 per cent in 1992 to 34.8 per cent) and a corresponding decrease in subjects initiated by the media (from 52.7 per cent to 37.2 per cent). The most dramatic changes are in the figures for ITV, with the BBC actually having slightly fewer party-initiated subjects than in 1992. The imbalance between channels over media-initiation noted in 1992[42] has been dramatically reversed, with the media initiating a far higher proportion of stories at the BBC than at ITV. This in part reflects ITN's decision not to commission opinion polls nor to give them the attention which they received in 1992. A further explanation may lie in the format of the extended *Nine O'Clock News*, opening up space for a wider range of stories than those covered by *News At Ten*.

It is difficult to say to what extent the rise in party initiation reflects a decline in media autonomy, a more professional approach to setting the news agenda on the part of the parties or a greater willingness for correspondents to adopt the party agenda as the basis for their own interpretive or strategy-oriented coverage. But, in contrast to 1992, Labour's disciplined campaign initiated a smaller proportion of stories than did the Conservatives' troubled one, so the last explanation seems most likely. This explanation is given considerable support in our coding for the favourability of stories towards parties or leaders (see Table 11.5).

Here, it is apparent that there has been a very considerable decline

Table 11.5: Tone of stories mentioning party leaders and/or parties – BBC/ITV 1992/97; Sky News 1997

Tone	BBC		ITV		Sky
	1992	1997	1992	1997	1997
	%	%	%	%	%
Favourability to Major/Conservatives					
Negative	18	31	30	26	31
Mixed	19	33	26	27	24
Positive	6	8	5	16	17
Straight	57	28	40	31	28
Total	100	100	100	100	100
No. of stories	128	222	101	141	159
Favourability to Blair (Kinnock)/Labour					
Negative	14	18	14	13	23
Mixed	15	31	23	26	18
Positive	5	22	5	25	28
Straight	66	29	57	36	31
Total	100	100	100	100	100
No. of stories	127	196	94	126	130
Favourability to Ashdown/Lib. Dems.					
Negative	4	3	2	2	7
Mixed	18	28	27	19	11
Positive	6	24	7	29	36
Straight	73	46	64	51	46
Total	100	101	100	100	100
No. of stories	103	138	83	97	81

in the number of stories coded as 'straight' and a commensurate increase in those which are evaluative, whether negatively, mixed or positively. Moreover, the BBC was consistently more evaluative and less 'straight' than ITV. So it would seem that, while the media may have made a lesser contribution to the election subject agenda than it did in 1992, TV coverage does seem to have become substantially more evaluative *within* stories. This broadly supports the idea of a shift towards a more 'interpretive' model of reporting, even though the majority of evaluative coverage in this election was not coded as 'negative'.

QUESTIONS OF BALANCE

All news programmes claim that the stopwatch does not *dictate* the news, but all pay attention to the times and keep tallies for the purposes of maintaining balance between the parties according to broadcasters' pre-agreed ratio.[43] 'Stopwatch' balance is a crude instrument, saying nothing about the nature of the news. Clearly, a 'bad news' story may hurt rather than help a party, the sort of balance a party could do without. But the balance requirement can have positive consequences for the parties too. Activities which might not meet normal news values may still run in the bulletins to satisfy the stopwatch. This is especially valuable to the Liberal Democrats and to the Scots and Welsh nationalists who can expect a much higher news profile in a campaign period than when more normal news criteria apply. However, the effect for the viewer may sometimes be to diminish rather than enhance understanding of issues. A strict interpretation of balance *within* stories (as opposed to *between* stories and over the bulletin as a whole) can have the effect of extending and fragmenting stories because of the need to include statements, sometimes poorly matched, from the various parties. The BBC, which habitually opened with a single story drawing together the activities of the main parties or examining their positions on the principal issue of the day, more often seemed to pay a penalty in loss of conciseness and clarity. By contrast, ITV tended to lead with a short tripartisan introduction from the anchor and then treat party activities as three separate stories, as it had in 1992.[44]

On the measures we have available, coverage of the 1997 campaign seems to have been reasonably balanced, especially at the BBC. There was less discrepancy between the parties over initiation of news stories than in 1992 (see Table 11.4) with all three news programmes showing party initiation in roughly the ratio we would have expected: the Conservatives, as the incumbents and with the most troubled campaign, having the most, Labour a little behind them in second place and the

Liberal Democrats a little behind them. Our figures for frequency of appearances by party leaders (Table 11.3) also suggests more balanced coverage than in 1992, at least at the BBC. For 1997, the BBC displays a near-perfect match for three leaders by frequency and has Ashdown lagging only a little behind by length (see Table 11.3). The figures for ITV are more closely comparable with those for 1992, except that it is Blair and not Ashdown who makes the fewest appearances (see Table 11.2). Sky, which we would expect to be the most driven by news values, is the most unbalanced, with Major receiving considerably more coverage by both measures.

Television's interpretation of balance was also criticised for adding significantly to the impression of a negative campaign. Politicians' soundbites, which frequently highlighted personal attacks, tended to be 'balanced' by a counter-attack from rivals, a particular problem given the inclusive structure of the BBC's opening stories. Both Paddy Ashdown and Tony Blair, who put much of the blame on the media,[45] voiced strong criticisms of the negative campaign. There is some evidence from the United States that negative campaigns do increase voter apathy and cynicism, but it is disingenuous of Blair to complain of television's negativity.[46] In the opinion of various commentators, this election seemed more negative, abusive and bitter than any in recent times,[47] but our content analysis of press releases, conference statements and leaders' speeches suggests that the parties were the principal culprits. 69 per cent of Labour's included attacks on the Conservatives with 33 per cent coded as predominantly negative. For the Conservative Party, which admitted openly that its strategy was based on attacking Blair and Labour, 81 per cent included attacks, mainly on Labour, and 58 per cent were coded as predominantly negative.

Against such a negative background, and with a higher proportion of party-initiated stories reaching the screen than in 1992, it is perhaps surprising that the increase in interpretive coverage which we uncovered (see Table 11.5) is not inflected more negatively. This finding sits uneasily with Patterson's plea for increased airtime in US news for politicians' voices to be heard to counteract cynical 'interpretive' election journalism.[48] The reality, in Britain at least, may be that while television coverage is becoming more interpretive, it is principally the politicians themselves who are becoming increasingly negative.

CONCLUSIONS

Our findings suggest that television performed its public service role with some credit in reporting the 1997 election. The campaign was covered very extensively and in considerable depth, and due attention was paid to substantive issues with a range which seems to have been broader than in 1992. We have also suggested that television achieved a considerable degree of fairness and balance between parties in its coverage, with the BBC scoring particularly well in our content analysis if not so well in the ITC's survey of viewers' opinions.

The broadcasters also entered the campaign with laudable intentions arising from a consciousness of their role in the democratic process. In many respects their coverage met these intentions. Coverage was not dominated by news values at the expense of an exploration of the issues on any of the channels; much less attention was paid to opinion polls than in 1992, particularly by ITV; care was taken, by the BBC and ITV at least, to ensure that the news went beyond a metropolitan focus and examined the issues in the regions as well. Despite intentions, however, there was a stronger focus on leaders and 'presidential' forms of campaigning than in the past, and this may only be partly explained by the parties' own campaigning techniques. Furthermore, there was a considerable increase in stories addressing campaign conduct and strategy, and in senior correspondents being cast as expert analysts. We have suggested that this reflects a more interpretive approach on the part of the broadcasters; a trend for which evidence has already emerged in the United States. The benefits of this are open to question: it was an expressed wish of the broadcasters to give a greater voice to the reporter and, in part, this may represent an attempt to combat the firmer grip which disciplined party communications attempt to exercise on the news agenda. On the other hand, the US studies suggest that more strategy orientated and evaluative coverage tends to increase the importance of campaign journalists at the expense of the politicians themselves, to encourage greater cynicism towards politicians and the political process and to produce more negative coverage. On the latter point, at least, we are reassured: the rise in interpretive coverage did not appear to coincide with increased negative evaluations on the part of broadcast journalists.

The questions of whether there was too much coverage, as viewers appear to have suggested, and whether this led to the particular decline in viewing figures for the *Nine O'Clock News* and even, indirectly, to the decline in turnout, are also difficult to answer. Assessments of the quantity of coverage must turn upon judgments of how public service television *ought* to perform at elections. As the public's most trusted source of political knowledge, it would be unreasonable to criticise the BBC for providing *too much* coverage. If the BBC's ratings decline was partly due to the extension of its coverage, then that decision can still be defended as a brave one in accordance with its public service role. If, though, it was also due significantly to its reporting approach, and in particular to its interpretation of the 'balance' requirement and its adoption of a more evaluative model, then it may indeed have conspired against understanding, with the result that this most public-spirited of media systems was in reality performing a public disservice. However, viewers generally found even the BBC's coverage to be accurate and interesting. The most likely reasons for reduced turnout are political. Turnout appears to have declined most spectacularly in safe seats; that is, where individual voters were most likely to feel that their votes made least difference to the result.[49]

NOTES

1 Margaret Scammell and Martin Harrop, 'The Press', in David Butler and Dennis Kavanagh (eds), *The British General Election of 1997* (London: Macmillan, 1997), pp. 156–85.

2 Richard Tait, 'Anatomy of a Turn-off', *Guardian*, 20 May 1997, p. 17.

3 See Mark Lawson, 'It Would Leave a Saatchi Gasping', *Guardian*, 22 April 1997, p. 18.

4 Peter Golding, David Deacon and Michael Billig, 'Dominant Press Backs "On Message" Winner', *Guardian*, 5 May 1997, p. 4.

5 Holli A. Semetko, Margaret Scammell and Peter Goddard, 'Television', in Pippa Norris and Neil T. Gavin (eds), *Britain Votes 1997* (Oxford: Oxford University Press, 1997), pp. 101–7.

6 J. Lewis, 'Always Wrong', *Broadcast*, 18 April 1997.

7 Scammell and Harrop, 'The Press'.

8 The project is supported by the Economic and Social Research Council through a grant to Margaret Scammell and Holli A. Semetko. It included newsroom observation at ITN, interviews with editors and producers at ITN and the BBC, and observation and interviews at the morning press conferences. Peter Goddard of Liverpool University monitored all election news and, with Katy Parry, conducted all the content analysis coding. Special thanks are due to the many news and campaign professionals who took time to be interviewed and provided valuable documentation and materials for this research. The content analysis covered the two most-respected British TV news programmes, the BBC's *Nine O'Clock News* and ITV's *News at Ten*, as well as a comparable hour from BSkyB's dedicated 24-hour satellite news channel, Sky News, in the period 1–30 April 1997. References to 'BBC', 'ITV' or 'Sky News' refer to these programmes unless otherwise stated. It was based on internationally established variables (see Holli A. Semetko, Jay G. Blumler, Michael Gurevitch and David H. Weaver, *The Formation of Campaign Agendas* (Hillsdale, NJ: Lawrence Erlbaum Associates, 1991)) comparable with those used to monitor television and press coverage of the 1992 election (see T. J. Nossiter, Margaret Scammell and Holli A. Semetko, 'Old Values versus News Values: The British 1992 General Election Campaign on Television', in Ivor Crewe and Brian Gosschalk (eds), *Political Communications: The General Election Campaign of 1992* (Cambridge: Cambridge University Press, 1995), pp. 85–107).

9 This has been called 'meta-coverage'. See David Deacon and Michael Billig, 'Between Fear and Loathing: National Press Coverage of the 1997 British General

Election', paper presented at the Elections, Parties and Public Opinion Conference, University of Essex, September 1997.

10 See Joseph N. Cappella and Kathleen Hall Jamieson, 'News Frames, Political Cynicism and Media Cynicism', *The Annals of the American Academy of Political Science*, Media and Politics Special Edition (1996), pp. 71–84; Thomas E. Patterson, *Out of Order* (New York: Vintage, 1994); Thomas E. Patterson, 'Bad News, Bad Governance', *The Annals of the American Academy of Political Science*, Media and Politics Special Edition (1996), pp. 97–108.

11 See also Chapter 12 by Jay G. Blumler and Michael Gurevitch, 'Change in the Air: Campaign Journalism at the BBC, 1997', in this volume, for a discussion of Hallin's findings of increasing 'analytical mediation' of news in the United States.

12 See David L. Swanson and Paulo Mancini (eds), *Politics, Media and Modern Democracy* (Westport, CT: Praeger, 1997).

13 A phrase coined by Jean Bethke Elshtain, quoted in Cappella and Jamieson, 'News Frames, Political Cynicism and Media Cynicism', p. 72.

14 Nossiter, Scammell and Semetko, 'Old Values versus News Values'.

15 See Chapter 17 by Stephen Perkins, 'Regulations, The Media and the 1997 General Election: The ITC Perspective', and Chapter 18 by Colin Munro, 'Legal Constraints, Real and Imagined', in this volume.

16 For a further discussion of 'stopwatching', see Richard Tait, 'The Parties and Television', in Crewe and Gosschalk, *Political Communications: The General Election Campaign of 1992*, pp. 59–61.

17 For an international comparison, see Holli A. Semetko, 'The Media', in Lawrence LeDuc, Richard G. Neimi and Pippa Norris (eds), *Comparing Democracies* (Thousand Oaks, CA: Sage, 1996). For the extent of coverage of earlier elections, see Nossiter, Scammell and Semetko, 'Old Values versus News Values', p. 87. For a more detailed discussion of the extent, range and philosophy governing television coverage in 1997, see, for example, Harrison, 'Politics on the Air', pp. 133–49, and Semetko, Scammell and Goddard, 'Television', pp. 101–7.

18 For our purposes, 'political' news stories were those in which British politicians or political parties were mentioned. The percentages for the BBC and ITN programmes excluding Sky News were even higher: 53.3 per cent (by number of stories) and 67.9 per cent (by time).

19 See, for example, Golding, Deacon and Billig, 'Dominant Press Backs "On Message" Winner'; Martin Bell, 'The Accidental Hero', *Guardian*, 6 May 1997, G2, pp. 4–5.

20 Pippa Norris, 'The Battle for Campaign Agendas', in Anthony King (ed.), *Britain at the Polls 1997* (Chatham, NJ: Chatham House, 1997).

21 See Norris, 'The Battle for Campaign Agendas'.

22 Norris, 'The Battle for Campaign Agendas'.

23 Holli A. Semetko and Klaus Schoenbach, *Germany's 'Unity Election': Voters and the Media* (Cresskill, NJ: Hampton Press, 1994).

24 Nossiter, Scammell and Semetko, 'Old Values versus News Values', p. 89.

25 But see Karen Sanders and Tim Bale, 'Every Movement, Every Fart, Every Scratch: The Symbolic Agenda of a British Satellite Broadcaster's 1997 General Election' (private paper). Among their findings were that Sky News was concerned to be seen as a 'serious player' in covering the election and that this, together with the common background of many Sky News journalists in BBC or ITN News, led to the adoption of a more or less 'public-service' approach.

26 The information from Michael Jermey throughout this section is derived from internal ITV election planning memos and from observation interviews in the

course of the campaign conducted by Holli A. Semetko. Peter Horrocks's and Sue Inglish's responses throughout this section are also from observation interviews in the course of the campaign conducted by Holli A. Semetko.

27 John Birt, 'Memo to BBC Journalists', BBC internal memo, distributed 2 May 1997.

28 See Ivor Crewe, 'The Opinion Polls: Confidence Restored?', in Norris and Gavin, *Britain Votes 1997*, pp. 61–77.

29 This 'tradition' is actually a relatively new development for British television; earlier observation studies at the BBC for the 1979 and 1983 elections found a marked reluctance to claim an independent agenda-setting role for TV journalism. See Michael Gurevitch and Jay G. Blumler, 'The Construction of Election News: An Observation Study at the BBC', in James S. Ettema and D. Charles Whitney (eds), *Individuals in Mass Media Organizations: Creativity and Constraint* (Beverly Hills, CA, and London: Sage, 1982), pp. 179–204; Jay G. Blumler, Michael Gurevitch and T. J. Nossiter, 'Setting the Television News Agenda: Campaign Observation at the BBC', in Ivor Crewe and Martin Harrop (eds), *Political Communications: The General Election Campaign of 1983* (Cambridge: Cambridge University Press, 1986), pp. 104–24.

30 Michael White, 'Shoot the Messenger … from a Flattering Angle', *Guardian*, 28 April 1997, G2, p. 24.

31 Scammell and Harrop, 'The Press', p. 175.

32 Nossiter, Scammell and Semetko, 'Old Values versus News Values', pp. 88–9.

33 See Butler and Kavanagh, *The British General Election of 1997*, pp. 105–8.

34 Cappella and Jamieson, 'News Frames, Political Cynicism and Media Cynicism', pp. 71–84.

35 Bell, 'The Accidental Hero', pp. 1–5 (esp. 4–5).

36 Sanders and Bale, 'Every Movement, Every Fart, Every Scratch'.

37 See, for example, Swanson and Mancini, *Politics, Media and Modern Democracy*.

38 See Tait, 'Anatomy of a Turn-off'.

39 See John Curtice's paper given at Political Studies Association conference, Keele University, April 1998.

40 The subjects were: Steven Norris (7 April; spoke for 193 seconds), Michael Portillo twice (9 April; 238 seconds and 28 April; 133 seconds), David Willetts (10 April; 182 seconds).

41 This approach was specifically requested of his team in March by Nigel Dacre, editor of ITN. See Michael White, 'Shoot the Messenger'.

42 Nossiter, Scammell and Semetko, 'Old Values versus News Values', p. 92.

43 See Perkins, 'Regulations, Media and the Election', and Tait, 'The Parties and Television'.

44 For a more detailed discussion on this point, see Semetko, Scammell and Goddard, 'Television', pp. 104–5.

45 See Semetko, Scammell and Goddard, 'Television', pp. 105–6.

46 See Stephen Ansolabehere and Shanto Iyengar, *Going Negative* (New York: The Free Press, 1995).

47 See, for example, Butler and Kavanagh, *The British General Election of 1997*, pp. 239–41.

48 Patterson, 'Bad News, Bad Governance', pp. 97–108.

49 John Curtice and Michael Steed, 'The Results Analysed', in Butler and Kavanagh, *The British General Election of 1997*, pp. 299–300.

12

Change in the Air: Campaign Journalism at the BBC, 1997

JAY G. BLUMLER and MICHAEL GUREVITCH

Democratic political communication systems are becoming more complicated as a result of changes in the media and society. With the advance of media abundance, there are more channels of communication, more news outlets of different kinds and more incessant competition between them. Inside news organisations, tensions are sharpening between professional cultures and institutional needs.[1] From the advance of modernisation, more fragmented social orders have emerged, full of interest groups and contending value orientations, in which the political role of the media has become more pivotal.[2] Individuals rely on them more often for social connectness and political awareness. Would-be opinion formers, political parties and their leaders rely on them more heavily to reach individual citizens and cultivate or restore public support. Expectations of media performance multiply and diversify.

Outcrops of this process were arguably noticeable in the British general election of 1997. The campaign was unprecedentedly long and lacked sparkle or suspense. But, in broadcasting terms, it was bifurcated, comprising on the one hand a highly visible, highly controlled, often deplored but inescapable surface and on the other hand a new and different undercurrent, less prominent and less remarked upon, but which may nevertheless contain a transforming potential.

Those two dimensions may be labelled 'professionalisation' and 'populism' respectively, and broadcasters strove to respond to both. The former embraced journalists and politicians as intricately intertwined actors, struggling round their implicit maxims – 'you say what I constrain you to say' and 'you report what I constrain you to report'. The latter added what the broadcasters sometimes called 'real people' to the equation, appearing in a variety of formats partly in an attempt to overcome the aridity of the former.

All this is to say that democratic political communication systems are continually evolving. Our own observation research at the BBC in successive elections has offered insights into the main changes over time in British campaign communication.[3] Our reports from the 1987 and 1992 elections, in particular, highlighted a disturbing trend. Despite the best efforts of BBC producers, it was proving more difficult to implement their public service remit in the face of the major parties' increasingly professionalised approaches to campaign publicity. The problem was reflected in our chapter titles – 'The Earnest versus the Determined' and 'Struggles for Meaningful Election Communication'.[474]

In 1992 we also criticised BBC campaign journalism on three grounds. First, it was too reactively bound to the parties' narrow issue agendas. Second, it was hamstrung by overly cautious applications of the norms of fairness and objectivity. Third, the role of the audience in its coverage was at best 'shadowy'. Supposedly paramount in a normative sense, audience needs and likely reactions tended instead 'to be assumed and taken for granted' and 'rarely entered into the editorial discussions we observed and overheard'. The producers themselves recognised this last failing. As one put it:

> We were in no position with our dispositions to understand what was moving voters. We were almost entirely focused on the press conferences, the leaders on the trail, reporting how the campaign was going, as if it were primarily a media-party based affair.

Between 1992 and 1997, changes external and internal to the BBC were more far-reaching than ever before. The aim of our research in 1997 was to identify the main changes and to consider some of their implications. How would the BBC reconcile its awareness of new conditions with its traditional public-service commitment to the provision of extensive, prominent and substantive campaign coverage? What adaptations to Britain's campaign communication system might be emerging as a result? Our exercise included policy interviews before and after the election, plus five days of campaign observation, divided between the newsroom at the BBC's White City Television Centre and its political programming base at Millbank in Westminster.[5]

EXTERNAL CHANGES

The external environment for political communication by British broadcasters was reshaped between 1992 and 1997 by three sorts of changes: of media system, in party publicity organisation, and of mass political culture. However, the impact of these developments on the BBC's campaign journalism varied.

Multichannel expansion

Public-service broadcasters throughout Europe have adjusted their schedules and programming, sometimes quite drastically, to the onset of multichannel competition.[6] Of course, satellite and cable inroads into the viewing audience are not so great in Britain as on the European mainland. They have been increasing steadily in recent years, however, and will continue to do so. The launch of Channel 5 even coincided with the start date for full-scale campaign coverage by the BBC. So what account did its policy for such coverage take of the ongoing expansion of the UK television system?

A well-placed executive's answer to this question was 'not much'. Audience fragmentation was still limited, and BBC research suggested that many in the audience continued to rely especially on the BBC for informed reporting of politics. When it was pointed out that the BBC could nevertheless come under competitive pressure, with more channels available to counter-programme against serious coverage approaches and with a weakening of political interest among many voters, our informant agreed, but maintained that it was premature to take this into account. This factor would significantly influence programming policy only when the amount of political viewing of BBC channels fell below a certain level.

This perspective was reinforced by our own observations during the campaign. Competitive worries and comparisons were rarely voiced. Instead we seemed to be witnessing a large operation unfolding confidently according to its pre-designed template.

Yet more professionalisation of party publicity efforts

This was probably the most media-oriented and media-based campaign yet. The entire round of daily campaign activities, from party press conferences in the morning, through ongoing responses to each other's messages to leaders' walkabouts and evening speeches, were ostentatiously geared to television. The morning press conferences were replete with graphics and videos, and the politicians on the podium took questions first from senior BBC and ITN correspondents. Moreover, the campaign began, of course, long before its official starting point: what Americans term 'the permanent campaign' is now entrenched on British shores. More than at most elections, this campaign was presented in terms of the leaders and their qualities. Negative campaigning was measurably dominant.[7] Publicity management by the parties' leading 'spin doctors' had become a prominent news topic in its own right. And the persuasion process had stepped up a gear, as the parties created rebuttal units to react rapidly to each other's claims and accusations. Although the professional model of modern campaigning was already well established in Britain by 1992,[8] its role at that time was 'curbed and tamed' by inherited influences of party organisation and elite political culture.[9] In the run-up to the 1997 election, however, it appeared that many of those traditional sources of inhibition had been swept aside – especially by the campaign strategies developed by 'New Labour'.[10]

The BBC's response to this trend took two distinct forms. At a philosophical level, its leading journalistic lights deplored the resulting coarsening of political discourse and the sterility of what they now called 'the soundbite culture'. Several said they hoped to put their minds to the task of political communication reform during a wide-ranging post-election review of news and current affairs programming:

> How to change the conventions of political discourse in mainstream news programmes is the challenge of the next five years.

> New ways of talking about politics have to be sought in the future.

> We need to evolve a new grammar of political communication.

At the level of daily campaign practice, however, BBC journalists seemed to take the intensification of the parties' publicity efforts largely in their stride. This is not to suggest that they failed to notice the parties' news-making tactics. They often mentioned the reactions from themselves, which, they thought, such tactics were designed to elicit (an 'I know, you know' syndrome!). Because both major parties often held 'rebuttal conferences' in addition to their regular morning press conferences, the journalists' news gathering load was heavier than in the past:

> All the parties are quicker off the mark in rebutting charges and allegations from their opponents. So the hamster wheel will revolve faster than before.

The exceptional length of the 1997 campaign was also regrettable. As a programme editor explained:

> The campaign has gone on for an inordinate length of time even before the official campaign began. It has been a very long campaign. And the parties' positions were well known in advance. It's as if we are all going through the motions in six weeks of this un-newsworthy toil and sweat.

But our overarching impression of party–BBC relations in the 1997 campaign was of two large, well-oiled, powerful and highly professional machines facing each other and carrying out their respective tasks competently and efficiently. A new element in this situation was said to be an unexpected reduction in the volume of complaints from parties ('There is much less heavy breathing than in 1992'). But in a situation of 'mutual professionalisation', the work of coverage may become less exciting and electric. 'The campaign has not fired us up', an editor declared: 'There have been very few exceptional days.' That tallies with our own impression. Although the journalists were evidently doing their job out of a profound sense of commitment, they rarely seemed galvanised. It may be significant that the only exception we witnessed to this mood of assured steadiness arose when John Major scrapped his professional script at a morning press conference to plead emotionally for breathing space from fellow Conservatives over the issue of Britain's relations with Europe.

Plummeting public regard for politics

The most formative influence on broadcasters' thinking, however, was evidence of increasing disenchantment among many members of the public with politicians, political institutions and political talk, which they 'knew' rubbed off onto their own political programmes, personalities and reports. A widespread and deeply held perception throughout British broadcasting one suspects, this was mentioned by many of our BBC interviewees:

> There is a widespread public disillusionment with political institutions.

> We are all increasingly aware that there is a degree of alienation from the political process and that applies to political coverage on our bulletins.

> A larger disenchantment with the Westminster process is all over the place. Our own research shows it.

Wry mentions of their own membership of 'the Westminster village', the 'Westminster culture', the 'Westminster hothouse' and even of being 'inside the Beltway shelter' (i.e. the Washington DC ring road; there's Americanisation for you!) also abounded.

The challenge of this development was best summarised for us by a Channel 4 broadcaster with many contacts in the corporation:

> If you're in the BBC, you know that a very important part of your remit is political coverage. But you also know from your research and other sources that it's a big turn-off. So that has started a big debate, at first intermittently, then more widely, about what can we change?

In fact, this did result in significant new ways of organising campaign discussion on BBC television and radio, which are dealt with later in this chapter.

INTERNAL DEVELOPMENTS

Continuity with the past

The provision of high-quality civic communication has long been a leading principle of BBC news and current affairs. This was still a major influence on its approach to the 1997 election.

As before, much time, effort, planning and thought (including editorial-level seminars), as well as financial and manpower resources, had been invested in coverage of the campaign. This was probably the most 'thought-through' approach to election reporting of any we had observed. Tight budgets, whatever their past and likely future grip, did not seem to apply during the campaign.

Also as in 1992, the flagship *Nine O'Clock News* bulletin was extended by 20 minutes and based on a three-part structure: part I reported the day's political events; part II reported non-election news; and part III presented other political packages – on the issues, from leader teams, opinion poll reports by Peter Snow and a miscellany of 'second-string' election news. The lunch-time *One O'Clock News* was also extended by a few minutes, though not the large-audience *Six O'Clock News*, where (it was said) 'we are trying to keep the election within bounds' – meaning that 'we will try to stop it taking more than half the programme'!

Four minor adjustments to this inherited model were made. First, the *Nine O'Clock News* usually closed with a two-way exchange between the news reader and the BBC's Political Editor, Robin Oakley, exploring how the respective parties seemed to have fared in the day's events – this as a regular feature rather than sporadically as in 1992 (with John Cole). Second, there were to be fewer opinion poll reports than in 1992 – the target being no more than two per week. Third, a different authority structure applied. At the top, a 'war cabinet', consisting of the Chief Executive of BBC News and the Heads of Television News, Radio News and Political Programmes, met by video-conference early every morning, when they reviewed the previous day's coverage, assessed forward prospects and considered any policy issues that might have arisen. Their conclusions were relayed in turn to two mid-morning team meetings – for news editors at the Television Centre and for political correspondents at Westminster. Finally, amidst what was still to be an analytical and issue-driven approach, there was a wish (in an editor's words) to 'lighten up' the coverage 'a bit' and inject some 'light and shade to engage the viewers' – such as through highly produced location reports rather than items from the studio. A Westminster desk segment, presented nightly by Anne Perkins at the top of part III, mixing 'duty items' (such as a minor party manifesto launch), oblique stories and less weighty pieces – like a broadsheet's inside-page diary – also stemmed from the concern to 'lighten up'.

But the overall public service rationale for the coverage was essentially unchanged. Over and over again our informants spoke of their commitment to such a philosophy in terms we found genuine and sincere:

> At a general election, public service comes into the equation. We don't have to justify the inclusion of stories solely by news values. The election *is* the story.

> We go into this election with a didactic purpose as well as a journalistic purpose. The two are interconnected, but as you know, our Director-General, he has a high purpose. That high purpose will be on display during this election.

To us, the apparent lack of concern about the possible impact on viewing levels was striking. That the *Nine O'Clock News* should be 45–50 minutes in length was 'never, never under debate', an executive told us. Despite risks of audience 'overkill', the fact that any significant reduction of time 'would severely constrain our ability to meet all our editorial obligations' was regarded as decisive. A producer concurred:

> It would be difficult to run the bulletin at the usual length in terms of the BBC remit. We would not be able to give viewers the sort of information that the BBC would like to provide.

An editor even spoke of the 'fantastic luxury' he enjoyed, since 'nobody would say that was a jolly interesting programme but the ratings went down'. And when evidence of a significant drop in the audience became available, the newspeople tended to rationalise, arguing that they were not going to be deterred from doing their duty as public service broadcasters. In a producer's words:

> We are relaxed about it. We have been told from the top that the BBC has a duty to do this.

After the election was over, however, opinion at BBC News veered towards the view that an hour of politics at 9 p.m. on BBC1 (often including party election broadcasts after the news) was about five or ten minutes too long.

But if the structure of BBC election news closely followed the 1992 pattern, much of its content was modified more substantially by three new developments. These were significant, not only for their impact on the coverage, but also because of their implications for the roles of the other principal 'actors' in political communication – politicians and voters.

The Westminster powerhouse

In 1997 a new centre of gravity for campaign coverage operated at the BBC's political programmes base at 4 Millbank, in the heart of Westminster. In addition to a head of political programmes, this had its own editor, a political editor (Robin Oakley), 11 other political correspondents, many producers, studios and other production facilities, including independent programme-making abilities and experience. Its scale and level of activity were little short of awesome. On entering the newsroom for the first time, one of us wrote, 'It looks like a powerhouse and you are struck by the available firepower.' BBC personnel – at Westminster and elsewhere – seemed to share this view:

> This is the greatest political machine in Britain. Once the question is known, the machine can be terrific.

Such a statement suggests that the BBC could rival the machinery of the political parties, even if its purpose was different.

Multiple roles were performed at this base: news-gathering, the construction and provision of packages, advising programmes, sometimes production itself. For the main television news bulletins and for some radio news programmes, most reports and packages on campaign events were prepared at Westminster. Much of part I of the *Nine O'Clock News*, specifically, emanated from there. All this contrasted with 1992, when its equivalent was more like an 'outpost', 'out on a limb', often 'deserted', as an editor declared.

Many advantages of this development were mentioned to us: closer or quicker access to press conferences and to leading politicians for interviews; the build-up of a large team of able, knowledgeable, authoritative and well-known correspondents; and the ease of forging a consistent editorial line across all political teams (without, it was claimed, smothering the variety of style and approach of different programmes). A bulletin editor was also impressed with the level of professionalism attained at Westminster and the speed with which requested stories could be delivered: 'They generate a lot of material [and] can always have a story up and running.' Significantly, it was also suggested that such a specialist centre was well placed to face up to, and read between the lines of, the parties' news-making manoeuvres. As a Millbank producer put it, 'The editorial confidence here has grown enormously; we have much more clout.' And as an executive argued:

> It's best to have this kind of specialist political journalism. In this world what you see is not what you get. What a politician says is not what he means. To be able to properly find your way through that particular kind of jungle, you really need people who are aware of the nuances and of the forces at play behind the scenes to properly interpret what is being said and what the real truth of the matter is.

This is not to imply that editors and producers at the Television Centre were out of the campaign frame. Editorial responsibility for all bulletin content, including election reports, lodged still with the programme editors. They had their own liaison teams of producers at Westminster (termed 'my eyes and ears' by more than one), who regularly consulted with the Millbank correspondents and producers over the significance of daily events, what the main themes and top stories of the day might be and how they might be dealt with. Much telephone communication was said to be 'flying back and forth during the day', and Television Centre personnel claimed that they could and did see everything that was available at Westminster.

So far as we could tell, all this worked efficiently, smoothly and harmoniously. But it also seemed to us that the key initiatives and input inevitably stemmed from Millbank. Robin Oakley, the Westminster Unit's political editor, had first refusal on all campaign material, and he and his colleagues formed an acknowledged core of specialist political judgement.

Did this have specifiable consequences for the content of election news? The role of the Millbank unit ensured that part I of the 9 p.m. bulletin usually focused on daily party initiatives, not neglecting but briefly summarising their policy elements and illustrating them with soundbites from the press conferences. Reports were often laced with the metaphors and language of conflict (sometimes described as 'bitter') and emphasised the parties' strategic aims and how they were faring. This was a view of the campaign from 'inside the belly of the beast'. Perhaps not surprisingly, an informed academic, who fully immersed himself in this material, found much of it 'negative, disputatious and repetitive'.[11]

More analytical 'mediation'

According to Hallin,[12] US television news is today 'more *mediated* than the TV news of the 1960s and 1970s'. In essence, less time has been devoted over successive campaigns to politicians' words and more to those of journalists. As Hallin elaborated:

> During the earlier period the journalist's role as a communicator was relatively passive. ... Today's television journalist displays a sharply different attitude toward the words of candidates and other newsmakers. Today those words, rather than simply being reproduced and transmitted to the audience, are treated as raw material to be taken apart, combined with other sounds and images, and reintegrated into a new narrative.

In his view, a combination of factors explained this trend: the availability of more sophisticated reporting techniques, the weakening of political authority and increased competition for audiences in the US television industry.

Strong signs of a similar trend, albeit in British garb, emerged in Britain's 1997 campaign. As ever since the 1960s, a substantive emphasis on exploring key election issues was a feature of BBC policy. As one news executive put it:

> Our campaign coverage policy, formed in advance of the campaign, was heavily biased toward issues. We had given much thought to that – how to deal with particular issues.

But its application was more 'mediated' this time, owing to three features of that policy.

One was to stretch the BBC's issue coverage beyond party bounds. In advance of the campaign, therefore, a grid of 20 issues was drawn up, based on survey data about concerns uppermost in British voters' minds, and circulated to all news programmes. Each was expected to include in their coverage, over the campaign as a whole, reports on a good number of the issues specified in the grid. For example, quite long packages of this kind (running for between five and eight minutes) appeared most nights in part III of the *Nine O'Clock News*, some pre-prepared, others produced in response to the daily flow of campaign argument.

Second, specialist correspondents – not only at Westminster but also from the BBC's Social and Economic Affairs Units – were given more prominent roles in election reporting and presentation. Issue packages usually opened with a so-called 'election briefing' – a graphic displaying in bullet points the main policies of the parties' manifestos on the problems concerned. Having thus dealt with the parties' stands, this left the BBC correspondent free to offer a wide range of commentary and analysis, including facts and figures, descriptions of typical problem situations, interviews with experts, professionals and ordinary people and a summary assessment of the feasibility of policies proposed for tackling the issue concerned.

Third, the specialist correspondents were encouraged to be more robust in their commentary than they had been in the past. The guideline was that although they should not express personal opinions, they could express professional judgements. As an executive put it:

> Our job is to make judgements about what is going on without being afraid it will cast a shadow over our impartiality. There is now an atmosphere of robustness.

In the words of a correspondent, 'Deconstructing things for the viewer's benefit is part of our job.' Fear of top-brass disapproval had also receded. 'They expect you to take the bigger picture and give a higher degree of analysis', another correspondent told us.

What explains this development? In part, it reflects the build-up of the specialist units of BBC News. These were said to be 'in the BBC's bloodstream now' and 'the bedrock of BBC journalism'. In part, 'robustness' offers opportunities for correspondents to catch the eyes of their superiors in hope of eventual advancement. Reporters are unlikely to be noticed, far less praised, simply for having stitched together the most suitable passages of politicians' direct speech.

But a key factor may have been the emergence among journalists of a set of pejorative impressions of what fully professionalised politicians are like as competing would-be persuaders. They tend to be perceived as inveterate over-simplifiers, inclined to ignore inconvenient facts and difficulties and to neglect longer-term perspectives for immediate advantage. An executive discoursed in this vein:

> although of course we have to report the campaign as it is in all its partisan rhetoric, one of the things we all hope will happen, which is consistent with our general editorial objectives now, is that we start to address at least some of the debates on the basis that these are, whatever the rhetoric may tell you, highly complex problems that any government will have difficulty tackling. ... It's the current version of the 'mission to explain', expressed in the idea that the audience is entitled to get across the range of outlets of the BBC sufficient context and analysis, which, translated into policy matters, often means 'understand that this is complex'. Whatever the politicians tell you, there is no free lunch there.

But why were BBC personnel less afraid that robustness would imperil impartiality? One reason was that all political parties were regarded as more or less equally prone to simplify. An executive illustrated the point by suggesting that neither Labour nor Conservative tax-and-spend policies stood up to close analysis. If so, he went on:

> it clearly doesn't stray into impartiality territory, in the sense that it is pro-Tory or pro-Labour, because the premise for my crude example is that they are both saying the same thing.

Another reason was a belief that the BBC was not alone in its critique of simplistic partisan approaches. As our executive informant added:

> Neither do I think it strays into impartiality difficulty, if you assume, which I do, that what we are reflecting is not an editorial position of the BBC, but what is demonstrably the reality of the underlying debate out there in the real world, in the professions, in Whitehall, in the think tanks and everywhere else.

As a result, even long-standing hesitations among BBC journalists about claiming an agenda-setting role for themselves were close to being discarded. As two different reporters put it:

> When it comes to the crunch, it is the BBC who will determine its agenda in an impartial way.
>
> So it's a different agenda, a more objective view of the agenda.

Another termed it 'analysis-setting – interpreting, in robust terms, whatever it is the politicians have said or done'.

OPENING UP THE CAMPAIGN DIALOGUE: POPULISM À LA BBC

British campaigns tended to be 'top-down' affairs in the past, presented by politicians and journalists for reception by voters. The few series in which ordinary people's voices could be heard – *Question Time*, *Election Call*, *The Granada 500* – have been regarded chiefly as supplements to the main streams of coverage. As we stated in our review of the 1966–92 observation reports, 'At every election, campaign communication was treated as the near-exclusive province of politicians and journalists – shutting out or marginalising other voices, such as party dissidents and representatives of cause and interest groups.'[13] In fact, proposals for widening access to holders of other views were rejected in 1987 because they (1) would have been unwelcome to leading politicians; and (2) would have unduly complicated the BBC's job of maintaining balance between the major parties' positions.[14]

Given perceptions of deepening public disenchantment with politics and politicians, however, it was widely accepted that the traditional model was no longer viable. All forms of political programming had to cultivate a popular touch:

> In the present climate, we can't just present politics in the old ways.

> I get the feeling, looking at the coverage in the round, that we are trying to make it a 'people's election'. Mostly, it is an attempt to weaken the notion of being one set of insiders talking to others.

> Politics has become a tainted profession [and] it is important for us not to go down with the sinking ship.

Attempts to break loose from the old system took four forms. First, more attention was paid to the accessibility of the language in which the news was written. As a news reader explained:

> There has been a growing perception, fed by market research, that many people are not digesting political reporting from the BBC as well as they might. It was not as accessible as it should be.

Thus, jargon and 'insider' terms should be avoided, and reports should be written as straightforwardly as possible.

A second 'key thing' (as an editor put it) was 'getting our people out into the country', i.e., showing correspondents less often at Westminster and more often in situations where important issues arise and people experience them. Reporters were urged 'to go out into the country at large, and make issue films' in hospitals, schools, fishing ports, farmyards, village halls, and so on.

Third, packages of issue analysis were to centre more often on the opinions and circumstances of ordinary people and others who have to deal, professionally or managerially, with the problems concerned. Politicians, then, would feature less prominently in such films than in the past. That is presumably why a social affairs correspondent spoke to us with pride about having produced what he called 'a people piece on social welfare' – an eight-minute film in which 'only me and real people appeared'.

Fourth, a host of attempts to promote dialogue between voters and politicians proliferated in the television and radio schedules – across all channels and not just those of the BBC. As a programme editor explained:

> The whole idea of bringing ordinary people more fully into the coverage has been enthusiastically taken up. I feel it is the most striking feature of our coverage this time compared to last.

This 'populist' thrust embraced a wide range of formats, subject-matter and casts of participants. It included conventional 'phone-ins, studio panels confronting party representatives and larger studio audiences putting questions to politicians through a moderator. In some cases, a broadly representative public element was involved; in others, it was more focused (e.g., on women, university students, etc.). In some cases, the debate ranged quite widely; in others it zeroed in on some bounded issue area (such as economic policy). Sometimes a several-sided exchange was organised, including not only voters, politicians and experts, but also officials and professionals involved in dealing with the problems at issue. For two programmes – *The ITV 500* and Channel 4's *Power and the People* – participating voters were briefed in advance by experts. Some of these programmes were deliberately given 'populist' titles – as in *The People's Agenda*, *The People's Election*, *Voters Can't be Choosers* and *Power and the People*. And although little room was available for such discussions in the BBC's television news bulletins, they featured regularly in its *Campaign Roadshows* (mid-afternoon thrice weekly on BBC2) and *Question Time*, in *Newsnight* and on *Breakfast News*, as well as in other current affairs programmes.

All this adds up to a systemic breakthrough of sorts with much corporate and personal momentum behind it. Unlike the United States, however, where the main vehicles of 'talk show democracy' have sprung up outside and even in opposition to the mainstream journalistic establishment, in Britain the new forms arose within and were adapted to the norms and procedures of public service television. As a senior executive cautioned:

> But beware. This is the BBC. We're very nervous about doing this sort of thing. The questions come through our presenters ... We do not open our wavelengths to just anybody. Whether that's good or bad, it's just not what we do. We're the BBC still and there's still this feeling. And also we're responsible for fairness, political balance and all of that. It's within our control ... We're still in the steering.

'Populism à la BBC' is therefore probably best characterised by three propositions:

1. *It was usually ascribed definite but ultimately limited redemptive powers.* It could improve the programming, making it seem more fresh, relevant and exciting. A producer explained:

> The advantage is that they [the politicians] lose control. It's not that one wants them to say stupid things. But the danger of the system in which they have become very accomplished, briefed, polished and

rehearsed – as well as because the rules of the game of Michael Heseltine v. John Humphrys have become so well established – is that everybody just knows that much of the banter is an artifice. But with ordinary voters, politicians cannot slap them down … It creates an edge for them.

It could improve the quality of political discussion, help politicians lift their rhetorical game and generate real exchanges. In an editor's words:

Using audiences, or using formats that involve non-politicians … breaks that slightly sterile insider debate, where everybody has been around the course so many times, and they all know each other's policy positions.

It could also serve an 'informing function' for BBC journalism itself, freshening its contacts with broader opinion circles and its sense of what issues really matter to people and in what ways. According to a news executive, for example:

The thing that is beginning to be clear is that even our terrific news-gathering specialism doesn't give you everything. There are people out there who know about their business, who we ought to be tapping into. The big way that became apparent to me was in our coverage of the European debate. Business in this country have a view about Europe that, frankly, we weren't reflecting. It's tapping into that sort of view that getting out more can achieve.

Despite these expected advantages, however, many of our informants declined to espouse more radical goals, like enfranchising the electorate or even promoting a 'people's agenda' for politicians to respond to. (We might have found a different ethos had we been observing Channel 4.) In most cases their goals fell short of those that have inspired the US public journalism movement.[15] In the main, BBC journalists seemed more concerned to democratise their *programmes* than the *politics of their country* – as the following comments show:

It's not really about saying it's an exercise in direct democracy or anything like that.

It would be a Platonic ideal if we could somehow wrap politicians and people together and make the country more involved in the process. We are in a sense only the messenger. But I don't feel it's the role of broadcasters to say there is a problem in the political process and we can solve it. That would be arrogant. We can say our perspectives are too bound by the Beltway, but to see ourselves as redeemers of the process is to arrogate too much power to ourselves.

2. *Discussion programmes based on popular participation would not be a guideline-free zone.* As the election approached, there was much concern to avoid any appearance of imbalance in the composition of voter panels and studio audiences. 'The problem', said one executive, 'is that voters are not impartial!' Producers were therefore expected to adopt methods of selection that could be defended as 'squeaky clean'. Recruitment of representative bodies of electors could be farmed out to a polling organisation. Or producers could undertake the task themselves, knowing what the BBC wanted – and wanted to avoid. Usually the aim was to exclude (rather than to balance) party members.

3. *The programmes were absorbed into the framework of rational civic discourse long characteristic of other forms of political discussion on the BBC.* The aim, then, was to generate more 'light' than 'heat' and to recruit people who could take part in relatively serious and policy-relevant discussions with politicians and other informed guests. One criterion was sheer ability to talk on one's feet. In a producer's words:

> The grammar of television, of broadcasting, is that only people who are articulate do it. That's a given.

Another was an ability 'credibly to take on a well-briefed minister or shadow spokesman … at either a concrete level or a general level'. Prior outline planning of how the discussion should proceed could also help. As another producer explained:

> It is more choreographed than it looks, based on the structure of questions to be raised and knowledge of somebody in the audience who can raise it.

If politicians were 'put on the spot' (a popular phrase among producers) by concerned voters, well and good, and of course spontaneity was valued. But these campaign programmes were not modelled on *Oprah*, or for that matter *Kilroy*, where the studio audience member is mainly a source of raw experience, strong views, pithy points, emotional expression and sharp conflict. As a producer stated, the aim was not to produce 'a free-for-all or anything like that'. And as another explained:

> the BBC's Producer Guidelines are anti-tabloid. We wouldn't seek out such emotionalism though we wouldn't stamp it out if it surfaced. But we want to have as much of the discussion as possible focused on the platforms on which these people are standing.

UNRESOLVED TENSIONS AND PROSPECTS

What type of balance sheet would suit this record? It would be subjective and perhaps shallow to tot up a list of seeming successes and short-comings, patting the BBC on the back here and kicking it in the pants there! A more appropriate summary verdict might be that, while its 1997 election coverage policy overcame all the old weaknesses of 1992, it was also caught up in a new set of tensions.

First, the significant drop in the audience for the *Nine O'Clock News* highlights a tension between 'public service' and 'public reception'. What is the meaning of 'public service' if a large section of the public declines to be served? No facile answer to this question will do. We should be thankful that the BBC still takes its political vocation seriously in a period when impoverished campaign communication styles are so prevalent throughout the democratic world. When, during the US presidential election of 1996, for example, the commercial networks faced similar conditions to those in which the BBC had to operate this year – concerted news management at the top and a disaffected public at the bottom – they almost shut up civic shop altogether, drastically reducing their coverage. A public service BBC must continue to reject such a path and look instead for fresh ways of providing a political menu worth sampling without putting people off.

Second, there is the abiding tension between 'access' and 'mediation'. Both are valid principles. On the one hand, the diverse groups of a pluralist society deserve opportunities to present their concerns and beliefs through the mass media on terms they could be expected to recognise as valid. On the other hand, especially in an age of media abundance and information overload, members of the public are entitled to help from an independent journalistic service in making sense of the many messages and claims that come their way. Some politicians would probably say that in the 1997 campaign the BBC leaned too far toward 'mediation'. But how many voters would welcome less fettered access for much of the material that the party publicity machines tend to produce these days? If the ills of 'the soundbite culture' are to be addressed in a project of political communication reform (as certain BBC informants hoped), then politicians and their publicity managers must be engaged in it as a joint task.

But third, there was a huge tension – a contradiction even – between the BBC's several editorial objectives for coverage of the 1997 campaign. The point is that pride of place was given at the top of the main news bulletins to what, by BBC journalists' own accounts (peppered eloquently throughout this report), was a thoroughly compromised and tainted process: 'arid', 'dysfunctional', 'insider'-driven, full of simplistic 'free lunches', full of 'artifice', unable to be taken at face value and therefore needing to be regularly deciphered! Of course, the rest of the coverage – the informed issue analysis and the injection of popular voices – was different, well intentioned and well done. But could that really be expected to compensate for the exposure of viewers to the 30-round heavyweight boxing match that was staged nightly at the top of the news?

Finally, there are intriguing unknowns about the future prospects of British public service populism. Many broadcasters liked its feel and flavour in the recent campaign and may be motivated to explore its potential further. It is also in tune with the *zeitgeist* of today's less deferential society, in which evidence of popular endorsement and responsiveness to public sentiment seem to count for more than they used to in British politics. But the 1997 exercises in audience participation rarely made waves beyond the ghetto of current affairs programming in which they were confined. Unbuttoned versions of the US kind might attract more notice but lose deliberative value. A not entirely fanciful answer to this dilemma (as well as to the first tension discussed above) occurs to us here. If the *Nine O'Clock News* was to be extended to 45 minutes again at the next election, perhaps discussions of the hustings issues of the day, centring on voters with politicians, specialist correspondents and others, should be incorporated into its part III!

NOTES

1 See David L. Swanson, 'The Political-Media Complex at 50: Putting the 1996 Presidential Campaign in Context', *American Behavioral Scientist*, 40 (1997), pp. 1264–82.

2 Paolo Mancini and David L. Swanson, 'Politics, Media and Modern Democracy: Introduction', in David L. Swanson and Paolo Mancini (eds), *Politics, Media and Modern Democracy: An International Study of Innovations in Electoral Campaigning and Their Consequences* (Westport, CT: Praeger, 1996), pp. 1–26.

3 Michael Gurevitch and Jay G. Blumler, 'Longitudinal Analysis of an Election Communication System: Newsroom Observation at the BBC', *Osterreichische Zeitschrift fur Politikwissenshaft*, 22 (1993), pp. 427–44.

4 Jay G. Blumler, Michael Gurevitch and T. J. Nossiter, 'The Earnest versus the Determined: Election Newsmaking at the BBC, 1987', in Ivor Crewe and Martin Harrop (eds), *Political Communications: The General Election Campaign of 1987* (Cambridge: Cambridge University Press, 1989), pp. 157–74; Jay G. Blumler, Michael Gurevitch and T. J. Nossiter, 'Struggles for Meaningful Election Communication: Television Journalism at the BBC, 1992', in Ivor Crewe and Brian Gosschalk (eds), *Political Communications: The General Election Campaign of 1992* (Cambridge: Cambridge University Press, 1995), pp. 65–84. A broader analysis of the problems arising from change in the relationships among politicians, journalists and citizens appears in Jay G. Blumler and Michael

Gurevitch, *The Crisis of Public Communication* (London: Routledge, 1995), esp. ch. 15, pp. 203–21.

5 The research was supported by the Leverhulme Foundation through a grant to Professor Dennis Kavanagh. We are enormously grateful to them and to the many BBC executives, editors, correspondents and producers, who allowed us to look over their shoulders and talked to us about their work in such helpful and often vividly interesting terms. We also thank Richard Ayre, Malcolm Balen, John Bartle, Peter Bell, Georgina Born, Bob Franklin, Dennis Kavanagh, Philip Schlesinger and David Swanson for perceptive reactions to a previous draft of this chapter.

6 Karen Siune and Wolfgang Treutzschler (eds), *Dynamics of Media Politics* (London: Sage, 1992).

7 Margaret Scammell, 'Old Values versus News Values: The Media in the 1997 British General Election', paper presented to annual meeting of the American Political Science Association, Washington, DC, 1997.

8 Dennis Kavanagh, *Election Campaigning: The New Marketing of Politics* (Oxford: Blackwell, 1995).

9 Jay G. Blumler, Dennis Kavanagh and T. J. Nossiter, 'Modern Communications versus Traditional Politics in Britain: An Unstable Marriage of Convenience', in Swanson and Mancini, *Politics, Media and Modern Democracy*, pp. 49–72.

10 Dennis Kavanagh, 'The Labour Campaign', *Parliamentary Affairs*, 50 (1997), pp. 533–41.

11 Martin Harrison, 'Politics on the Air', in David Butler and Dennis Kavanagh (eds), *The British General Election of 1997* (Basingstoke: Macmillan, 1997), pp. 133–55.

12 Daniel C. Hallin, 'Sound-bite News: Television Coverage of Elections, 1968–1988', *Journal of Communication*, 42 (1992), pp. 5–24.

13 Gurevitch and Blumler, 'Longitudinal Analysis of an Election Communication System'.

14 Blumler, Gurevitch and Nossiter, 'Struggles for Meaningful Election Communication'.

15 Jay Rosen, *Getting the Connections Right: Public Journalism and the Troubles in the Press* (New York: Twentieth Century Fund, 1996).

Television and the 1997 Election Campaign: A View from Sky News

ADAM BOULTON

Nineteen ninety-seven was the second British general election campaign covered by Sky News. With the impending arrival of BBC News 24 we were also acutely aware that it would be the last campaign in which we would have a free run at continuous 24-hour coverage. Under the slogan 'The election station – you won't miss a thing', we set ourselves the task of providing the most comprehensive coverage and analysis of election news. Within the framework of multi-channel broadcasting on cable and satellite, we were not troubled by competing demands from non-news programming, assuming that those viewers who opt to watch our channel automatically expect extensive high-quality coverage of British politics.

Within Sky News and across the whole of the BSkyB network a number of issues concerning our coverage of the general election were of importance. What impact would the election have on audience figures? Would saturation coverage cause ratings to fall or, as in the 1992 campaign, would we be able to tap into a bigger pool of viewers eager for the latest political news, unable to satisfy themselves with the services available on conventional generalised terrestrial channels? Next came questions of programming content. In addition to our regular pattern of hourly and half-hourly news bulletin format, what special programming could be made to deal with the specific circumstances surrounding the election? How could we stimulate extra public interest? A third concern lay in our relationship with the various political parties. The parties would be calling national press conferences and conducting their own constituency campaigns. Decisions had to be made about how we reported the formal campaign and about how we resolved the conflicting agendas set by the politicians and the news instincts of an independent news organisation. Additionally, there would be more informal communications between ourselves and the parties, usually covered by the fashionable word 'spin'.

Finally, there were the legal requirements surrounding election coverage. Special consideration had to be given to respecting the Broadcasting Act and the Representation of the People Act (RPA). Given the intricacies and the ambiguities of these laws, this was no simple matter.

AUDIENCE

Judged by audience figures, Sky News can to be said to have had a good election, according to the rates of viewing recorded by the independent television ratings agency BARB, which is used by all British broadcasters.

While print journalism exaggerated the so-called 'big turn-off' of terrestrial news bulletins during the campaign (both BBC and ITN reported declines in their regular audiences in 1997), Sky News recorded a significant upsurge in regular viewing during the election campaign and its aftermath, recording the best sustained viewing ratings up to that point in the year.

A similar pattern had been noted in 1992, when the election coincided with a general increase in the Sky News audience share in homes with satellite and cable television. In 1997 BSkyB's penetration into the total viewing public was much greater overall, but the election still saw an upsurge in regular audiences.

On average just over one million viewers in the United Kingdom tune into the service each day; over the election period this increased to 1.55 million on Thursday 1 May, 1.73 million on Friday 2 May, 1.71 million on Saturday 3 May, 1.89 million on Sunday 4 May. Overall, during the election week (28 April–4 May), over 4.7 million viewers in the United Kingdom tuned to Sky News (one million more than usually tune in weekly, on current average, in the United Kingdom).

The four weeks leading to the election achieved figures as follows: week ending 6 April, 4.35 million; week ending 13 April, 3.41 million; week ending 20 April, 3.78 million; week ending 27 April, 4.1 million. This amounts to a weekly average over four weeks of 3.91 million; an average weekly reach for Sky News is 3.7 million. Over the same period the average weekly reach figures for the BBC's *Nine O'Clock News* were 6.8, 4.9, 4.3 and 4.1 million – a weekly average of five million individuals, representing a 20 per cent drop, of approximately 1.2 million individuals, on the monthly average for March 1997, the period immediately before the campaign.

Shortly before midnight on election day, 1 May, Sky News was attracting an average audience of 211,000 individuals, with the average audience holding at 99,000 until 3 a.m. (In normal times the regular daily peak audience is 66,000.)

In terms of share of viewing, Sky News outstripped Channel 5 on

Thursday and Friday 1 and 2 May accounting for 1.9 per cent and 2.4 per cent of all viewing in multi-channel homes compared with 1.4 per cent and 1.5 per cent on Channel 5. Throughout the night (Thursday/ Friday) there was a net flow of viewers from BBC and ITV coverage to Sky News. (For example, at 10.35 p.m. 54,000 viewers switched out of BBC 1 into Sky News, with another 63,000 switching in from other channels at 10.43. By definition the flow in the other direction was smaller.)

This increase in average viewing confirmed the general trend for Sky News audiences to increase at the time of major news events. A dramatic geometric increase could perhaps be foreseen for sudden and unexpected news such as the death of a public figure, terrorist disruption or an exciting trial. Such fidelity to a dedicated news channel also seems to hold for predictable events such as elections, perhaps bearing out one of our slogans 'there when you need us'. A similar trend is experienced on the US 24-hour news channel CNN (Cable News Network). Presumably because viewers realise that there are no programming obstacles to reporting events as they happen, dedicated channels appear to become addictive and habit-forming.

Sky News carries out no equivalent research on its substantial audience overseas, which is estimated at a maximum potential of 430 million in 70 countries. More than five hours of Sky News election night coverage was carried live on our sister channels Fox News in the United States and Foxtel in Australia, as well as on Star channels in Asia.

PROGRAMMING

While Sky News's potential universe of UK viewers is limited to cable and satellite receivers (roughly 25 per cent of TV reception points), the opt-in nature of viewing means that the audience is largely self-selecting, composed of youngish AB (professional and managerial) adults and 'opinion formers'. We worked on the assumption that our viewers require information and coverage first, spoon-feeding not at all. The channel is covered by the same regulations of due impartiality and balance as BBC and ITV stations; Sky is regulated by the ITC and subject to the RPA. (These are responsibilities we take seriously; we cancelled a publicity poster due to be launched coincidentally on the day the *Sun* came out for Tony Blair. Parodying the 'demon eyes' campaign with pictures of our presenters, its slogan in red writing was 'Time for a change? elect Sky News'. We did not want to lay ourselves open to mis-interpretation.)

From its inception in 1989, Sky News as a channel has been

committed to public interest broadcasting and to interesting the public (for example, we voluntarily carry party political and party election broadcasts). In domestic political coverage we regard ourselves as a 'television wire service'. We experience no problems of access to political events or interviewees – in the 'Media' *Guardian* of 17 February 1997 Alistair Campbell referred to 'the five big political broadcasters – Robin Oakley, John Sargeant, Mike Brunson, Elinor Goodman, Adam Boulton ...'.

For Sky News election coverage could be an organic part of our normal work rather than an add-on. We amalgamated our normal Westminster political newsroom with the main newsroom at Osterley for the duration of the campaign. These co-ordinated reporting coverage throughout Britain, including the two correspondent teams with each of the party leaders (each included one of our lobby correspondents). The political editor stayed in Westminster co-ordinating live coverage and liaison with party headquarters. We carried the morning news conferences by Labour, the Liberal Democrats and the Conservatives live – as well as any later events and a large selection of evening speeches. *Tonight*, my regular weekday 30-minute news analysis programme, was expanded to two (different) hour-long editions at 6 p.m. and 11 p.m. (*Tonight* carried extended interviews with each of the party leaders, who also took phone-calls from the public.)

The dominance of live events and rapidly up-dated news reports sent in by satellite in our news coverage has resulted in a transfer of a substantial part of the burden of editorial control from producers and the central newsdesk to the reporters and commentators themselves. Reporters are acutely aware of these extra responsibilities, which depend on a framework of trust and support from news executives, who have to make themselves immediately available for consultation at all times. They also have to monitor all output to ensure that the coverage can be constantly fine-tuned. Unlike the traditional news bulletins, our authority depends on our being prepared to update, modify and if necessary correct a constant stream of reporting. As an extra insurance we built frequent two-ways with our own experts into all our programming. I and Professor Michael Thrasher of the University of Plymouth were available to provide context at all times. For example, as a daily feature, Thrasher used his psephological expertise to explain why the politicians were concentrating on particular places.

OPERATIONS

All arrangements for programming were made unilaterally by Sky News. Operational coverage in the field necessitated co-operation with the parties and with the BBC and ITN. We took two of the highly priced places on each of the battle buses, but like other broadcasters kept the bulk of our reporting and technical teams moving around the country under their own steam. Sky News declined to join in the pool of satellite up-links shared by the BBC and ITV, since we felt it would be unable to satisfy the quantity and the timing of our needs. Instead we organised our own fleet of satellite trucks. However there was extensive pooling with the BBC and ITN for coverage of setpiece events; each of us took responsibility for the coverage and broadcast of conferences and live injects from one of the party headquarters. Similar arrangements for shared multi-camera coverage were entered into at other events around the country.

So what impact did these different constraints and emphases have on Sky News's coverage of the 1997 election campaign?

MORNING CONFERENCES

The political parties can be congratulated on the morning conferences during the campaign. In spite of their obvious desire to set their own agenda, all of them laid themselves open to the questions and issues which journalists wanted to raise. In Labour's case this was a substantial improvement on their performance in 1992, when spin control was perhaps a less mature science and there were frequent crude attempts to exclude questions and questioners.

In 1997, I was one of the group of television reporters called at practically every news conference. This did result in an embarrassing moment at Labour's manifesto launch, when Tony Blair called me by name while looking to the opposite corner of the giant ballroom at the Institute of Civil Engineers. In his defence it should be said that he knew I was there because he had just given a private pre-launch briefing to Michael Brunson, Robin Oakley, Elinor Goodman and me. There was much criticism of the so-called 'boys' club' of regular questioners by the newspaper feature writers visiting to write colour on the election. I make no apology; I see it as my job to ask questions and have stood on many doorsteps where print journalists have hung back, waiting for the 'electronics to do the business'.

By and large we are skilled questioners who see it as our job to raise the issues of the day. And we weren't even a boys' club – it was an intervention from Elinor Goodman that sparked John Major's 'don't bind my hands' outpouring. One of the most effective techniques can be for questioners to probe the same area repeatedly, and in 1997 there did seem to be a greater willingness among the journalists to build on colleagues' questions. This was the first time Sky News broadcast the morning conferences in their entirety, but by doing so, we gave viewers one of the best possible bases on which to formulate their opinions about the parties and their policies.

SOUNDBITES AND SPIN DOCTORS

There has been much discussion of the use of spin doctors during the campaign. But outrage can be overdone; I can see no problem with the increasingly professional presentation of policy by the parties. I regarded it as part of my job to have frequent contact each day with advisors and, yes, I even found them 'helpful' in clarifying the positions of their political masters. However, this does not mean that I was blind to their interests being different from mine. Experience reveals who can be trusted and which spokespeople reflect the views of the hierarchy and which don't; reading mood can be as important as content. What is more, we have our own chance to spin the spin doctors, who closely monitor the concerns of the commentators, often responding privately. In 1997 Labour's machine took this a step further, both measuring the specific responses of reporters against general profiles of them which they had built up privately and playing the work of different television journalists to their focus groups to help decide future media strategy.

The 'downside' of this relationship is the possibility of favouritism and of threats. I felt the brunt of this from both sides myself on one particular campaigning day. As part of its so called 'fifth term' strategy to prevent voters switching back to the Tories at the last moment, Labour were pushing a headline that the Conservatives would abolish the state old-age pension. From phone calls, letters and conversations I was aware that this had struck a raw nerve with the public. I also felt that it was a defining moment in the election, since many voters seemed ready to accept Labour's bold claims, ignoring Tory protestations that a Labour government would also radically overhaul the benefits system.

At the conferences I questioned both Tony Blair and John Major bluntly about their pension policy and their presentation of it; afterwards both interventions were met with full rebuttals in private. The suggestion to Blair that his was a 'pathetic scare tactic', resulted in a frank exchange of views with Alistair Campbell, David Hill and Peter Mandelson. The response from the Tories was even firmer. I suggested to Major that Peter Lilley's trailed reforms had opened the party to attack – and raised with him Labour counter-claims that Tory campaigners were using the underhand tactic of 'push-polling' (where a party provides negative information about opponents, then asks a question to elicit a response favourable to their side). Major's 'Adam, I never expected that from you', was followed by detailed clarification from

Danny Finkelstein, and later in the morning Peter Lilley phoned from his tour in Bristol to make sure that I understood his policy.

Most serious of all, a senior Cabinet minister in the campaign team suggested to me after the election that that question had permanently damaged my relations with the Major camp. Much of this can probably be put down to the heat of political battle, but this was merely an extreme example of a daily pattern of on and off the record exchanges between campaigners and journalists. Anecdotally, one could say that television and politicians are involved in mutual backscratching.

Dealing with such spin reporters at Sky had one significant advantage over many of our colleagues; it was firmly established with the parties that there was no point in going over our heads. Extended executive hierarchies can lay broadcasting organisations open to such pressures. I am profoundly grateful that my chief executive Sam Chisholm left distinguished complainants in no doubt that they should sort our their differences not with him, but with Nick Pollard, the head of Sky News, and myself. Nick Pollard's idea of setting up an open log of spin complaints proved to be a very effective prophylactic.

There has been much hand-wringing about the 'Americanisation' of British election coverage. While this may be a blow to the self-esteem of certain broadcasters, is democracy being damaged? Television journalists should perhaps adapt themselves to changing times. For the second election running, this was a campaign in which extended interviews with the leading politicians failed to contribute significantly to developing the sum of public knowledge. Perhaps that is because the fight is fairer, with politicians more skilled in the techniques of television and radio, especially in prevarication. Political parties have become more skilled in distilling their message and sticking to the line. Perhaps this means that horizons are narrowed – but doesn't it also mean that they will be held more bindingly to their pledges? Don't such messages help the not-so-enthralled voter to make a choice? And doesn't such presentation also bring about uncalculated revelations? Don't the differing public reactions to Labour's attacks over 'Jennifer's ear' and pensions encapsulate the different outcomes in 1992 and 1997?

DEBATES

Viewer involvement and public access were fashionable buzzwords in 1997 for television companies concerned that the general public were jaded by conventional political coverage. With live coverage, debates and the use of phone-ins already built into our election programming, such concerns came as no surprise to us at Sky News. We were the only network to go to Birmingham, Belfast and Edinburgh to present audience discussions with local party leaders in a national context.

And yet, all of us in television news must accept that we failed to deliver perhaps the greatest political event in television history, even though Major, Blair and Ashdown had all agreed in principle to a live debate. This is not the place to go over the ins and outs of the negotiations from which Sky News was, in any case, mostly excluded. But for the future it is worth noting that the competing interests of individual companies obstructed a considered and common approach on behalf of British television news which probably could have secured the prize.

Because Sky News is not universally available, Sam Chisholm stated years in advance that we would not bid to stage any leaders' debate exclusively. Following the rekindling of the debate by John Major in March 1997, Nick Pollard, the head of Sky News, contacted the BBC and ITN, offering our assistance in staging debates on a pooled, general access basis. We cited the success of the US Presidential Debates Commission in securing debates in every presidential election since its foundation. The BBC and ITN effectively rejected our proposals, choosing to engage in their own secret and ultimately fruitless talks.

Subsequent discussions have revealed that concerns to secure the debates in the public interest were significantly hampered by the television companies' private calculations. The BBC was anxious to be in the driving seat for the debates to justify its claim to be the public service broadcaster par excellence. ITV needed to secure an exclusive debate of its own if the network were to provide peak-time space for its transmission. Both attitudes were more suited to the broadcasting of the 1960s and 1970s than to today's multi-channel television and radio environment. Instead of facing up to a clear statement from the television industry of how and why debates should take place, politicians found themselves locked in intricate lobbying by different companies at the very time when they were trying to run national election campaigns. They can scarcely be blamed for failing to agree to the BBC's and ITN's approaches.

This recipe for failure seems set to be assembled again (with Prime Minister Blair likely to be much more reluctant) unless individual companies behave maturely and come together well in advance of the next election to table common proposals, which would be likely to prove an offer politicians would be unable to refuse.

ELECTION LAW

Any intelligent television journalist can work within the constraints of due impartiality and balance. In fact, for me, they are a major reason for choosing a career in broadcasting rather than print. However, the technicalities of the RPA are now a clear impediment to good television journalism. In particular, the ban on constituency coverage until nominations close, and the effective power to veto coverage handed to individual non-cooperative candidates, is depriving viewers of a whole dimension of local, constituency-based coverage. It is ridiculous that television and radio, covered by an over-arching obligation to fairness, are prevented from reporting on constituency races while local papers can effectively turn themselves into bonus literature for favoured candidates. At a national level these regulations make it all but impossible to focus on a balanced cross-section of candidates in any discussion of issues. The laws leave television with little option but to concentrate on leaders and national figures, however much this may be lamented.

CONCLUSIONS

In future, more and more of the public are going to get their election news from Sky News and stations like it. Already academic analysis of BBC and ITN election output is focused on only a small portion of the media battlefield where politicians are now conducting their campaigns. From party leaders down, they devote much of their energies to 'secondary outlets' in the knowledge that many voters are already opting out of conventional national media news coverage without ceasing to consume print, television and radio. So far Sky News and other new generation channels have willingly accepted and developed the public service responsibilities passed on from the BBC and through ITV.

But the expansion of media for political communication is not going to end here. The rapid development of political on-line services, the imminent multiplication of digital channels and the systemic convergence of electronic media will all mean that the public will be getting political information on-screen from many sources other than conventional television stations. Already party web-sites, 24-hour television and radio news channels, and local and cable broadcast services mean that the totality of election broadcasting is beginning to match the diversity of print. By the next general election party web-sites could effectively be party political channels outside the reach of current legislation. Even with Sky News's voluntary decision to broadcast party election broadcasts, viewers can already watch television around the clock without seeing one. Where does this leave the legislators' strictures for fairness and balance? Should PEBs be turned into commercial-trailer-length bites carried by compulsion on all channels? Perhaps Lord Neill's inquiry can start to confront some of these questions.

More importantly still, what about the growing number of voters likely to opt out of political coverage, failing to exercise their civic responsibility as some would see it? More people will switch to channels like Sky News, and there will be more pressure to rein back political coverage on conventional terrestrial channels, which in any case will each have a diminishing share of the total audience. It will no longer be possible to force the bulk of the electorate to tune in, thanks to freedom of choice and technological innovation.

Politicians, journalists and academics have not yet even begun to suspend current prejudices and predilections, as a necessary first step to addressing these issues. For Sky News, covering the substance and the context of electioneering and satisfying viewers will almost be the easy part.

14

The Debate that Never Happened: Television and the Party Leaders, 1997

RICHARD TAIT

The 1997 general election set a number of records – the biggest swing to Labour, the largest number of Liberal Democrat MPs elected for 70 years, the disappearance of Conservative MPs in Wales and Scotland. But it also set records of another sort, which should concern anyone with an interest in the health of British democracy.

Despite, or because of, a six-week campaign, the turnout of 71.6 per cent was the lowest for 60 years, and despite, or because of, more extensive television coverage of the campaign than ever before, the audience, and that means the voters, showed less interest in the election than the politicians expected. A survey of 4,000 viewers by the commercial television regulator, the Independent Television Commission (ITC), found that four out of ten viewers said they actively avoided the coverage by changing channels or switching off their sets.[1]

Ironically, it was also an election where the broadcasters came closer than at any time in the history of television to persuading the party leaders to take part in a series of debates which could have done something to both increase public interest and improve turnout.

In 1992 I argued that the decline in television audiences for election coverage was likely to happen and also highlighted the pressures politicians put on television coverage of the election.[2]

Some of the problems I identified in 1992 have, if anything, got worse rather than better. The vast investment in instant rebuttal computers has reinforced the parties' attachment to sound-bite politics.[3] The fragmentation of the television audience with the growth of satellite and cable has continued to erode the audience share of those television channels which offer public-service programmes such as news and current affairs.

In part, the audience avoided politics on television because the expansion of multi-channel television made it easier for viewers to escape from coverage of the election. On the election night itself, a third of the total audience preferred entertainment, films and sport to the election night programmes of the BBC, ITV and Sky.

It is in this context that the failure of the parties to agree to a series of television leaders' debates must be seen as a wasted opportunity of epic proportions. The broadcasters believed that the first ever leaders' debates would have attracted vast audiences – 15 to 20 million people on a Sunday evening at the height of the campaign. Many of those viewers would have been voters who had hitherto paid little attention to the campaign. The debates would have given the campaign a focus – a clear point where important policy issues which had been raised in the daily coverage would be debated face to face by the party leaders. The fact that the campaign would provide the raw material for the debates would also have added to viewer interest in the daily coverage.[4]

Instead, the failure of the negotiations and their aftermath deprived the public – and the politicians – of a really valuable event. The rows about the terms, the name calling and recriminations and the arrival on the scene of the Tory 'chicken' followed by a menagerie of other silly animals ensured that, far from enhancing the public's interest in politics and politicians, the reputations of both were further damaged and diminished.

What I propose to do in this chapter is to analyse why the debate did not take place. As one of the negotiators who tried on behalf of ITV to find an acceptable formula for the debate my conclusions are based on both my own private contacts and my discussions with colleagues such as Nigel Dacre, Editor of ITN's news on ITV, and Marion Bowman, the Deputy Controller of Factual Programmes at ITV, about their experiences in the formal negotiations. I cannot speak for the BBC, who were engaged in a parallel process but my impression is that their experience was very similar to ours.

The story of the debate that never happened is an essential case study for those who wish to understand what is wrong with the current relationship between the politicians, the broadcasters and the public. As someone who believes it is in the public interest for that relationship to be radically reformed, I will also draw some conclusions and recommendations as to how to avoid a similar result when the next general election is called.

There was nothing unusual about the initial sparring ahead of the 1997 general election. Peter Mandelson, Labour's campaign manager, told the Westminster Media Forum in November 1996, 'If we get a "yes" from Number Ten we should be ready to move.'[5]

The broadcasters, notably the BBC and ITN, had been in informal discussions with the parties about the possibility of leaders' debates from the autumn of 1996. I think it is fair to say we were not sanguine about the likelihood of such debates taking place. The form had been pretty well established for nearly 40 years – the broadcasters propose a leaders' debate and the incumbent prime minister says no. The argument was usually that the prime minister should not give a national platform to his or her opponent which might undermine the prestige of premiership. The only exception to that rule was in 1979.

What made 1997 different was that by January it was clear that John Major was seriously considering whether to trade that aura of incumbency for the chance to get to grips with his main opponent at length on the main policy issues of the election – what he called 'a proper, significant detailed debate on the issues'. It was clear that the Conservative strategists were not unanimous that this was the right approach, and that ambiguity was to play an important role in the final failure to reach agreement, but it was the most positive response from 10 Downing Street for nearly 20 years. Both the BBC and ITN therefore did not waste much time in approaching the three main party leaders to see if a debate or series of debates could be agreed.

As far as ITN was concerned, we were clear that this was a debate which should be carried on the channel which could offer the biggest possible audience – ITV, for which ITN is the news supplier. ITV asked ITN and London Weekend Television to produce the proposed programmes, and the three organisations set up a steering group to monitor the negotiations, keep our regulator, the ITC, informed, and, we hoped, see the project through to a successful conclusion.

From the start we were very aware of the difficulties involved. The parties were not prepared to discuss the issues around a table. Initially they were anxious to keep secret the fact that negotiations were even taking place. We made it a principle to deal with the three main parties simultaneously and on an equal basis.

However, from the start of the negotiations it proved very hard to get all three parties to move at the same pace, and this, together with the fact that the election was now imminent, put the whole venture under time pressures which would have required goodwill, flexibility and a willingness to compromise on the part of the three parties to ensure agreement in time. In the event, all three qualities proved to be in short supply. The leaders' debates were to fall victim to a culture of political intervention in the smallest details of television coverage.

In 1992 I drew attention to the tendency of political parties to set unfair preconditions to participation in studio discussions and debate. In the period since, these attempts, if anything, got worse.

One incident from the 1997 election campaign may help illustrate the problem of parties getting involved in the detail of programme makers' plans to an unhealthy degree. *Channel Four News* had invited the then Chancellor of the Exchequer, Kenneth Clarke, and his then shadow, Gordon Brown, to debate the economy live. Clarke was in Nottingham. His minders said he would debate with Gordon Brown as long as Brown was not present in the studio and next to Jon Snow, which they thought would give Brown an unfair advantage. *Channel Four News* said that should not be a problem since the Shadow Chancellor, on previous form, was likely to be too busy to leave his Millbank campaign headquarters for ITN's main studio.

The team was confident that he would want to be interviewed at ITN's Westminster studios nearby. However, whether by accident or design, Gordon Brown's minders decided on this occasion that the Shadow Chancellor *could* come to ITN, and rejected indignantly any suggestion that they should both be interviewed at remotes. The debate collapsed and each side blamed the other and complained about what they saw as ITN's appalling behaviour.

There are a couple of points about this sorry incident which I believe are relevant to an understanding of why the leaders' debates never happened. The first and most important issue is that no-one outside the hothouse which politicians and broadcasters inhabit would have the slightest idea what the row was about. The second is that the result was that a debate between Clarke and Brown, two of the most confident and affable media performers in British politics, did not take place. An intelligent interested audience was deprived of the chance to hear them debate some of the central issues of the campaign because of a trivial dispute about studio arrangements.

The same culture affected the negotiations over the leaders' debates. We got hints that two of our proposed presenters, Sue Lawley and Jonathan Dimbleby, might pose problems for one or other of the leaders. We responded that they were part of ITV's election night team and not negotiable. All three parties wanted discussions on the set and style of the programme – one even wanted to have the right to give its detailed agreement on podium style and height. The parties seemed on occasions to regard the negotiations as almost an extension of inter-party warfare and accused us, whenever we proposed something they did not like, of favouring their opponents.

It rapidly became clear that there were also at least two serious obstacles to agreement: the role of the Liberal Democrats and whether there should be a studio audience. Liberal Democrat participation in the debate meant that one of the more archaic rules governing the broadcasting of politics during elections made its unwelcome appearance as a hindrance to agreement. The 5–5–4 rule is a convention which allocates the time given to each of the three main UK parties in election coverage on the basis of the allocation of party electoral broadcasts.

It resulted in the practice known as 'stopwatching', whereby television news and current affairs programmes judged the balance of their coverage by counting the exact number of minutes and seconds of coverage.[6] In 1992, ITN, with the support of the ITC, abandoned the use of the stopwatch in news, though not in current affairs.

The leaders' debates were clearly current affairs and not news, so the 5–5–4 rule applied.[7] This posed a problem to the producers, who wanted both to include Paddy Ashdown in the programme *and* to give a substantial amount of time to a head-to-head between John Major and Tony Blair.

The initial proposal which both we and the BBC came up with was to restrict the amount of three-way debate, to give a little under two-thirds of the time to a Major–Blair debate and give Ashdown the further opportunity to comment on the issues in a one-on-one interview which would take up most of the rest of the time. It solved the stopwatch problems and we thought it would produce a programme with the maximum argument between the two people most likely to become prime minister. In terms of a compelling programme with the capacity to engage a mass audience, it seemed an effective format.

We were conscious of how in some countries the leaders' debates had become formulaic and over controlled – at worst little better than a series of prearranged sound bites. We were also conscious of the debate going on in public and behind the scenes inside the parties, over whether taking part in television debates was a good idea – and if so, for whom?[8]

There was no question of the legality of our proposal – and no question of its not meeting ITV's regulatory obligations. Our advice was that it was up to the broadcasters how a debate programme was structured, so long as the party leaders all had a fair opportunity to put forward their policies. But the Liberal Democrats rejected it on the grounds that they wanted more interaction for Paddy Ashdown, and after a delay were backed in their rejection of the format by the Labour Party. So we set about trying to find ways in which the format could be adjusted to meet their objections.

The Labour Party had initially appeared not to take the prospect of the Conservatives agreeing to a debate too seriously; they tended – or claimed – to see the floating of the possibility of a debate as a tactical ploy by the Conservatives to distract the electorate from more important issues – notably sleaze.

In the early negotiations they focused largely on the issue of the involvement of an audience. The Conservatives had originally argued that they did not want an audience, citing the recent ITV monarchy debate as a reason to avoid public participation. They argued that in this live programme on the future of the British monarchy, the audience had got out of control and had destroyed any chance of a serious debate on the complex issues at stake. The Conservatives did not want the image of an incumbent prime minister facing raucous or even abusive reactions from a hostile audience. We persuaded them to accept an invited audience, and then negotiations centred between both parties over whether the audience could ask questions. Eventually all the parties agreed to that as well.

As the weeks went on it seemed hard to get the parties to address the central issues with sufficient urgency. Of course, as the election loomed they had other pre-occupations – like planning the campaign. I remember one important meeting at a party's offices taking place in a corridor as all the conference rooms were full of election planners.

The Conservatives needed persuading that our original formula, let alone our revisions, would work and were clearly having an internal debate about whether the gamble was worthwhile. The Liberal Democrats were not prepared to show too much flexibility on Paddy Ashdown's role until they could see that the other two would compromise. The Labour Party took a long time to respond in detail.

However, on 18 March the BBC and ITV dispatched formal proposals to the parties and intensive negotiations began. On 20 March, with the longest general election campaign in recent years about to begin, Labour set out its response. Its letter to ITV was a detailed and thoughtful one, but it set out a preference for a very different programme compared with the one we had been proposing for the previous two months.

We wanted two 90-minute debates – Labour needed to be persuaded of the need for two and thought the length should be more like conventional current affairs programmes – which are usually less than an hour. We suggested four broad subject ranges over three hours – the economy, social issues, Europe and the constitution. Labour suggested adding transport, agriculture, employment and foreign affairs to what would perhaps be a single, shorter programme. But at least we knew where we stood.

For the final stage of the process the parties appointed official negotiators: Lord Holme for the Liberal Democrats, Lord Irvine for the Labour Party and Michael Dobbs for the Conservatives – three experienced and able operators. But if the parties had been busy in the run-up to the campaign, now the campaign had started two new factors entered the equation. First, the campaign planners were understandably reluctant to disrupt their carefully crafted schedule for debates that might not happen. Second, whether there should be debates and on what terms began to emerge as a campaign issue in its own right.[9] The parties would not have been human if they had not begun to adopt a twin-track approach – negotiating on behalf of their leaders, but also preparing an exit strategy which would ensure, if possible, that their party avoided blame if the debates did not go ahead.

It is a tribute to how effectively the ITN, ITV and BBC negotiators did their job that by the middle of the first week of the campaign most of the outstanding issues had been resolved. We had agreed or felt confident of agreement on the presenters, the role of the audience, the dates and times of the programmes. We had the real possibility of a series of debates. Our final proposal had sections where all three leaders debated and sections where John Major and Tony Blair debated head to head. It would have been a real debate, with each leader having the right to challenge the ideas and the policies of his opponents. There would have been a studio audience, who would ask some of the questions. The one issue which was proving obstinate was the exact allocation of time between the three-way debate and the Blair–Major debate.

Then on Thursday 27 March Labour set a deadline of the end of that day for reaching agreement – the Conservatives attacked them and the Tory chicken was launched on its short political career. Labour and the Liberal Democrats accused Michael Dobbs of offering a deal on time which they could accept and then, under pressure from above, reneging on it. Dobbs denied the charge. The negotiations were over, and although we and, much later in the campaign, *The Times* tried to revive them, the chance had passed.

It was wholly understandable that all three parties should want to discuss the detail of the proposal and suggest ways in which the programme could be improved. The parties were perfectly entitled to fight their case and press for whatever advantage they could from the terms of the debate. But the failure of the negotiations to achieve a sensible compromise suggests that each party pushed its particular interests too far.

The broadcasters too have lessons to learn from the failure to reach agreement. BBC and ITV were negotiating separately for the prize of being the network to broadcast the first debates. I am sure that we were right to do so on this occasion, and that the process benefited from having two broadcasting organisations each putting forward ideas to the parties. I think the politicians did try to play us off against one another, but our proposals were very similar and we knew that if the leaders ever were to agree to take part, the most likely arrangement, whatever was being said to us, would have been one debate on ITV and one on BBC1. There were informal contacts between the BBC and ITV, particularly in the latter stages of the process, and one possibility is that next time the broadcasters may try to mount a joint approach, although there are some complex obstacles in the way.

One obstacle is that commercial channels are very unlikely to want to hand over prime-time slots to a 90-minute programme that is being shown without commercial breaks on all channels. One idea which could have worked would have been for the BBC and ITV each to produce and host one debate, perhaps giving free access to any other broadcasters who wanted to carry it. That would have required agreement and co-ordination in format and subject area, but could have been achieved.

Some have suggested that the negotiations should be handed over to a neutral third party, who would set up the debates and hand them over to the broadcasters. This happens, for example, in the United States. While I would welcome the involvement of anyone with an interest in the issue to join in a public debate about how the leaders' debates should organised in the future, I think there are real regulatory and practical objections to handing over the negotiations and the production to a third party.

First, terrestrial television is closely regulated. Both the BBC and ITV are under the obligation to be impartial and fair in their coverage of public affairs, which means they need to assure themselves that any negotiations with the parties have been fair and meet their codes, guidelines and obligations. This is not something which can be carried out by third parties. Second, a third-party negotiator would run the risk of being stuck in the middle between the broadcasters and the politicians and a convenient scapegoat if things went wrong. At some point, the broadcasters and the politicians would have to sit down and reach agreement on the regulatory issues, which are also the issues which are of most concern to the politicians.

The experience of Peter Stothard, Editor of *The Times*, is instructive. Late in the campaign he offered to stage leaders' debates which his newspaper would sponsor and we could broadcast as a way of breaking the log jam. A few days later, having endured in concentrated form the arguments and disputes with which some of us had lived for several months, he withdrew from the field. All the parties publicly welcomed his initiative – but they were not prepared to move from their existing positions.

In the aftermath, each party sought to blame the other – in particular, the Tories accused Labour of 'chickening out' and even some Labour supporters expressed disquiet.[10] Others pointed to parallels with 1979, when the then prime minister Jim Callaghan, behind in the polls, challenged Margaret Thatcher, the leader of the opposition ahead in the polls, to a debate and she declined. I think, however, it is simplistic to single out any of the parties for particular blame.

The simple truth about the debate that did not happen is that politicians left it far too late in the parliament to consider a new, and to them, worrying concept. All three parties did not want the debates enough to make the fairly minor concessions which would have allowed them to take place. Labour was already winning the election so perhaps did not think a debate had much value. The Conservatives and the Liberal Democrats disliked one another too much to make common cause to put any real pressure on Labour to agree to a format. Everyone was far more conscious of the potential for the debate to go wrong than of the case for taking part as a contribution to the democratic process. The broadcasters failed to convince the politicians that the public interest would have been served by their taking part despite their reservations about the format.

Broadcasters cannot make politicians do what they do not wish to do – in essence all we did was invite the three most influential figures in the 1997 general election to talk to one another about the issues which most affected the electorate.

If a great opportunity was wasted, at least we now have a base for the future. All three parties have agreed to the principle of participation in debates, although I suspect that the broadcasters will still have great difficulty, as in 1997, in persuading whoever is the front-runner going into the campaign to take the risk of agreeing to participate. I hope, rather than believe, that the politicians now realise that there is probably one last chance – the next election – to establish televised leaders' debates as a valuable and valued part of the campaign, before the fragmentation of the television audience makes it impossible to attract the 15–20 million people who would have watched political and television history being made on the nights of 20 and 27 April, had the politicians decided to take part.

NOTES

1 Jane Sancho-Aldridge, *Election '97: Viewers' Responses to the Television Coverage* (London: ITC, 1997).

2 Richard Tait, 'The Parties and Television', in Ivor Crewe and Brian Gosschalk (eds), *Political Communications: The General Election Campaign of 1992* (Cambridge: Cambridge University Press, 1995), pp. 59–64. For television audiences in 1997 see Richard Tait, 'Anatomy of a Switch Off', *Guardian*, 20 May 1997.

3 See Chapter 17 by Stephen Perkins, 'Regulations, the Media and the 1997 General Election: The ITC Perspective', in this volume.

4 See Chapter 12 by Jay Blumler and Michael Gurevitch, 'Change in the Air: Campaign Journalism at the BBC, 1997', in this volume.

5 Speech on 19 November 1996 to the Westminster Media Forum (an all-party group of MPs that meets regularly to discuss media issues). My colleague Stewart Purvis spoke at the same meeting and reported Mandelson's comments.
6 See Tait, 'The Parties and Television', pp. 59–62.
7 It is possible that the 5–5–4 rule might not necessarily have applied quite so rigidly – at one point in the negotiations the Liberal Democrats sounded prepared to trade time for concessions on structure. But the attitude of the parties did not encourage the broadcasters to suggest too much relaxation of the rule. Cf. Chapter 18 by Colin Munro, 'Legal Constraints, Real and Imagined', in this volume.
8 See Martin Walker, 'Good and Bad News for Major in American TV Debates', *Guardian*, 17 March 1997.
9 See Perkins, 'Regulations, Media and the Election'.
10 'Stand Up and Debate, Tony', *New Statesman*, 4 April 1997.

PART V:

THE REGULATION OF TELEVISION IN ELECTIONS

15

Debate on Section 93 of the Representation of the People Act In Favour: The Case for the Society for the Prevention of Cruelty to Candidates

AUSTIN MITCHELL

Let us be clear about why television journalists like Ivor Gaber want Section 93 of the 1983 Representation of the People Act repealed to take away the ability of candidates to veto coverage of their constituency by refusing to appear. It is not to help politicians or the people. The Unhappy Medians want to increase their own power and give themselves the ability to do what they want in the way that suits them. They say they will give us an impartial, insightful picture of the campaign and yet manage to make it more interesting and lively. 'Trust us' is their plea.

I don't. They are not impartial political scientists like the members of the Political Studies Association and myself; they are journalists, a much lower form of life. Their aim is not to give us a balanced, fair picture, but to maximise interest, create rows, highlight the quirky, generate internal argument within parties and generally to lever open with their electronic tin opener the united front parties need to display in election campaigns. Nor is it correct that repealing Section 93 will produce a bonanza of brilliant, analytical broadcasting which will grip the attention of the nation in the way election broadcasting does not do now. If the people aren't interested, it is because too much is crammed down their sets already. Adding new coverage of lunk-heads versus nonentities in safe seats, for instance, will not to create more interest.

The Unhappy Medians really want more power, and this is really another weapon in the long war between parties and the media which has been going on since the media smashed the silly old by-election coverage rules, adopted John Humphrys's harassment as an interviewing style, got themselves into parliament and then jazzed up coverage there.

The media have been winning the war for years. Their victory is symbolised by the massive mausoleum at 4 Millbank. Once television coverage of politics came from two studios in a basement bunker where politicians had to let themselves in and turn on lights and camera. Now there are half a dozen studios and as many more for sound in a massive media complex employing at least 200 of the brightest and the best. All of these want to justify their existence by getting more politics on television than anyone except a masochistic PPE (Politics, Philosophy and Economics) graduate could want. They have to expose political foibles, create rows, do down ministers and exploit any available sensation to provide the stories that will justify their numbers and salaries. Biting the hand that feeds them is their way of life. They've even created the College Green parliament as a much livelier battle-ground than the boring old palace across the street. They made media stars out of egomaniac Tory dissenters and shattered the precarious unity of John Major's Tory party. Now they want to do the same for Labour, a process we are resisting by threatening non-co-operation and playing so hard to get so that I've never known so many ministers so unwilling to come on television (apart from the pat-ball play of news interviews which are really statements with noises off) since Nero burned Rome.

Naturally the parties resent this growing media dominance. They have become much better at media management and have far more money to do it with. They are, therefore, anxious to ward off the huge new media clobbering machine with its growing power and particularly to keep it out of their own protected game preserve: the election campaign. Elections are crucial: a life and death war for power. The stakes are huge for parties and candidates. So they don't want to submit to the media dominance which is the norm elsewhere, and will resist anything which diminishes their power. Which is why both parties covertly set out to wreck the televised leader debates we so desperately need in this country. They had to show willing while behind the scenes they manoeuvred and made impossible conditions in order to avoid it, a process the media facilitated by stupidly failing to agree in advance on a common framework to be imposed on the parties as an offer they couldn't refuse.

The parties have been becoming much more skilled at campaign management, much of it copied from the United States, where the Clinton technique of taking the north for granted to concentrate on winning the south naturally appealed to a Labour party trying to do the same here. Australia was another influence, with the winning 1996 technique of making opposition invisible so there was nothing to distract from government and its failures. Our 1997 campaign is viewed, particularly by those who ran it, as brilliant. In fact, it was nervous, over-cautious and ritualistic and ended in disaster: a huge majority and nothing for them to do because the manifesto was minimalist.

Campaign managers, spin doctors, media advisers and pollsters are the new, self-made stars of politics. They like to present themselves as masterminds, managing events behind the scenes, even if much of their effort is devoted to building their own egos, helped by a credulous media, keener on covering them than the boring politicians they nominally work for. They view campaigns as a battle with rallies, sorties and constant offensives, using candidates as a karaoke chorus. The media are the enemy: uncontrollable, potentially destabilising, so they have to be kept at bay. Campaign managers are control freaks, aiming to smash, disrupt, wrongfoot and clobber the enemy. Candidates are the same on their smaller stage. To ask either to expose themselves to unprotected sex via whatever whims the media want to pursue is silly. The media's job is to relay their messages, not destabilise their game.

I admire Peter Mandelson as the Machiavelli of New Labour and Tony Blair's Tamagochi and agree with him on this issue, speaking from the more lowly point of view of the candidate. Indeed, the only thing that is different is that while campaign managers want to keep the media out, I am desperate to get them in. It is next to impossible for the average candidate to attract the media interest necessary to give elections life and interest. I have struggled for too many elections to get photographers, television journalists, even newspapers, to display any interest in Grimsby, its problems, its uniqueness, its campaign, its issues or the beauty, intelligence and stature of its candidates, particularly one of them.

If only media people were the prodigies of democratic education Ivor Gaber portrays them as being they would swarm to Grimsby. In fact, they follow fashions, cover only the glamorous, the fashionable and, I can add with increasing bitterness, the young, the female and the new. They are obsessed with the marginal seats, where the parties present them with a stultifyingly boring campaign of clones mouthing karaoke, all kept on song by tight discipline, rip'n'read scripts and instructions to 'stay on message'. No one comes to Grimsby. Except John Prescott, who flew over in a helicopter, and a BBC journalist who got off the train by mistake before he could go on to Cleethorpes.

Repeal of Section 93 of the RPA will make it easier for the electronic media to look at categories across the campaign: women candidates, gays, raving lunatics or clones. Yet they can, and do, do that already and anything more is a small gain for them compared with the major loss of power to candidates, particularly sitting members. We need the power of veto because it is our only one. The law may be clumsy and inefficient, and it is clearly frustrating for the media. Yet it permits a balance of terror which gives a candidate some say. Take the occasion in 1983 when I refused to appear on a BBC Radio Humberside round table discussion and phone-in with the other candidates because the BBC excluded Europe. This was an issue I felt strongly about, and one on which the other candidates all thought the same but knew little. I refused to appear. They sulkily wrote back suggesting it should go ahead with an empty chair which might have put in a more consistent and solid performance. I stuck to my guns. They climbed down. I clobbered two uninformed twerps on Europe with the help of a few carefully inspired callers, some speaking in Dr Strangelove terms.

The same goes for television. I want my brief moment of fame to be treated in a way which helps me not the media. That does not include being shouted at by any lunatic they care to select. The right of veto extends to all candidates, even the ones with no chance. I would be furious if one stopped me being covered when I want to be. Yet they have all paid their deposits and surely have a right to put their views if they want to, though it has often proved easy to persuade them to waive their rights. This happened in the Grimsby by-election, when I was desperate to appear on what was really a national campaign.

Candidates have all too little power. We are treated like clones. It is difficult to get anything onto the media. Television does not want us. Local radio takes us on sufferance for a few dutiful and carefully balanced appearances. The local press doles out column inches and would not allocate anything extra even if I ran naked through the streets of Grimsby or bit the Liberal Democrat. So you plough your lonely furrow and try to meet people who obstinately refuse to come out, attend meetings, or read literature even though it now contains more photos than words. It is an impossible job. Don't take away from us the one power we have got to disrupt the self-interested, even malevolent, plans of the media.

There is a case for revising the Representation of the People Act, particularly in respect of by-elections, which we try and treat as just another constituency when, in fact, they are a national campaign focused on one place and swamped by huge expenditures so extravagantly fiddled as to bring the law into disrepute. Yet once you start to change the Act you open up a whole can of worms and disturb a settlement which may be cumbersome, but does work. Media people may think election campaigns are for them. They feel contempt for the politicians who provide them with raw material they ritually abuse. They may want the law changed to make it easier to do this. Yet there is no head of steam behind the demand; indeed the public consider that too much time and attention is devoted to both politics and elections. More important, any change in the law would have to be agreed between parties and passed by Parliament, processes dominated by the politicians the Unhappy Medians want to humble. We're not keen to lose the one little bit of power we do have to put a spanner in their works.

16

Debate on Section 93 of the Representation of the People Act
The Case Against: Scrap It

IVOR GABER

I am speaking to this motion, not as an impartial academic observer with an interest in this area, which I like to think I am; nor as a harried television executive having to explain yet another breach of the regulations, which I am not; but as a humble political producer, which I was for *Channel Four News* during the last election and have been for BBC, ITN and Sky in previous elections. I shall not speak, at least not for long, on the grand themes of democracy and the people's right to know. I want to talk about the plain stupidity of the Representation of the People Act and how it not only fails to achieve what it intended to achieve but is anti-democratic and, perhaps worst of all, produces dull political programming, something which broadcasters fear and which impoverishes the political process.

The aim of Section 93 is to prevent any candidate from gaining an unfair advantage over any other candidate as a result of getting partial radio or television coverage on radio. Does it even succeed in that? Just try asking the hapless soul who had to represent Labour in Huntingdon last time round, or, for that matter, the Conservative candidate in Sedgefield.

However, let me begin by quoting the relevant clause. I have read this clause many many times and still find it opaque on an almost heroic scale.

93. (1) In relation to a parliamentary or local government election –
(a) pending such an election it shall not be lawful for any item about the constituency or electoral area to be broadcast from a television or other wireless transmitting station in the United kingdom if any of the persons who are for the time being candidates at the election takes part in the item and the broadcast is not made with his consent; and
(b) where an item about a constituency or electoral area is so broadcast pending such an election there, then if the broadcast either is made

before the latest time for delivery of nomination papers, or is made after that time but without the consent of any candidate remaining validly nominated, any person taking part in the item for the purpose of promoting or procuring his election shall be guilty of an illegal practice, unless the broadcast is so made without his consent. [152 words]

In English that means that first of all, during an election period, it is unlawful to broadcast a programme in which a candidate 'takes part', if the candidate does not consent. In other words, the candidate agrees to be interviewed, the candidate does not like the way the interview has gone so the candidate withdraws his consent for the entire item to appear. Fair enough, if you are the candidate! Secondly, there is a draconian ban on any such programmes being broadcast before nominations have closed. And once nominations have closed, it is illegal to broadcast a programme in which a candidate takes part, i.e. is interviewed, unless *all* the candidates either take part or agree, in writing, not to be part of the programme (fat chance).

That is the law; what does it mean in practice?

First, it affects journalists who work in local and regional television and radio far more drastically than it affects national broadcasters. Put simply, it means that if you want to do a broadcast about a particular constituency you can … as long as you interview *all* the candidates or *none*. Interviewing all the candidates is possible, as long as you can find them, but makes for less than riveting television. Moreover, the problem is getting worse. The number of candidates contesting elections is rising. In 1945 the average was fewer than three per constituency. In 1992 it was almost six and in 1997, with the advent of the Referendum and UK Independence parties, it was eight. So the answer is not to interview *all* candidates (although you are allowed to hear them talking, more of that later).

If a journalist does a general political report, but in a particular constituency, broadcasters try to avoid showing any posters urging people to vote for any of the local candidates (which explains why, when everyone else is putting up political posters, TV cameramen can often be seen taking them down … although frequently they forget, or there is no time, so posters do appear in shot and Section 93 is breached). Also they try not to film local candidates, if the report is not about his or her particular constituency – although this is not always possible, as we shall see.

In practical terms, this amounts to constituency reports in which broadcasters film candidates allegedly 'not taking part'. In other words, they are not formally interviewed (which is taking part), but as a producer I do go out with them 'on the 'doorstep' to 'overhear' their conversation with Joe and Josephine public – although here something very odd happens. When a party is doing well it is only too delighted to allow us to go out with them, but by some strange coincidence we always seem to end up in areas where voter after voter tells them how much they are looking forward to voting for them – this time this happened with all our Labour reports. Meanwhile the Conservatives tell journalists that their voters dislike speaking in front of the cameras – that old spiral of silence again – and so it would not be appropriate to film them on the hoof. But, they insist, broadcasters will get a good sense of the campaign by filming their candidate interacting with party workers. And if broadcasters then decline – they run away, literally.

In other words, the Act enables parties to exercise total control and makes it quite impossible for broadcasters to give a real account, in both words and pictures, of what is actually taking place on the ground.

There are other problems. When covering politics there are many ways in which newspapers are the better medium – ideas, back-stabbing and gossip do not make for good television – but in one important way the electronic media excel. Television enables the electorate to meet their candidates, to get to know them, to develop a feel for their personalities and for their ideas – to decide, in other words if they like them, if they trust them. Alas, Section 93 makes this impossible. That is because the words 'taking part' have been construed to mean 'no interviews'. We are forced to rely on other people to speak for the candidate. If, for example, television does a constituency report about a marginal seat, the parties on the ground can usually be relied on to offer one of their local bigwigs or even a smallerwig, like the assistant agent, or when really desperate a nearby MP who is not part of the main central campaigning team because he is too lowly or just too much of a loose cannon. Usually, however, the party's central media operations will have organised someone from their campaigning team to be available, someone 'prominent' who is not a candidate, such as an MEP. Ironically, parliamentary elections give MEPs far more publicity than they get at European elections.

More often than not, however, and for this the media are to blame, what is offered is the party leader making a flying visit. Posters can be removed but candidates cannot. Broadcasters find themselves in the ludicrous situation that they can speak to anyone about a constituency, except the candidates. And the anyone they speak to has usually been provided by the party's media machines, thus greatly increasing the power of those whose power requires no further increase.

There are wider effects. For example, the Act stops broadcasters doing a piece looking at women candidates, candidates from ethnic minorities, gay candidates and so on. This is because if broadcasters tried to include interviews with women, blacks, gays and so on they would either have to desist from making *any* reference to where the candidates were standing, which would be plain silly *or* interview all the candidates standing against them which would be plain impossible.

Perhaps the most telling incident arising from the idiocy of Section 93 came during the last election at Tatton. Could broadcasters do a constituency report about Tatton, interview the candidates, find out where they stood on various issues? Yes, if they had been prepared to interview all 10 candidates (eight of whom garnered a total of just 2.4 per cent of the vote). However, the Conservative candidate, whose name escapes me at the moment, would almost certainly have refused to take part and refuse to give his consent to the broadcast going ahead in his absence. So in fact the answer was no. The only significant coverage of that contest was the so-called battle of Tatton Heath when Christine Hamilton, spectacularly failing to understand Section 93, staged a confrontation with Martin Bell and proceeded to speak on behalf of her husband, MP Neil Hamilton, because, she said, the Act precluded him from speaking. It did not, although maybe that was just her excuse. It did not because the confrontation was a 'real' event staged in front of the cameras – no one did a one-to-one interview.

But if life under Section 93 is difficult for a national broadcaster, the situation is far worse for local television. If local television wants to do a constituency profile, something that should be the bread and butter of local coverage, they find it almost impossible to gain the necessary consents. Patrick Burns, a Midlands editor of the BBC, describes one aspect of the unequal struggle to try and track down a fringe candidate, who does not live in the constituency and has no recognisable address where he can be found: 'Perhaps the single most irritating recurring theme is the sheer amount of time and effort that skilled BBC journalists, and for that matter ILR and ITV journalists, have to spend chasing the invisible man or woman. Skilled journalists' scarce time would be better used actually preparing and telling the story of the election to the electorate.'

At local level there is also a temptation for an established high-profile sitting candidate to say: 'What's in it for me, sharing the limelight with people who are far less well known? I remain well-known if there is no programme; the others remain unknown. Why should I only have equal airtime and share the spotlight with unknowns?' There is a distinct suspicion that candidates, on occasions aided and abetted by the political parties, are tempted to take this line.

This issue was considered at a gathering, not dissimilar to this one, after the previous election. At the end of the debate one of the party's media managers who had listened to the deliberations was asked if he had any sympathy for the views of those who wanted to change the law. In his usual calming tone Peter Mandelson said:

> The law has got nothing to do with it. Problems arise because of the requirements and dictates of broadcasters. They ride rough-shod over politicians, campaigners and managers and employ various forms of 'hooligan' tactics [laughter] to make politicians and election campaigns do and perform as they require. I support legal ways of allowing managers or candidates or anyone, to withstand the pressures. My personal view is that it is in the nature of broadcasters to promote the view that they are hard done by, that their lives are miseries, that they are constrained and controlled by the law and by the political machines – and I just don't buy it.

I disagree. The panoply of formal and informal controls that govern broadcasters' political coverage outside elections and which require them to show 'due impartiality' are more than sufficient to ensure that their election coverage remains impartial. Section 93 is a hindrance to good political broadcasting and good democratic practice. I say, Mr Mandelson notwithstanding, scrap it.

17

Regulations, the Media and the 1997 General Election: The ITC Perspective

STEPHEN PERKINS

Twenty-seven small fragments of output – the party election broadcasts (PEBs) – and one small but deadly fragment of legislation – Section 93 of the 1983 Representation of the People Act (RPA) – generated virtually all the problems for the ITC during the 1997 general election. Many hundreds of hours of other coverage passed by pretty quietly, from our point of view. Nevertheless, I want to make a few observations about campaign coverage as a whole, our research on it, and the leaders' debate, before returning to those particular problem areas. I will also give some indications of where changes are being or should be made before next time.

There is no doubt that broadcasters had to work harder than ever before to engage the attention of viewers and voters at this election. A variety of factors were at work. First and most obviously, Labour's victory had been signalled from the start of and indeed long before the campaign itself. Unless opinion polls were entirely disregarded (and broadcasters did try, after getting their hands burnt in 1992) there did not appear to be much of a 'horse-race' to follow. Second, the sheer length of the campaign itself – six weeks in total – made it difficult to maintain public interest. Third, there was much greater scope for 'election avoidance' on television. Though some viewers might have doubted it, it was perfectly possible even on the four main terrestrial channels to avoid all election coverage. By April 1997, 25 per cent of homes had access to cable and satellite television, and Channel 5 also arrived on the scene early in the campaign. This was bound to affect audience sizes for election programmes, and it did (though that is not to imply there was no election coverage on the new channels). All this raises the question of how far there was a deeper level of disaffection with the political process, reflected for example in the reduced turnout. That question will be answered more in the groves of academe than the groves of broadcasting regulation. Suffice it to say that those who identify such alienation sometimes allege that broadcasting helps generate it. They refer to the condition known as 'Millbank syndrome', which afflicts politicians, spin-doctors and journalists alike, and leads them to assume that voters are as interested in their laddish games as they are themselves.

PROGRAMMES

Against this background, audiences for election programmes on commercial television held up reasonably well. Ratings for *News at Ten*, for example, were down seven per cent on the same period last year (although the BBC's greatly and nobly extended *Nine O'Clock News* fared rather less well). The quality held up pretty well too. It seems to me that policies played a greater part in this election than for some years past. Education, health and Europe came through quite strongly – not just taxation and sleaze. This was widely reflected in programming from Channel 4's discursive *Midnight Special* series, through the extended packages in *News at Ten*'s special report slot, to Channel 5's excellent *Minute Manifestos*. ITV's major peak-time contributions – *The ITV 500* – were also arranged around policy issues. Sky News devoted the most time to the election; apart from some very effective reporting, they were certainly the only ones offering live coverage on a Sunday of a Tony Blair education seminar in Milton Keynes. Sky also broadcast the only piece I saw on Mebyon Kernow, the Cornish independence party.[1]

On the debit side, and returning to the theme of Millbank syndrome, I would suggest there was too much, too near the top of too many bulletins, about the parties' tit-for-tat point scoring from the morning press conferences. Intriguingly, Alastair Campbell seemed to endorse that point.[2] I can also testify personally that it was possible to tire of the nightly reports from the Major/Blair/Ashdown battlebuses.

RESEARCH

Other viewers thought so too, according to the ITC's specially commissioned research.[3] Depressingly, but unsurprisingly, a half or more felt there was too much across all channels of nearly every aspect of coverage: party leaders, commentators, polls, press conferences, you name it. The only partial exception to this was party policies, where a significant minority (19 per cent) felt there was too little. However, even here, 65 per cent thought there was the right amount or too much. Four in ten actively avoided election programmes by switching over or switching off.

More encouragingly, levels of concern about unfairness or partiality were low. Such concern as existed was mainly in relation to the amount of airtime devoted to Plaid Cymru, the SNP, the Referendum Party and the Green Party. Between eight and ten per cent of ITV viewers believed these parties had too little coverage. The expectation among some viewers that coverage of these parties throughout the United Kingdom could match that of the government and official opposition was obviously unrealistic. In the ITC's view, the nationalist parties received a fair measure of coverage on the networks and much more, obviously, in the relevant ITV regions themselves. Other solutions – such as a *Scottish News at Ten* – may be found as devolution progresses. As for the smaller UK parties, they did not fail to get their message across on television. But we believe that the serious and significant political positions taken up by a number of these parties could merit more attention in future.

Overall, 56 per cent of viewers in the ITC research said coverage had given them what they wanted and 27 per cent disagreed.[4] Other factors influencing those who disagreed included negative campaigning (Millbank syndrome again?) and the lack of involvement of women in both the broadcasting and political roles. This echoes research published before the election by the Fawcett Society.[5] Women were less interested in the coverage generally. The young – notably first time voters – were also among the least interested. A particular policy area which viewers felt received insufficient treatment was the environment.

It seems that politicians have still not learned that scoring a hit off an opponent might not always be a great hit with viewers. As for broadcast journalists, perhaps just once in a while they could have hijacked a party press conference on to green issues rather than, say, sleaze. In particular, more thought should be given to making programmes relevant to women and the young. It would be in the interests of broadcasters and parties alike.

'DUE IMPARTIALITY'

Our research showing that viewers generally found election programmes fair and impartial was confirmed by the ITC's postbag, or rather the lack of one. The last *ITV 500* before election day attracted eight complaints, a Michael Brunson interview with Tony Blair got two, and a handful of other programmes one each. None was upheld by the ITC. We did not hear in this context from any of the parties. Interestingly, the Labour Party's well-publicised complaint to the ITC about a *News at Ten* interview with John Major in 1996 did *not* develop into a trend.[6]

The absence of 'impartiality' problems – at least as far as the main parties were concerned – vindicated the decision of ITN and other commercial broadcasters to 'go off the stopwatch', as in 1992. The stopwatch in this sense meant that coverage of parties in news and other programmes should be allocated in the ratio of party election broadcasts – down to the very last second.[7] This convention dated from a time when the extent of broadcast cross-examination of a politician might be to invite him to 'share his thoughts with the nation'. It failed to take account of the fact that, nowadays, not all journalistic exploration of a party's policies will necessarily count in that party's favour. Nowhere has the stopwatch principle ever appeared in legislation, or the ITC Programme Code. Broadcasters would still be advised to keep a watch going; they need to know what they have broadcast, and prevent the ratio going adrift by a matter of hours, rather than seconds. However, we believe that news journalism can properly and impartially be guided by news values. And we would not insist on observance down to the last second in other kinds of election programme. What the Broadcasting Act and the Programme Code do insist on is that for any 'major matter' (like an election) 'justice is done to a full range of significant views and per-spectives' over the period.[8] That, to us, is the best yardstick. Apart from PEBs and the RPA (see below), the Code places virtually no additional regulatory restraints specific to elections. This is in stark contrast to most other countries' systems.

THE LEADERS' DEBATE

In 1992 the ITC retained the former Independent Broadcasting Authority's role as 'publisher' of the terrestrial commercial channels. The ITC's role now is as licensor and post-hoc regulator. In other words, we do not get involved in the content of programmes before they go out (or, as the case may be, don't go out). However, with an event of considerable importance, such as a leaders' debate, it was perhaps inevitable that we would be called on to give guidance. It was the Liberal Democrats who first sought this from us. We felt the suggestion in some quarters of a simple 'head to head' between the leaders of the two largest parties was not on. Given the significance of such a debate, if it happened, it seemed to us almost inconceivable that the remainder of a broadcaster's campaign coverage could retrieve 'due impartiality' towards the third main UK party.[9] That was not to say that an invitation to the third party need be on the same terms as the other two. And in the event that a party declined a reasonable offer of participation this need not, in the ITC's view, prevent the programme going ahead.

The ITC was not party to the SNP's unsuccessful action in the Court of Sessions against STV and Grampian, although the SNP did raise the matter with us. The concerns of the SNP and Plaid Cymru were not, of course, what caused the leaders' debate to founder.[10] Nevertheless, if the debate or debates had been planned over a longer period, better proposals to ensure fairness to the nationalists could have been drawn up. That is one reason why we believe that work on a structure for leaders' debates at the next election should start now. The 1997 debates were a huge missed opportunity – most of all for viewers and voters.

PARTY ELECTION BROADCASTS

Most broadcasters would grudgingly accept that a measure of unmediated access to the airwaves by parties is a necessary thing during an election, if less so at other times. And attractive as political advertising might be to commercial channels' bottom lines, most broadcasters also agree that if PEBs help to ward off demands for paid commercials, that is a good thing. The system for the allocation of PEBs dates back many decades (with one significant difference this time, explained below). Nevertheless, the 1997 general election saw the ITC and the BBC taken to court in a dispute over allocation, while issues of content in other PEBs led to unprecedented problems.

The principles of allocation are the same for all the terrestrial networks (cable and satellite channels are not required to take PEBs, although Sky News did so voluntarily). In 1997, as in previous elections, the government and official opposition received five each, the Liberal Democrats, SNP and Plaid Cymru four, three and two respectively. The ITC settled a dispute in the SNP's favour, requiring Channels 4 and 5 to take the nationalist parties' broadcasts. The rules stated that any other party fielding 50 or more candidates would also get one broadcast. Eight 'minor' parties qualified in this way: an unprecedented number. The Pro-Life Alliance, British National, Liberal and Socialist Labour parties all put up just over 50 candidates (the minimum entry cost being 50 deposits of £500, a total of £25,000). The Greens achieved nearer 100, UK Independence and Natural Law nearly 200 each, while the Referendum Party was way out in front with 547. The BBC, ITV, Channel 4 and Channel 5 proposed to award all these parties one broadcast each, according to the rules. The Referendum Party then complained to the BBC, and about the commercial channels' decision to the ITC. The ITC upheld the broadcasters' decision, so the Referendum Party sought judicial review of the BBC and us.

The Referendum Party lost. The court decided that neither the ITC nor BBC decision had been irrational or procedurally flawed. The ITC's principal argument was that, although fielding greatly in excess of 50 candidates might be one factor in favour of a party receiving more than one broadcast, it was not sufficient on its own. The court also heard that, unlike previous elections, the Committee on Party Political Broadcasting had played no part whatever in the allocation decisions. This Committee consisted of representatives of the broadcasters, and of the parties in the House of Commons (apart from the Northern Ireland ones). Hitherto, allocation decisions had been agreed with the parties on the Committee, the broadcasters deciding on their own initiative only in the event of disagreement. The Committee had not met since 1983 and liaison had taken place through 'the usual channels'. However, as a result of an initiative by the BBC, the arrangement had been dispensed with for 1997 and the broadcasters had drawn up the allocation.[11] The Referendum Party was therefore unable to sustain its separate arguments that the involvement of the Committee had been improper, and that its MP Sir George Gardiner had been improperly excluded from that Committee's deliberations (when there had not been any). It is a small triumph for transparency, and dare I say for democracy, that broadcasters will now take these decisions entirely independently of politicians.

Just as with allocation, the content of PEBs was far from trouble-free. Minor flurries included a Labour broadcast featuring the chairman of Granada Group, Gerry Robinson. This had to be followed in the northwest of England by an announcement pointing out that Robinson's views were not those of Granada Television. Thirteen viewers complained to us about a Conservative broadcast envisaging a bleak future under Labour. The ITC turned down the complaints, on the grounds that this was 'no more than an imaginary, if partisan, look into the future', and therefore the kind of proposition PEBs were entitled to put.[12] However, much more serious issues arose over the content of PEBs and the extent to which broadcasters are responsible for that content.

Individual PEBs are, rather obviously, not expected to be 'duly impartial'. Impartiality is achieved across the whole series. Alleged 'facts', notably statistics, may be deployed in a highly partisan way, and viewers generally understand and expect that. The most difficult issues arise over 'taste and decency'. The Pro-Life Alliance and BNP broadcasts were prime examples of this.

Broadcasters including the BBC decided collectively that images in the Pro-Life Alliance broadcast were unacceptable for transmission at any time. These images, I understand it, showed dead foetuses. The Alliance submitted a revised version, with the images blurred beyond recognition. This was broadcast. Thirty-two complaints either objected to censorship *or* felt the broadcast even as re-edited had offended against taste and decency. The ITC replied to complainants that the broadcasters had succeeded in bringing the PEB into line with the Programme Code, and that we would not censure our licensees for the measures they had taken to achieve this.[13]

The decision to 'censor' part of a PEB is not one to be taken lightly, but it seems to have been abundantly clear that the Pro-Life broadcast could not be transmitted in its initial form, and that broadcasters had responsibilities to prevent it from so being. The BNP (British National Party) broadcast called for much more difficult and finer judgements to be made. This is perhaps demonstrated by the fact that the BBC and commercial broadcasters arrived at different decisions. Small but important changes required by the latter included removal of shots of identifiable black people who had not given consent to appearing, and of shots of a specific, named, multi-racial school in east London. Again, as with the Pro-Life Alliance, it is worth stressing that only visual images were involved, and the spoken message was not edited.

Nevertheless, 84 complaints about the BNP's PEB were received. Many objected to the BNP's being allowed a broadcast at all. Others objected to specific content, in particular a sequence that queried whether a multi-racial society was 'what our war heroes fought for' and a reference to BNP policy to 'stop immigration and help immigrants return home'. The ITC concluded that broadcasters had acted responsibly and well, and that the PEB had not breached the Code. The most offensive images had been removed, and the party's policy on immigration had been communicated briefly and without strident language.[14]

This outcome was, of course, a pragmatic compromise, and will not have satisfied everyone by any means. The other alternatives would have been worse. Refusing access to a political party on principle, rather than because of the content of its broadcast, would be in conflict with basic democratic rights. At the other extreme, unmitigated freedom for parties could lead to an entirely unacceptable level of offence. Intervention by broadcasters to meet taste and decency concerns runs the risk that a party's views may be sanitised, and therefore become more acceptable. But that is the least problematic alternative. The ITC has since introduced a revised Code, which makes clearer where broadcasters' responsibilities begin and end.

THE REPRESENTATION OF THE PEOPLE ACT, SECTION 93

My remarks about the RPA will be brief. It is true that the scope of Section 93 is often exaggerated by broadcasters, and a great deal of ITC time was spent giving guidance on what was and was not possible. I make no complaint about that – it is our job. Nevertheless, giving candidates the right of veto over constituency coverage in which any other candidate takes part remained a major obstacle to free reporting. It was also grossly unfair to those candidates who were willing to take part. It bit on coverage of communities, of geographical and other kinds. Regional ITV companies ran extensive and by and large excellent coverage. But local broadcasters were inhibited from addressing many local topics effectively: the row over plans for a new hospital in Norwich, where two candidates were involved; a constituency in Northampton not covered because a sitting MP would only discuss one policy issue and refused to speak on others; Westcountry Television unable to examine the issues arising from Labour's local 'women-only' candidates, because it would have involved interviewing 20 other candidates as well. The Asian viewers' channel Zee TV ran a good deal of election programming, including interviews with many Asian candidates of various parties. It was absurd that they were unable even to mention the constituencies involved.

The ITC believes that broadcasters can be trusted to provide constituency coverage that is fair to all candidates, without the RPA. In the event that the test of 'due impartiality' was failed, sanctions are available to the ITC to deal with it. The BBC has similar responsibilities. Renewed attempts are being made to have Section 93 reformed or repealed, and we are happy to join with broadcasters in these.

NOTES

1 See Chapter 13 by Adam Boulton, 'Television and the 1997 Election Campaign: A View from Sky News', in this volume.
2 Reported in the *Independent*, 14 April 1997.
3 Jane Sancho-Aldridge, *Election '97: Viewers' Responses to the Television Coverage* (London: ITC, 1997), pp. 20–1.
4 Sancho-Aldridge, *Election '97*, p. 45.
5 Helen Garner, *Watching Women – Election 1997* (London: Fawcett Society, 1997).
6 The ITC felt Trevor McDonald's interview with John Major had been 'a little too friendly and relaxed for a major setpiece interview with a party leader', but that it had not been in formal breach of the Programme Code. See *Programme Complaints and Interventions Report* (ITC, September 1996), p. 3.
7 See Richard Tait, 'The Parties and Television', in Ivor Crewe and Brian Gosschalk (eds), *Political Communications: The General Election Campaign of 1992* (Cambridge: Cambridge University Press, 1995), pp. 59–60.
8 *The ITC Programme Code* (ITC, 1995), p. 15.
9 See also Chapter 18 by Colin Munro, 'Legal Constraints, Real and Imagined', in this volume.
10 See Chapter 14 by Richard Tait, 'The Debate that Never Happened', in this volume.

11 See also Munro, 'Legal Constraints'.
12 *Programme Complaints and Interventions Report* (London: ITC, April 1997), p. 2.
13 *Programme Complaints and Interventions Report* (London: ITC, May 1997), p. 5.
14 *Programme Complaints and Interventions Report*, pp. 3–4.

18

Legal Constraints, Real and Imagined

COLIN MUNRO

Elections, including general elections, are held in the shadow of the legal rules which apply, at least some of which are designed to encourage the fairness of the contest. In the United Kingdom, in the absence of a written constitution, the legal rules have to be gathered eclectically from a mixture of sources in legislation, principally on electoral law or concerning the media.

From a position of some detachment, one is struck by the very different attitudes of different players to such constraints as are provided by the law. Politicians, whose experience will often extend to periods out of office, are apt to see some merit in rules promoting, to a degree, the fairness of contests. Journalists and programme makers, by contrast, seem to feel that legal requirements hang over them like an incubus, and impede their ability to report elections properly.

Some of the darker suspicions entertained by broadcasting staff can be shown to be misplaced. However, whether their apprehensions are real or illusory, it cannot be denied that legal issues and litigation were recurrent themes in the 1997 election campaign.

As regards litigation, it is arguable that the groundwork was laid by a decision some two years before.[1] In April 1995, there were elections for the new local authorities across Scotland. The BBC in London had decided to broadcast a lengthy interview with the Conservative prime minister on a *Panorama* programme, which was to be screened in Scotland as well as elsewhere, three days before polling day. Despite warnings from Scotland, the Corporation persisted in their intention, perhaps insensitively and certainly imprudently. When aggrieved politicians from two other parties raised a challenge, Court of Session judges were sufficiently persuaded of an injustice to grant interim interdict to prevent the interview from being shown in Scotland before polling day.

Whether that decision was legally right or wrong, the litigants' success was always likely to encourage other challenges in the courts, especially in an era when parties and pressure groups increasingly regard legal actions and threats as tactical weapons.[2] Besides, the corpus of broadcasting law had been revised in 1990 and 1996, with one of the express aims being to clarify and strengthen the requirement of impartiality.

It may, therefore, be readily understood why litigation featured prominently in the 1997 general election. The focus for most of this litigation was broadcasting law, although some other aspects of electoral law and arrangements, including boundary changes and candidacy rules, provoked challenges as well.

ELECTIONS AND MEDIA LAW

The emphasis within litigation attests to the perceived importance of broadcasting, as does the regulatory framework within which it operates.[3] By contrast, the print media are virtually unregulated. Newspapers are free to editorialise, and they are under no legal obligation to be fair or balanced in their coverage. Our conception of the freedom of the press, rightly or wrongly, is one which holds that a newspaper may be as politically biased as it (or its proprietor) chooses. This view is not only accepted so far as the law is concerned, but also within the system of self-regulation. The Press Complaints Commission, like its predecessor the Press Council, regularly 'upholds the right of the press to be partisan on matters of public policy'.[4]

With broadcasting, the case is altered. Broadcasting, like the press, is exempted from the election expenditure limits rules, so that editorial coverage of the campaign does not have to be attributed to any candidate's expenses return, even if some item is arguably broadcast 'with a view to promoting or procuring the election of a candidate at an election'.[5] The exempt status of broadcasting, not entirely clear previously, has been statutory since 1969.[6]

However, the broadcasters' exemption from one aspect of election law comes at a price. So far as individual election contests are in issue, there is a strict and limiting rule for broadcast items 'about the constituency or electoral area', which was introduced in 1969 as an additional safeguard.[7] It is provided, first, that it is unlawful to broadcast any item about a constituency if any candidate takes part but does not consent to the broadcast. Second, it is an offence for a candidate to take part in an item and consent to it being broadcast before the close of nominations. Third, after the close of nominations, a candidate commits an offence by taking part in an item about a constituency so as to further his chances of election, unless the broadcast has the consent of all the other candidates.

More generally, and perhaps more importantly, there are other exclusionary rules and constraints on what may be broadcast. An exclusion of great significance is the ban on political advertising. No BBC service funded by the licence fee or grant-in-aid may carry advertising. Statutory provisions prohibit the inclusion of political advertisements in other television and radio services.[8] It should be noted that, because the exclusion is so broad, there are no problems over defining parties or election campaigns, and there is no obvious means of circumvention.[9] Another kind of exclusion seeks to preclude what we might regard as 'the Berlusconi problem'. Bodies of persons whose objectives are wholly or mainly of a political nature or that are affiliated with or controlled by such bodies are disqualified from holding licences granted by the Independent Television Commission or the Radio Authority.[10] The BBC, Channel 4 and S4C are established as public corporations, but by convention enjoy substantial political independence.

Beyond these 'brightline' rules, there lie the more nebulous but crucial rules designed to constrain the broadcasting companies to be fair in their coverage of politics and elections, in news and current affairs and general programming. These rules are found in the Broadcasting Acts 1990 and 1996, and in the BBC's Charter and Agreement.[11] The broadcasting service providers are not allowed to 'editorialise' or express their own views on matters of controversy in the way in which newspapers can. They are also required to preserve 'due impartiality' as respects political controversy and current public policy. Commercial television and radio have long been under such obligations as a matter of law. The BBC accepted the same obligations on a voluntary basis initially, but they became semi-official when they were appended to successive versions of the Licence and Agreement, and they are explicitly incorporated in the new Charter and Agreement which came into force in 1996.

In 1996 too, the Corporation became for the first time obliged to elaborate the requirement of impartiality in a code.[12] Chapter 2 of its *Producers' Guidelines* is used to fulfil this function, and there are also chapters in the *Guidelines* about politics and broadcasting during elections.[13] Similarly, the Independent Television Commission and the Radio Authority are statutorily obliged to formulate and publish codes on the same requirement.[14] Thus, along with the broad rules, there is a growing body of 'soft law' concerning impartiality. These fairness rules were crucial to two of the cases heard during the 1997 election campaign: the SNP case and the Referendum Party case.

FAIRNESS AND TELEVISED DEBATES: THE SNP CASE

For a few weeks in the run-up to the general election, there seemed to be a real prospect of a 'head-to-head' or televised debate between the

main party leaders.[15] However, after a period of positioning and postur-
ing, the talks broke down amidst mutual recriminations. How sincere
the Labour and Conservative Parties were is perhaps debatable, but
evidently a central stumbling block was the difficulty of deciding what
was needed to satisfy the fairness rules in broadcasting law. The Liberal
Democrats threatened to bring a legal challenge, if they were dissatisfied
with the role envisaged for Paddy Ashdown in any leaders' debates
arranged.

In the event, the Liberal Democrats' threats were not carried out, but
there was litigation north of the border, where the Scottish National
Party has long been sensitive to the treatment it receives (or does not
receive) from the broadcasting organisations.[16] Accordingly, in *Scottish
National Party* v. *Scottish Television plc and Grampian Television plc*,[17] the
party and its officials sought an interim interdict in the Court of Session
because of fears that their leader, Alex Salmond, was going to be
excluded from such a debate or debates, if they occurred. When they
tried to have their fears confirmed or denied, the BBC quite reasonably
told them that no final decision had been reached. However, the two
Channel 3 companies which broadcast in central Scotland and the north
of Scotland in effect confirmed that, if such debates were arranged,
Salmond would not be a participant in them. Accordingly, the SNP
moved against these companies, aiming to interdict them from broadcasting such programmes in Scotland before the date of the general
election.

Under Section 6 of the Broadcasting Act 1990, the Independent
Television Commission (ITC), the regulatory body for commercial
services, must 'do all that they can to secure' that every licensed service
complies with the requirement to preserve 'due impartiality as respects
matters of political or industrial controversy or relating to current public
policy'. In application of the requirement, it is provided that 'a series of
programmes may be considered as a whole'. The Commission is also
required to give further guidance as to application in a code and to 'do
all that they can to secure that the provisions of the code are observed
in the provision of licensed services'.

These were the key provisions. For the SNP, it was submitted that in
Scotland, where the party counted as one of the main parties, there
would be partiality in the result if they were excluded from a programme
which would have a special impact. Although arrangements had not
yet been finalised, their counsel used a sheaf of press cuttings to try to
show that they had a 'reasonable apprehension' that such a programme
would be broadcast.

Counsel for Scottish Television argued that the legislation should be
interpreted as imposing requirements on the service as a whole, so that

it was misconceived to focus on any single programme. Moreover, the provisions were designed to confer discretion on the service providers as to precisely how the requirements were met. Besides, his client had not been involved in any negotiations over the party leaders' debate (these having been conducted by the ITV network) and had taken no decision to broadcast such a programme if it were made. The petitioners' argument, he submitted, was premature, the basis of their averments merely hypothetical. For Grampian Television too, counsel argued that the petition should be dismissed for irrelevance, contending that the provisions on 'due impartiality' implied a measure of discretion and that courts should not interfere with the exercise of discretion except upon the well-established grounds of illegality, irrationality, or procedural impropriety.[18] But he also submitted that the petition should be dismissed as incompetent, since the duty imposed on the company was either to be treated as a statutory duty, in which case the application for judicial review would have been the appropriate procedure, or else was a duty in the licence, in which event it was for the Independent Television Commission to enforce as the licensing body, and the SNP and other private persons lacked title to sue.

There were other arguments about the balance of convenience in the circumstances, with the petitioners claiming prejudice to Scottish voters if a partial debate were shown, and the respondents claiming prejudice to Scottish viewers if they were deprived of a debate between potential prime ministers, which Salmond was not. No counsel referred to the European Convention on Human Rights, although not long previously the Inner House had accepted that the Convention should have the same relevance as in English law,[19] so it could have been argued that the court should be strongly disinclined to impose any prior restraint on freedom of expression.

The Lord Ordinary, Lord Eassie, refused the petitioners' motion, on account of irrelevance. He noted that in all the circumstances the petitioners' case was 'largely, if not entirely, hypothetical' and observed that the courts were not there to decide matters which were merely hypothetical. While the hypothetical nature of the matter was sufficient reason in itself, he also accepted the arguments of counsel for the television companies concerning the interpretation of the provisions, so that the requirement of impartiality was to be viewed in the round and was not properly applicable to a single programme, and concerning the discretionary nature of the decision, which would only be reviewable on the usual grounds. The judge considered, on the procedural point, that an application for judicial review would have been the appropriate procedure, rather than the one which had been used. He was not, however, persuaded that enforcement of the duties on licensees could only be at the behest of the ITC, especially as the powers of the commission did not, as he understood the matter, allow them to prohibit a particular programme.

Thus, the legal constraint apprehended was more imaginary than real, and more generally, the decision had some very welcome aspects for broadcasters.[20] The recognition that due impartiality is to be tested against the service as a whole allows them some flexibility, as does the acknowledgement that they have been entrusted with a measure of discretion with which courts should not lightly interfere. Although the BBC's position is constitutionally different, both of these points could be argued to apply to it in much the same way. In fact, there was not long to wait before the arguments became very relevant, for a week or so later the BBC and ITC were respondents in another proceeding, in the English High Court.

ALLOCATION OF PARTY BROADCASTS: THE REFERENDUM PARTY CASE

The fairness rules which constrain coverage of politics in news and other programmes are also the rules which have to be followed when determining the entitlement of parties to free airtime. While paid political advertising is excluded, domestic broadcasters have long made it their practice to allocate slots of airtime to the main political parties, free of charge, for their use in propagandising. There are annual series of party political broadcasts, supplemented at appropriate times by party election broadcasts.

But how, in the absence of specific guidance in legal provision, is entitlement to what is effectively free advertising time to be determined? With only the broad fairness rules to guide them, the broadcasters have had to grapple with this awkward question from year to year, and it is scarcely surprising that the issue has occasionally given rise to litigation.[21] Perhaps finding strength in unity, the BBC and commercial broadcasters have tended to consult together and come to the same decisions. They have also consulted with representatives (such as the chief whips) of the main British political parties represented in parliament (that is Labour, Conservative, Liberal Democrat, SNP and Plaid Cymru), through joint participation in an unofficial and ad hoc (and rather shadowy) body called the Committee on Party Political Broadcasting.

For the 1997 general election, the BBC proposed to allocate to the Referendum Party one television and one radio party election broadcast, each of five minutes' duration. It allocated more and, in the main, longer broadcasts to the three main political parties: five ten-minute television slots each for the Conservative and Labour Parties and four for the Liberal Democrats, and four ten-minute radio slots for the Conservatives and for Labour and three for the Liberal Democrats. In addition it allocated three five-minute slots for the Conservative and Labour Parties and two for the Liberal Democrats on Radio 2. There were additional allocations to the nationalist parties in Scotland and Wales and, like the Referendum Party, any party which was contesting 50 or more seats was allocated a single television broadcast. There were similar decisions on allocations made by the ITV Network Centre (which also represented Channel 4 and Channel 5) and approved by the ITC.

Sir James Goldsmith's Referendum Party was sufficiently aggrieved by its proposed treatment to initiate judicial review proceedings against the BBC and the ITC. On 11 April, with polling day just under three weeks ahead, their application for leave was granted by Mr Justice Sedley, who was unimpressed by arguments that the broadcasters' decisions were irrational, but considered that the applicants might have a tenable case on an argument that the broadcasters (or the ITC anyway) had unlawfully delegated the exercise of the decision-making to the Committee on Party Political Broadcasting, or in making their decisions had unlawfully deferred to it and its chosen criteria.

A week later, after a Divisional Court (Lord Justice Auld and Mr Justice Popplewell) had heard the parties' arguments, the application for judicial review in *R. v. BBC and ITC, ex parte the Referendum Party* was rejected.[22] In fact, the delegation point which Geoffrey Robertson QC, as counsel for the applicant, had developed at the leave stage of proceedings, was dropped at the hearing or at least transformed. The applicants had been persuaded, and now acknowledged, that the broadcasters were the decision-makers. It is of interest to note that, apparently upon legal advice, the broadcasters in 1995 and 1996 were endeavouring to make clearer that they did not merely *propose* allocations to the Committee on Party Political Broadcasting, but actually *decided* themselves. The rather skeletal accounts of the decision-making process which are published are at least consistent with such an implication.[23]

A somewhat different argument about procedural impropriety was, however, put forward, to the effect that the applicants had been denied an adequate opportunity to make representations. The Referendum Party had sought to nominate to the Committee Sir George Gardiner (the dissident former Tory MP who, following his deselection, had resigned from the Conservative Party and joined the Referendum Party in March, shortly before the announcement of the election). As no meeting of the Committee was subsequently held, the party had been unable to put its case at that forum. In fact their difficulty, and the difficulty with this argument, was that it was the long-established practice of the Committee, so far as possible, to work without meetings. In any event, the court was satisfied there had been no procedural deficiency, because the party had been able, by correspondence and meetings, to make representations to the broadcasters.

The applicants' other challenge was based on irrationality. The party was expecting to field candidates in 547 out of 659 constituencies, had a budget of about £20 million for the campaign, and on recent opinion poll indications had the support of over 3 per cent of the electorate, and growing. The nub of their case was that the criteria used to determine the allocation of broadcasts were unfair, particularly to a new party. The ITC, for example, in writing to them, had explained that 'the allocation of additional PEBs should be related to electoral support, normally at the previous General Election ...'. A Canadian decision, holding that the use of a formula for allocation of broadcasting time favoured existing parties at the expense of emerging parties and was discriminatory under the Charter of Rights and Freedoms, was persuasive.[24]

Some of these points certainly deserved consideration, and they are arguably stronger because of the broadcasting authorities' persistent reticence about the criteria which they do employ. Over the years their decision-making has been far from transparent in this regard. However, the conventions and practices which have guided them may be inferred, even if they are not fully published or readily disclosed. Evidently, the principal criterion consists of votes cast for a party at the previous general election, but there are some other conventions applied, such as equality of time between the government and the official opposition.

If entitlement to party election broadcasts was judged solely by party support at the previous general election, the broadcasters' practice would merit (and would probably have received) condemnation. However, their practice has in fact been rather more flexible: in 1987, for example, on the strength of by-election performances as well as opinion poll evidence, the SDP/Liberal Alliance were allocated equal numbers to the Labour and Conservative Parties. David Pannick QC (for the BBC) and Christopher Clarke QC (for the ITC) were able to persuade the Divisional Court that several relevant factors were properly taken into account, and the court, noting that impartiality did not entail parity of treatment between parties of different strengths, did not consider that the broadcasters' decisions in 1997 affecting the Referendum Party were irrational.

With the failure of the applicants' arguments, another defence mounted by the BBC did not have to be considered fully. The interesting legal point involved in it was the susceptibility of the BBC to judicial review which, as Lord Justice Auld observed, has not been the subject of decision in England. Lord Justice Auld thought that an earlier Northern Irish case[25] in which the corporation was held unsusceptible to review was distinguishable, having been decided at a time when impartiality was not an obligation found in the Licence and Agreement. The obligation as it is found now in the Agreement was described by him as 'undertaken contractually to the Government', but having trailed some of the arguments on either side, he left it for another court in an appropriate case to consider and decide on the Corporation's susceptibility to review.

CONTENT OF PARTY ELECTION BROADCASTS

The 1997 election gave rise not only to disputes about *entitlement*, but also to some disputes about the *content* of party election broadcasts. Many people, in advance of the 1997 election, would have been under the impression that the content of the broadcasts (and party political broadcasts at other times) was entirely a matter for the party concerned. But, if so, the events of the April campaign will have disabused them of such a notion. Three of the party broadcasts gave rise to difficulties for the broadcasters, and in two of the three cases the issue ended up in the courts.

Only very occasionally in the past have proposed party election (or political) broadcasts caused any problem, and such problems as have arisen have usually been informally resolved. Perhaps it is significant that a wider range of parties than ever before benefited in 1997 from the practice of allocating one television broadcast to any party fielding 50 or more candidates.

It has often been assumed that the political parties have full editorial control over their free air time. But, more accurately, the proposition is only true up to a point. As things stand, the broadcasting companies are the publishers, and therefore remain legally responsible for what is broadcast. As publishers, even if not originators of the material, they could be liable in civil or criminal law for ordinary wrongs such as libel and contempt of court. In addition, they are obliged to comply with the requirements of broadcasting law and thus must not, for example, broadcast anything which 'offends against good taste or decency or is likely to encourage or incite to crime or to lead to disorder or to be offensive to public feeling'.[26]

It was that particular clause which was involved in the dispute between broadcasters and the Pro-Life Alliance. The Pro-Life Alliance, given a five-minute television slot, proposed to promote its anti-abortionist views with a film which included footage (from a US documentary) of an abortion clinic and the mutilation and disposal of

aborted foetuses. The BBC regarded the sequence as 'totally unacceptable on taste and decency grounds', and asked for scenes amounting to
2 minutes, 13 seconds to be cut. On similar grounds, executives from
the Independent Television Association, Channel 4 and Channel 5
reached the same decision. The Pro-Life Alliance sought judicial review,
but Mr Justice Dyson, having viewed the proposed transmission,
accepted submissions that the Corporation was entitled to conclude that
the images would grossly offend against good taste and be offensive to
public feeling.[27] With the contentious footage obscured, the party's
election broadcast was screened on the following day. The Alliance
circumvented the court's decision to an extent, by putting clips of
banned footage on the Internet, and also responded to requests from
some foreign television companies which were interested in broadcasting the original film.

The broadcasters, who had been united on the Pro-Life Alliance's
film, diverged in the same week on attitudes to a British National Party
broadcast. Channel 4 refused to transmit the broadcast, on the ground
that some footage was in breach of consent requirements in the ITC
Programme Code, which provides that: 'When coverage is being given
to events in public places, editors and producers must satisfy themselves
that words spoken or actions taken by individuals are sufficiently in the
public domain to justify their being communicated to the television
audience without express permission being sought'.[28] Other channels
showed the broadcast.

Defamation risks were involved in the other dispute, over a Sinn
Féin election broadcast to be shown only in Northern Ireland. The BBC
asked the party to cut two sequences of film from their proposed
broadcast, as being potentially libellous. One sequence showed the
Ulster Unionist leader, David Trimble, speaking on a mobile 'phone at
Drumcree, immediately followed by scenes of police officers batoning
people on the Garvaghy Road. The second sequence showed the (then)
Democratic Unionist MP, William McCrea, sharing a platform with a
leading Loyalist, Billy Wright, at a rally in Portadown. Refusal to cut
these sequences led the BBC to refuse to transmit the broadcast in its
original form, which led to a judicial review proceeding in the Northern
Ireland High Court. There Mr Justice Kerr declined to hold that the
BBC's decision was irrational.[29] The broadcast was shown with the
contentious sequences removed.

PROSPECTS OF REFORM

The rash of problems with the contents of party broadcasts inspired
some thoughts of reform. The broadcasting companies are able to seek

indemnities from the parties anyway, so perhaps it might be argued by the Pro-Life Alliance or others that there is the worst of both worlds. As far as the broadcasters are concerned, their uneasy and ambiguous position as publishing conduits could be resolved if there were legislation to place responsibility for what is broadcast in these slots entirely on the parties.

There are other, more important issues which arise. Arguably legislation should also give more precise guidance about issues of entitlement or should create a body or mechanism in order to do so, if the fairness rules are to be maintained. The uncertainty of application which is inherent in the present law can sometimes work to the advantage of the media. But sometimes, as with the party leaders' debate that never was, the cloudiness of the law is liable to obstruct the free gaze of the democratic process, or its imagined effects are unnecessarily inhibiting. Aside from the substance of legal requirements, litigation showed that there are also issues about justiciability which are far from fully resolved. Which bodies are susceptible to review, in which circumstances, and at whose behest, are all questions that call for further elucidation.

If the fairness rules remain, is there any need or justification for the retention of the provision concerning broadcasts 'about the constituency'? The provision gives every candidate a power of veto over certain kinds of broadcasts and causes broadcasters considerable practical difficulties. Here again the provision's constraints, when properly analysed, are less far-reaching than journalists sometimes believe, but this in itself is indicative of its chilling effects, which are disproportionate.[30] If there remains concern over the possibility of unfairness to individual election candidates, it is arguable that some minor additions to the codes on impartiality could adequately meet it.

There are larger issues in the background, such as whether, in a spirit of deregulation, rules such as the fairness rules are necessary at all and whether political advertising should be banned.[31] Even if there were fewer reasons to object to newspaper coverage of the 1997 election campaign, there may be those who consider it 'a little more possible to contemplate a libertarian ideal for television, but even more necessary to consider a public service ideal for the press'.[32] However, while the familiar, terrestrial television channels remain dominant and the concept of public service broadcasting retains influence, then caution is likely to prevail, in view of the perceived impact of television.

If the prospect of change lies within sight in the middle distance, it may be hastened not only by technological developments and changing patterns of media ownership and use, but also possibly by legal developments. In Canada, a temporary prohibition on advertising at election periods has been found to be in breach of the guarantees on freedom of expression and freedom of association found in the Canadian Charter of Rights and Freedoms.[33] In Australia, even in the absence of a set of constitutional guarantees, a prohibition on the broadcasting of political advertising at election times, found in national legislation, was held invalid by the High Court of Australia, because it substantially interfered with the freedom of political discourse which the court found was implied in their Constitution.[34] As the provisions of the European Convention on Human Rights are, under the Human Rights Act 1998, to be directly enforceable in the domestic laws of the United Kingdom, there is every reason to suppose that in the next few years some of the legal constraints on political communications at election times will be challenged as being unjustifiable or unnecessary. Perhaps paradoxically, those legal requirements, which not only constrain but in some respects serve to protect broadcasters, may be more sympathetically regarded when courts threaten to intervene to discard or re-write them.

NOTES

1 *Houston* v. *BBC* (1995) SLT 1305. See Colin Munro, 'The Banned Broadcasting Corporation', *New Law Journal*, 145 (1995), pp. 518–20; John MacInnes, 'Astonishingly Stupid: The Panorama Affair', *Scottish Affairs*, 12 (1995), pp. 1–8.

2 See Carol Harlow and Richard Rawlings, *Pressure through Law* (London: Routledge, 1992).

3 For an account at an earlier period, see Colin Munro, 'Legal Controls on Election Broadcasting', in Ivor Crewe and Martin Harrop (eds), *Political Communications: The General Election Campaign of 1983* (Cambridge: Cambridge University Press, 1986), pp. 294–305.

4 From an adjudication in Press Complaints Commission, *Report No. 34* (1996), p. 11.

5 Representation of the People Act 1983, s.75.

6 There was litigation in *Grieve* v. *Douglas-Home* (1965) SC 313.

7 Representation of the People Act 1983, s.93 (replacing Representation of the People Act 1969, s.9).

8 Broadcasting Act 1990, ss.8, 60, 92.

9 Broadcasting authorities have also tended to interpret the exclusion broadly. The rejection of an Amnesty International advertisement was held by the Court of Appeal not to be unlawful in *R.* v. *Radio Authority, ex parte Bull* [1997] 2 All ER 561, a few months before the election.

10 Broadcasting Act 1990, ss.5, 88 and Schedule 2, as amended by Broadcasting Act 1996, s.73 and Schedule 2.

11 The Charter is Cm 3248, the Agreement is Cm 3152.

12 By section 5.3 of the Agreement.

13 Published by the BBC and obtainable from its bookshops (or at the web-site: www.bbc.co.uk).

14 Broadcasting Act 1990, ss.6 (3), 90 (5). The ITC *Programme Code* and the Radio Authority *Programme Code* are published by these bodies in compliance with the statutory requirement.

15 See Chapter 14 by Richard Tait, 'The Debate that Never Happened', in this volume.

16 In 1996 the SNP brought judicial review proceedings (unsuccessfully) in the Court of Session regarding television coverage of the annual party conferences: see Colin Munro, 'SNP v. BBC – Round Two', *New Law Journal*, 146 (1996), pp. 1433–4. Earlier litigation on behalf of the party includes *Wolfe* v. *IBA* (1980, unreported) and *Wilson* v. *IBA (No. 2)* (1988) SLT 276.

17 Unreported, at time of writing. The author was present at the proceedings.

18 The grounds of review were summarised paradigmatically in this fashion by Lord Diplock in his speech in *Council of Civil Service Unions* v. *Minister for the Civil Service* [1985] AC 374.

19 *T, Petitioner* (1997) SLT 724.

20 The precedential value of judicial opinions in the case (and in the case described in the next section) is weakened because of the nature of interim proceedings. That said, proceedings aimed at prior restraint of the media are typically of this kind and assistance is frequently derived from earlier cases.

21 *Wilson* v. *IBA* (1979) SC 351 concerned party political broadcasts in the run-up to the referendum on the Scotland Act 1979. *Wilson* v. *IBA (No. 2)* (1988) SLT 276 concerned the SNP's entitlement to party election broadcasts. For the use of litigation and threats by the SDP and the SDP-Liberal Alliance in the 1980s, see Ivor Crewe and Anthony King, *SDP: The Birth, Life and Death of the Social Democratic Party* (Oxford: Oxford University Press, 1995), ch. 14.

22 Available on LEXIS (Butterworths' telepublishing law database), but not otherwise reported at time of writing.

23 The BBC's *Producers' Guidelines* (at Chapter 18) outlines the Corporation's practice, and likewise (rather more fully) the ITC's *Programme Code* (at section 4).

24 *Reform Party of Canada* v. *Canada (Attorney-General)* (1993) 7 Alta. LR (3d) 1.

25 *Lynch* v. *BBC* [1983] NILR 193, in which a smaller party's complaint over exclusion from an election forum programme was rejected.

26 Broadcasting Act 1990, s.6 (1) (a). The same obligation appears in the Agreement applicable to the BBC.

27 *The Times*, 25 April 1997.

28 Section 2.2.

29 *The Times*, 26 April 1997.

30 There is some danger of inadvertent breaches, as shown by the circumstances of the election petition in *Hobson* v. *Fishburn* (1988), *Guardian*, 1 November 1988. But the provision only applies to broadcasts 'about a constituency', and even then only if some candidate actively participates: *Marshall* v. *BBC* [1979] 1 WLR 1071.

31 For an argument that political advertising should be allowed, see Margaret Scammell, 'Political Advertising and the Broadcasting Revolution', *Political Quarterly*, 61 (1990), pp. 200–13.

32 William L. Miller, *Media and Voters* (Oxford: Clarendon Press, 1991), p. 205.

33 *Somerville* v. *Canada (Attorney-General)* (1996), 136 DLR (4th) 205.

34 *Australian Capital Television Pty Ltd* v. *Commonwealth of Australia (No. 2)* (1992) 108 ALR 577.

Index

Books of Related Interest

Conscience and Parliament

Philip Cowley, *University of Hull (Ed)*

How does the British policy process deal with 'conscience' issues?
Does parliament still decide? What influences MPs?
This book considers how the British policy process deals with
'conscience' issues, those social issues which have strong moral
overtones. It covers eight of the main topics to have been discussed
by parliament in the last quarter of a century – abortion,
censorship, divorce, Sunday trading, homosexuality, war crimes,
disability rights and animal welfare.

Contents: Abortion *Susan Millns and Sally Sheldon*. Homosexuality
Melvyn D Read and David Marsh. War Crimes *Gabriele Ganz*. Divorce
Philip Cowley. Sunday Trading *Melvyn D Read*. Disability Rights
Matthew Bailey and Kevin Shinkwin. Animal Welfare *Robert Garner*.
Censorship *Martin Durham*. Voting Without Party? *Charles Pattie,
Ron Johnston and Mark Stuart*. Conclusion *Philip Cowley*.

224 pages   1998
0 7146 4836 1   cloth
0 7146 4388 2   paper
The Library of Legislative Studies

FRANK CASS PUBLISHERS
Newbury House, 900 Eastern Avenue, Newbury Park, Ilford, Essex, IG2 7HH
Tel: +44 (0)181 599 8866 Fax: +44 (0)181 599 0984
NORTH AMERICA
c/o ISBS, 5804 NE Hassalo Street, Portland OR 97213 3644
Tel: (800) 944 6190 Fax: (503) 280 8832 E-mail: orders@isbs.com
Website: http://www.frankcass.com E-mail: sales@frankcass.com

British Elections & Parties Review, Volume 8

The General Election of 1997

David Denver, *University of Lancaster,*
Philip Cowley, *University of Hull,*
Justin Fisher, *London Guildhall University,*
Charles Pattie, *University of Sheffield (Eds)*

The Review brings together in one volume the very latest and most sophisticated research on the 1997 General Election, and the reference section provides a chronology of the political year, opinion poll results and details of by-elections.

Contents: New Labour, New Tactical Voting? The Causes and Consequences of Tactical Voting in the 1997 General Election *Geoff Evans, John Curtice and Pippa Norris.* Political Change and Party Choice: Voting in the 1997 General Election *Harold D Clarke, Marianne Stewart and Paul Whiteley.* Sex, Money and Politics: Sleaze and the Conservative Party in the 1997 Election *David M Farrell, Ian McAllister and Donley T Studlar.* Euroscepticism and the Referendum Party *Anthony Heath, Roger Jowell, Bridget Taylor and Katarina Thomson.* New Labour Landslide – Same Old Electoral Geography? *R J Johnston, C J Pattie, D F L Dorling, D J Rossiter, H Tunstall and I D McAllister.* Split Ticket Voting at the 1997 British General and Local Elections – An Aggregate Analysis *Colin Rallings and Michael Thrasher.* Between Fear and Loath: National Press Coverage of the 1997 British General Election *David Deacon, Peter Golding and Michael Billig.* Does Negative News Matter? The Effect of Television News on Party Images in the 1997 British General Election *David Sanders and Pippa Norris.* Triumph of Targeting? Constituency Campaigning in the 1997 Election *David Denver, Gordon Hands, Simon Henig.* Labour's Grass Roots Campaign in the 1997 *Paul Whiteley and Patrick Seyd.* Remodelling the 1997 General Election: How Britain Would Have Voted Under Alternative Electoral Systems *Patrick Dunleavy, Helen Margetts, Brendan O'Duffy and Stuart Weir.*

312 pages   1998
0 7146 4909 0   cloth
0 7146 4466 8   paper

FRANK CASS PUBLISHERS
Newbury House, 900 Eastern Avenue, Newbury Park, Ilford, Essex, IG2 7HH
Tel: +44 (0)181 599 8866 Fax: +44 (0)181 599 0984

NORTH AMERICA
c/o ISBS, 5804 NE Hassalo Street, Portland OR 97213 3644
Tel: (800) 944 6190 Fax: (503) 280 8832 E-mail: orders@isbs.com

Website: http://www.frankcass.com E-mail: sales@frankcass.com

Parliaments and Governments in Western Europe

Philip Norton, *University of Hull (Ed)*

The relationship between parliament and government is fundamental to a political system. In this volume, a distinguished team of specialists explore that relationship and consider to what extent parliaments have the capacity to constrain governments. Are there particular institutional features, such as specialisation through committees, that enhance their capacity to influence public policy?

Contents: The Institution of Parliaments *Philip Norton.* Old Institution, New Institutionalism? Parliament and Government in the UK *Philip Norton.* The German Bundestag: Influence and Accountability in a Complex Environment *Thomas Saalfeld.* The Italian Parliament: Chambers in a Crumbling House? *Vincent Della Sala.* Parliament and Government in Belgium: Prisoners of Partitocracy *Lieven de Winter.* A Changing Relationship? Parliament and Government in Ireland *Eunan O'Halpin.* Relationship between Parliament and Government in Portugal: An Expression of the Maturation of the Political System *Cristina Leston Bandeira.* The European Parliament: Crawling, Walking and Running *Mark P Shephard.* Do Parliaments Make a Difference? *Philip Norton.*

Volume 1   232 pages   1998
0 7146 4833 7   cloth
0 7146 4385 8   paper
The Library of Legislative Studies

FRANK CASS PUBLISHERS
Newbury House, 900 Eastern Avenue, Newbury Park, Ilford, Essex, IG2 7HH
Tel: +44 (0)181 599 8866 Fax: +44 (0)181 599 0984

NORTH AMERICA
c/o ISBS, 5804 NE Hassalo Street, Portland OR 97213 3644
Tel: (800) 944 6190 Fax: (503) 280 8832 E-mail: orders@isbs.com

Website: http://www.frankcass.com E-mail: sales@frankcass.com

Britain in the Nineties

The Politics of Paradox

Hugh Berrington, *Emeritus Professor of Politics, University of Newcastle upon Tyne (Ed)*

This volume looks at the striking changes in British politics and government since the accession of Mrs Thatcher and in particular at the last six or seven years. Its aim is to explore some of these recent changes and to emphasise the recurring paradoxes in the political developments of the last 20 years, for example, the changes of sides by the main parties on Europe.

Contents: Britain in the Nineties: The Politics of Paradox. An Introduction *Hugh Berrington*. Power in the Parties: R T McKenzie and After *Dennis Kavanagh*. Europe, Thatcherism and Traditionalism: Opinion, Rebellion and the Maastricht Treaty in the Backbench Conservative Party, 1992-1994 *Hugh Berrington/Rod Hague*. From Hostility to 'Constructive Engagement' The Europeanisation of the Labour Party *Philip Daniels*. Narratives of 'Thatcherism' *Mark Bevir/R A W Rhodes*. Institutions, Regulations and Change: New Regulatory Agencies in British Privatised Utilities *Mark Thatcher*. The Judicial Dimension in British Politics *Nevil Johnson*. The Periphery and its Paradoxes *William L Miller*. The British Electorate in the 1990s *David Denver*.

240 pages   1998
0 7146 4880 9   cloth
0 7146 4434 X   paper
A special issue of the journal West European Politics

FRANK CASS PUBLISHERS
Newbury House, 900 Eastern Avenue, Newbury Park, Ilford, Essex, IG2 7HH
Tel: +44 (0)181 599 8866 Fax: +44 (0)181 599 0984

NORTH AMERICA
c/o ISBS, 5804 NE Hassalo Street, Portland OR 97213 3644
Tel: (800) 944 6190 Fax: (503) 280 8832 E-mail: orders@isbs.com

Website: http://www.frankcass.com E-mail: sales@frankcass.com

Regional Dynamics

The Basis of Electoral Support in Britain

William Field, *Georgian Court College, Lakewood*

> '... a pioneering book ...'
> **Vernon Bogdanor, Oxford University**

> '... a sophisticated and balanced evaluation'
> **Parliamentary Affairs**

Many have noticed the 'North-South divide' in British politics. In this book, William Field points out that this divide marks the resurgence of a core-periphery cleavage which was also dominant in British politics in the years before 1914. He shows how astonishingly similar the geographical pattern of the vote was in the general election of 1987 to that in the two general elections of 1910, the last before the outbreak of the First World War. Many of the same constitutional issues – devolution and reform of the second chamber – were coming to the fore then as now.

Are we now seeing the resurgence of a pattern which, from the end of the First World War to the 1980s, was submerged by the politics of class? Is the decline of class leading to the resurrection of older cleavages? Was 'Thatcherism', so dominant in British politics in the 1980s, more a consequence of profound social and geographical changes than a cause? William Field examines these questions, and brings to his analysis a deep understanding of statistics and a rigour not always found in historical analysis.

224 pages   1997
0 7146 4782 9   cloth
0 7146 4336 X   paper

FRANK CASS PUBLISHERS
Newbury House, 900 Eastern Avenue, Newbury Park, Ilford, Essex, IG2 7HH
Tel: +44 (0)181 599 8866 Fax: +44 (0)181 599 0984

NORTH AMERICA
c/o ISBS, 5804 NE Hassalo Street, Portland OR 97213 3644
Tel: (800) 944 6190 Fax: (503) 280 8832 E-mail: orders@isbs.com

Website: http://www.frankcass.com E-mail: sales@frankcass.com

National Parliaments and the European Union

Philip Norton, *University of Hull (Ed)*

> '... a solid comparative collection, providing up to
> date and in-depth illustration of the potential, and
> problems, involved in thinking about parliamentary
> democracy in established EU member countries.'
> **International Affairs**

> '... to anyone seriously interested in the question of
> which Parliament should be legislating for Europe the
> book is a must'
> **The European**

This volume provides, for the first time, the material that is essential
for an informed debate. It discusses how national parliaments have
adapted to the effects of the Single European Act and the Maastricht
Treaty. Detailed studies of ten national parliaments lead to conclusions
as to how they have adapted, or not adapted to European integration.
The authors look at each parliament from the time of membership,
identifying the key stages of institutional change. These case studies
are complemented by an analysis of how national parliaments are
viewed by institutions of the European Union that set the agenda for
change and face the problems of remedying the perceived
'democratic deficit' within the EU.

198 pages   1996
0 7146 4691 1   cloth
0 7146 4330 0   paper
The Library of Legislative Studies
A special issue of The Journal of Legislative Studies

FRANK CASS PUBLISHERS
Newbury House, 900 Eastern Avenue, Newbury Park, Ilford, Essex, IG2 7HH
Tel: +44 (0)181 599 8866 Fax: +44 (0)181 599 0984

NORTH AMERICA
c/o ISBS, 5804 NE Hassalo Street, Portland OR 97213 3644
Tel: (800) 944 6190 Fax: (503) 280 8832 E-mail: orders@isbs.com

Website: http://www.frankcass.com E-mail: sales@frankcass.com

Remaking the Union

Devolution and British Politics in the 1990s

Howard Elcock, *University of Northumbria at Newcastle and*
Michael Keating, *University of Western Ontario (Eds)*

This volume addresses the issues arising from the recent devolution referenda by exploring the historical development of the proposals, the importance of national and regional identities, the changing policies of the political parties and the approaches of business and other major groups towards devolution. It also looks at the impact on electoral reform coming from the proposal that proportional representation be used to elect the regional assemblies and how the new assemblies are to be financed. Finally the book discusses the implications of a devolved British state where different countries and regions achieve different levels of autonomy at different paces.

240 pages 1998
0 7146 4876 0   cloth
0 7146 4430 7   paper
Cass Series in Regional and Federal Studies Volume 3
A special issue of the journal Regional and Federal Studies

FRANK CASS PUBLISHERS
Newbury House, 900 Eastern Avenue, Newbury Park, Ilford, Essex, IG2 7HH
Tel: +44 (0)181 599 8866 Fax: +44 (0)181 599 0984

NORTH AMERICA
c/o ISBS, 5804 NE Hassalo Street, Portland OR 97213 3644
Tel: (800) 944 6190 Fax: (503) 280 8832 E-mail: orders@isbs.com

Website: http://www.frankcass.com E-mail: sales@frankcass.com

The New Roles of Parliamentary Committees

Lawrence D Longley, *Lawrence University, USA and*
Roger H Davidson, *University of Maryland (Eds)*

Parliaments had been expected to decline in significance in the later part of
the twentieth century, but instead they have developed new and vital
political roles and have innovated in their institutional structure - most
recurrently in newly organised or invigorated parliamentary committees,
not only in a few parliaments, but as a global phenomenon.

Even as newly democratic parliaments throughout the world experiment
with more elaborate committee structures, those with older, highly
developed committee systems are reaching for more varied and flexible
alternatives. In short, parliamentary committees have emerged as vibrant
and central institutions of democratic parliaments of today's world and
have begun to define new and changing roles for themselves.

Contents: Parliamentary Committees: Changing Perspectives on Changing
Institutions *Lawrence D Longley and Roger H Davidson*. Parliamentary
Committees in European Democracies *Kaare Strom*. Norwegian
Parlimentary Committees: Performance, Structural Change and External
Relations *Hilmar Rommetvedt*. Changing Parliamentary Committees in
Changing East-Central Europe: Parliamentary Committees as Central Sites
of Policy Making *Attila Agh*. Committees in the Post-Communist Polish
Sejm: Structure, Activity and Members *David M Olson, Ania van der Meer-
Krok-Paszkowska, Maurice D. Simon, and Irena Jackiewicz*. US Congressional
Committees: Changing Legislative Workshops *Colton C Campbell* and *Roger
H Davidson*. Nascent Institutionalisation: Committees in the British
Parliament *Philip Norton*. Political Reform and the Committee System in
Israel: Structural and Functional Adaptation *Reuven Y Hazan*. Committees
in the Russian State Duma: Continuity and Change in Comparative
Perspective *Moshe Haspel*. The Organisation and Workings of Committees
in the Korean National Assembly *Chan Wook Park*. Parliamentary
Committees: A Global Perspective *Malcom Shaw*.

264 pages   1998
0 7146 4891 4 cloth
0 7146 4442 0 paper

FRANK CASS PUBLISHERS
Newbury House, 900 Eastern Avenue, Newbury Park, Ilford, Essex, IG2 7HH
Tel: +44 (0)181 599 8866 Fax: +44 (0)181 599 0984

NORTH AMERICA
c/o ISBS, 5804 NE Hassalo Street, Portland OR 97213 3644
Tel: (800) 944 6190 Fax: (503) 280 8832 E-mail: orders@isbs.com

Website: http://www.frankcass.com E-mail: sales@frankcass.com